HYBRID

MUSE

The Hybrid Muse

POSTCOLONIAL POETRY IN ENGLISH

Jahan Ramazani

The University of Chicago Press

CHICAGO AND LONDON

Jahan Ramazani is professor of English at the
University of Virginia. He is the author of *Poetry
of Mourning: The Modern Elegy from Hardy to
Heaney*, which was a finalist for the National
Book Critics Circle Award, as well as *Yeats and
the Poetry of Death: Elegy, Self-Elegy, and the
Sublime*. He is also editing the third edition
of *The Norton Anthology of Modern and
Contemporary Poetry*.

The University of Chicago Press gratefully
acknowledges the support of the John Simon
Guggenheim Memorial Foundation toward
the publication of this book.

The University of Chicago Press, Chicago 60637
The University of Chicago Press, Ltd., London
© 2001 by The University of Chicago
All rights reserved. Published 2001
Printed in the United States of America

10 09 08 07 06 05 04 03 02 01
1 2 3 4 5

ISBN: 0-226-70342-8 (cloth)
ISBN: 0-226-70343-6 (paper)

Library of Congress Cataloging-in-Publication
Data

Ramazani, Jahan, 1960–
    The hybrid muse : postcolonial poetry in
English / Jahan Ramazani.
        p.   cm.
    Includes bibliographical references (p.   ) and
index.
    ISBN 0-226-70342-8 (cloth : alk. paper) —
ISBN 0-226-70343-6 (pbk. : alk. paper)
    1. Commonwealth poetry (English)—His-
tory and criticism.   2. English poetry—20th
century—History and criticism.   3. Yeats,
W. B. (William Butler), 1865–1939—Criticism
and interpretation.   4. Ramanujan, A. K.,
1929—Criticism and interpretation.   5. Bennett, Louise, 1919—Criticism and interpretation.   6. p'Bitek, Okot, 1931—Criticism and
interpretation.   7. Postcolonialism—English-
speaking countries.   8. Postcolonialism—
Commonwealth countries.   9. Decolonization
in literature.   10. Walcott, Derek. Omeros.
I. Title.

PR9082 .R35   2001
821'.00917242—dc21
                                00-069077

For Caroline
with love

CONTENTS

ACKNOWLEDGMENTS   Editors and publishers have kindly granted permission to reprint material that first appeared in condensed form as "The Wound of History: Walcott's *Omeros* and the Postcolonial Poetics of Affliction," *PMLA,* vol. 112 (1997), and in a contribution to the millennium issue of *PMLA,* vol. 115 (2000), reprinted by permission of the copyright owner, Modern Language Association of America; "Is Yeats a Postcolonial Poet?" reprinted by permission from *Raritan: A Quarterly Review,* vol. 17, no. 3 (Winter 1998), copyright 1998 by *Raritan;* "Metaphor and Postcoloniality: The Poetry of A. K. Ramanujan," *Contemporary Literature,* vol. 39, no. 1 (1998), reprinted by permission of the University of Wisconsin Press; "Contemporary Post-colonial Poetry," in *A Companion to Twentieth-Century Poetry,* ed. Neil Roberts (Oxford: Blackwell, 2001), reprinted by permission of the editor.

For fellowships that enabled me to complete this book, I am delighted to have the opportunity to thank the John Simon Guggenheim Memorial Foundation and the Virginia Foundation for the Humanities. At the University of Virginia, my work on this book was aided substantially by a Sesquicentennial Fellowship; summer research awards; the Dean of Arts and Sciences, Melvin Leffler; and Chairs of the English Department, Patricia Spacks, Gordon Braden, and Michael Levenson.

My personal debts are more numerous than I can tally. I am deeply grateful to Susan Gubar, Hillis Miller, Marjorie Perloff, and Helen Vendler for lending me their bountiful, indeed invaluable, support as I undertook this project. For extending to me the benefit of their expertise in graciously answering questions and in suggesting exciting new lines of research, I thank James Arnold, Paul Breslin, Elizabeth Cullingford, Robert Hamner, Susan McKinnon, Tejumola Olaniyan, Charles Pollard, Benjamin Ray, Herbert Tucker, Reetika Vazirani, and my brother Vaheed.

My students have taught me a great deal about the pleasure and meaning of postcolonial poetry. My parents, Nesta and Ruhi, have continued to guide, buoy, and nourish me. I appreciate the shrewd insight and wit of Alan

Thomas at the University of Chicago Press. He engaged wise and generous readers, from whom I learned much and to whom I offer heartfelt thanks in their anonymity.

Finally, I dedicate this book to the person who has given me readings more probing and imaginative than I could have wished, conversations more stimulating and rewarding. My constant companion in parenting not only books, Caroline Rody has inspired, refreshed, and sustained me.

CHAPTER ONE

 Introduction

In recent decades, much of the most vital writing in English has come from Britain's former colonies in the so-called Third World. For readers of fiction, the geographic explosion of anglophone literature is by now self-evident: postcolonial novelists such as Chinua Achebe, V. S. Naipaul, Salman Rushdie, and Jamaica Kincaid have redrawn the map of English-language fiction in our time. By comparison, the notion of "contemporary poetry" remains strikingly provincial in the anglophone West. With the exception of Derek Walcott's work, contemporary poetry is typically limited to the United States, Britain, and Ireland, perhaps with some inclusion of former white settler colonies such as Canada. Whether favoring poetry that is postmodern or postconfessional, neoformalist or avant-garde, ethnic or mainstream, most anthologies, critical essays, and conferences reassert these boundaries. In recent years, conceptions of American poetry have expanded to include minority writers of African, Asian, and Latino descent, and the domain of British poetry has also begun to include "black British" writers. But the story of the globalization of English-language poetry remains largely untold.

Yet a rich and vibrant poetry has issued from the hybridization of the English muse with the long-resident muses of Africa, India, the Caribbean, and other decolonizing territories of the British empire. Postcolonial poets have dramatically expanded the contours of English-language poetry by infusing it with indigenous metaphors and rhythms, creoles and genres. The Indian poet A. K. Ramanujan imports the metaphoric compression of literary Tamil into English, the Jamaican poet Louise Bennett the phonemic wit and play of Jamaican creole words like "boonoonoonoos" for "pretty" or "boogooyagga" for "worthless." The Ugandan poet Okot p'Bitek adapts graphic idioms, images, and rhetorical strategies from Acoli songs: his spurned character Lawino complains—in language unprecedented in English poetry—that her husband's tongue is "hot like the penis of the bee" and "fierce like the arrow of the scorpion, /

Deadly like the spear of the buffalo-hornet."[1] At the same time, postcolonial poets have brilliantly remade the literary language and forms of the colonizer. Wole Soyinka engrafts resonant Elizabethan English onto Yoruba syntax and myth, Derek Walcott turns the Greek Philoctetes into an allegorical figure for postcolonial affliction, and Lorna Goodison adapts Western figures of femininity, such as Penelope and the Mermaid, to a Caribbean geography and history. Belonging to multiple worlds that are transformed by their convergence, postcolonial poets indigenize the Western and anglicize the native to create exciting new possibilities for English-language poetry.

In light of these achievements, why is postcolonial poetry so much less visible than fiction and drama? T. S. Eliot's remark in "The Social Function of Poetry" (1945) remains suggestive more than half a century later: "No art," he said, "is more stubbornly national than poetry." For Eliot, "Poetry is much more local than prose," partly because "poetry has primarily to do with the expression of feeling and emotion." This way of thinking about poetry can be traced back hundreds of years to European romanticism and the belief that the nation defined and expressed itself through its poetry, the ultimate embodiment of the *Sprachgeist*.[2] If poetry purifies the dialect of the tribe, then the poet or critic may feel little need to bother with the dialects of alien tribes. But the idea of a national literature was already being stretched by Eliot's own transnational affiliations and practices, dramatized by the rapid cartographic displacements in *The Waste Land* from London to Mylae, Carthage, Smyrna, and the Himalayas. Further attenuated by poets of ethnic and racial minorities, the nationalist paradigm faces yet more erosion with the emergence of "world poetry" as a rubric. But here, too, both change and recalcitrance are evident. When three major anthologies of world poetry— one avant-garde, the other two mainstream—were published between 1996 and 1998, the popular academic journal *Lingua Franca* translated the results in a world map "scaled according to the number of poets represented" in the anthologies. Although the map presumably showed the new global face of poetry studies, all of Africa, India, and the Caribbean could have fit within a quarter of the space allotted to the United States or Europe. Thus, neither the mainstream nor the postmodern version of world poetry has transfigured the geography of English-language poetry. A much earlier calculation of relative literary worth, Macaulay's infamous 1835 minute on Indian education, is a benchmark of how much such attitudes have and have not evolved: "A single shelf of a good European Library," he reckoned, "was worth the whole native literature of India and Arabia."[3]

At opposite ends of a polarized field, two recent American anthologies of contemporary poetry provide further clues as to why poetry studies has remained particularly resistant to internationalization. If the assumption is made, in the words of a widely used mainstream anthology, that "what distinguishes the work of contemporary poets . . . is especially the presence and vitality of the personal element," then a principal reason for inattention to postcolonial poets becomes clear, since personal "expression of feeling and emotion" is obviously inadequate as a paradigm for their work.[4] Nor are the terms of valorization for postmodern poetry germane. The signal ideas vaunted in a representative anthology are the "empty sign," "empty words," the "aleatory," writtenness, inorganicity, and the effacement of the signified.[5] But the idea that the poetic "I" represents either an inviolably private interior or an ideological sham bears little on the first-person pronoun in a short poem about the linguistic tear of the Middle Passage by a writer of Guyanese origin, Grace Nichols:[6]

I have crossed an ocean
I have lost my tongue
from the root of the old one
a new one has sprung

Neither poetry conceived as the lyric expression of personal feeling nor as the postmodern negation of commodified language is sufficient to help us enter into the work of Louise Bennett, Okot p'Bitek, or A. K. Ramanujan, whose poetry mediates between oral practices and imported literary forms; reclaims indigenous histories, landscapes, and traditions; and constitutes "imagined communities" in the wake of their threatened colonial destruction.[7]

If the field of contemporary poetry has been unreceptive to the expansion of English-language poetry beyond the West, then perhaps postcolonial studies could be presumed to embrace this body of work. Unfortunately, it hasn't. In contrast to the many volumes on fiction and even drama, there are no books on postcolonial poetry of the Third World.[8] The same pattern holds for critical essays on postcolonial literatures: each of two significant volumes, for example, contains five essays explicitly on fiction but none on poetry.[9] Similarly, one of the most cogent book-length overviews of postcolonial studies cites no poems as examples.[10] At a time when "world," "Third World," "non-Western," and "postcolonial literatures" in English have become ever more prominent in the globalizing curricula of secondary schools and colleges, how can we explain this relative neglect? Although critical interest in poetry has suffered a general decline in recent decades, assumptions within postcolonial studies compound the problem. On the one hand, postcolonial criticism is largely grounded in mimetic presuppositions about literature. But since poetry mediates experience through a language of exceptional figural and formal density, it is a less transparent medium by which to recuperate the history, politics, and sociology of postcolonial societies; it is less favorable than other genres for curricular expeditions into the social history of the Third World; and, consequently, it is harder to annex as textual synecdoche for the social world of Nigeria, Trinidad, or India.[11] On the other hand, postcolonial theory has been preoccupied with continually interrogating itself, rehearsing questions about its complicity in European discourses, the (non)representability of "other" cultures, and the definition of its primary terms, including "nation," "hybridity," "the other," and "postcolonial" itself. While theoretical inquiry is not necessarily inimical to poetry (informing, indeed, my analysis), the genre also demands specifically literary modes of response and recognition—of figurative devices, generic codes, stanzaic patterns, prosodic twists, and allusive turns.

Postcolonial studies and poetics nevertheless offer a potentially valuable blend of strategies for exploring this important and varied body of work. Poetics helps to reveal the literary energies of these texts, which aesthetically embody the postcolonial condition in particular linguistic and formal structures. The best postcolonial poems are resonant and compelling in no small part because of their figurative reach, verbal dexterity, tonal complexity, and their imaginative transformation of inherited genres, forms, and dramatic characters. In turn, the concept of postcoloniality—decolonizing indigenous cultures once subjugated under colonial rule and responding to its continuing aftermath—provides a comparative framework more bounded and historical than "world poetry" but less restrictive than "national" or "regional" poetry. Although the terms "postcolonial," "Third World," and "non-Western" have often been criticized for erasing cultural and historical differences, they can be useful in highlighting similarities and differences among various cultures still grappling with their colonial histories.[12] They can help to illuminate the robust variety of indigenous cultures living in the shadow of empire, whereas more local perspectives often make it difficult to recognize such cross-cultural relationships. Further, even supposedly particularist frameworks cannot help but yoke together heterogeneous experiences under labels of region (Asia), nation (India), religion (Islam), or some combination (Muslim India). Criticism and anthologies tend to focus on a national or regional group of writers, such as West Indian poets, African poets, Indian poets. A poet like A. K. Ramanujan is almost always read as

"Indian," Louise Bennett as "Jamaican" or "West Indian," Okot p'Bitek as "African," "East African," or "Ugandan." These contexts are indispensable, but they are not exhaustive, so I use the postcolonial horizon in concert with them to reveal the cross-cultural dimensions of the poetry.[13] A few proleptic examples may be illustrative. Boldly mocking Jamaican racism, emigration, and even independence, Louise Bennett participates in both a Jamaican performance tradition and a transnational poetics of postcolonial irony. A. K. Ramanujan compares an artificial waterfall inside a Chicago bank to "wavering snakeskins" and thus borrows an ancient Tamil metaphor, but we miss something unless we also notice that his double vision is also more broadly postcolonial. Okot p'Bitek was trained at Oxford as an anthropologist specializing in East African oral literature, yet his poetry instances a postcolonial ambivalence toward the discipline, both appropriating ethnographic modes of representation and fiercely rejecting British anthropology's Eurocentric values and Christian bias in the 1960s.

The scope of "postcoloniality" is vast, so in this study I circumscribe it with the specificities of English colonial history, language, and literature and focus on three major areas of the anglophone Third World: India, Africa, and the Caribbean. I also leave aside the white settler colonies or "dominions" of Canada, Australia, and New Zealand because their dominant literary practices and economies have more in common with the West's than with the anglophone Third World's. Despite critical efforts at establishing a unitary vocabulary for all varieties of postcoloniality, enormous differences in the colonial experience of these First World countries and in their ties with the "motherland" set them apart.[14] An island with a long and violent colonial history, Ireland is a fascinatingly ambiguous case, now of the First World but once kin to the Third. Exploring the controversial question of whether Yeats should be read as a postcolonial poet, I discuss this liminal example to reexamine some of the major concepts through which postcoloniality has been defined and debated: after colonialism, anticolonialism, nationalism, the Third World, and hybridity.[15]

In place of a general survey of regions and trends, I try to make vivid the achievement of postcolonial poetry in English through case studies of four Third World poets and an Irishman. I begin with reinterpretations of poets well-known to Western readers—W. B. Yeats (1865–1939) and Derek Walcott (b. 1930)—and then turn to authors known chiefly among followers of regional or national traditions: A. K. Ramanujan (1929–93), Louise Bennett (b. 1919), and Okot p'Bitek (1931–82). Though a small sampling, the preeminent anglophone poets of Ireland, Saint Lucia, India, Jamaica, and

Uganda represent a wide range of literary practices and proclivities, from the literary internationalism of Yeats and Walcott to the "folk" orality of Okot and Bennett, from Walcott's massive epic and Okot's long poems to Bennett's pithy ballads, Yeats's concentrated lyrics, and Ramanujan's ruminative texts. Arrayed chronologically, their work spans much of the twentieth century, with Yeats publishing perhaps his best poetry in the 1910s, 1920s, and 1930s, Bennett publishing hers in the 1940s, 1950s, and early 1960s, Okot his in the mid- and late 1960s, Ramanujan his in the 1970s and 1980s, and Walcott—to single out his masterpiece from over half a century of achievement—in 1990.

In view of their regional, historical, and aesthetic differences, what could these widely diverse poets have in common? To begin with, they were all born to colonial populations under British rule and continued to write in the aftermath of political decolonization. They all had a British colonial education, which Walcott has called "the greatest bequest the Empire made": "Precisely because of their limitations our early education must have ranked with the finest in the world."[16] This gift may also have been the greatest curse of empire, purveyed by missionaries and by imperial governments as a tool for altering native minds and even turning them against themselves. Educated as imperial subjects yet immersed in indigenous traditions and customs, these postcolonial poets grew up in the potentially productive tension between an imposed and an inherited culture—productive, that is, for the powerful literary mind that can create imaginative forms to articulate the dualities, ironies, and ambiguities of this cultural in-betweenness. Poetry—a genre rich in paradox and multivalent symbols, irony and metaphor—is well-suited to mediating and registering the contradictions of split cultural experience. These poets respond with emotional ambivalence and linguistic versatility to the experience of living after colonialism, between non-Western traditions and modernity, at a moment of explosive change in the relation between Western and "native" cultures.

Postcolonial studies offers the metaphor of "hybridity" as a potent lens through which to explore interculturation in the postcolonial world. Since the term can be misleading if it muffles the power differences between cultures or oversimplifies the multilayered deposits within any single culture, I use it to describe the intensified hybridization of already mixed and politically unequal cultures, where "native" represents a prior knotting together of diverse strands, as does the amalgamation "British."[17] A number of theorists have deepened our understanding of postcoloniality as interstitial, beyond identitarian boundaries. In influential variations on postcolonial hybridity, Edward Said has theorized the "global," Homi Bhabha "the Third Space," Stuart Hall "diaspora identities," James Clifford "traveling cultures," Gayatri Spivak "the 'native' informant," and Mary Louise Pratt "contact zones."[18] Other writers have revealed the hybridity of specific postcolonial regions. "Cultural traditions in India are indissolubly plural and often conflicting," Ramanujan observes.[19] Kwame Anthony Appiah highlights the "extraordinary diversity of Africa's peoples and its cultures," and Paul Gilroy "the stereophonic, bilingual, or bifocal cultural forms" of the African diaspora.[20] The Martinican novelist and theorist Edouard Glissant has formulated the "cross-culturality," the Barbadian poet and historian Edward Kamau Brathwaite the "creolization" of the Caribbean.[21] Although Mikhail Bakhtin relegates poetry to the status of purified, monologic utterance, postcolonial poetry instances the "artistic hybridization" he identifies with the novel. To the extent that postcolonial poems unconsciously mix the "sociolinguistic . . . world views" of colonizer and colonized, they are what he defines as "organic hybrids." They are also often what he calls "intentional hybrids," in which different "socio-linguistic points of view" are "set against each other dialogically," with an emphasis on the "collision" between First World and Third.[22]

Members of a small educated elite, anglophone poets of the Third World are perhaps especially hybridized by their intensive exposure to Western ideas and values through higher education, travel, even expatriation. Journeying in their midtwenties to the metropole, Bennett studied at the Royal Academy of Dramatic Art in London and Okot p'Bitek at Oxford's Institute of Social Anthropology. Further complicating the matrices of identity, many postcolonial poets have an oblique relation to the native culture that they are assumed to represent. Both Yeats and Walcott grew up in predominantly Catholic countries but belonged to Protestant minorities. Ramanujan spoke Tamil at home, along with English, in an area where Kannada was the regional language. These intercultural and intracultural dynamics—whether experienced as a condition of tragic mixture and alienation or as the comic integration of multiple energies and sources—have fueled some of the most powerful poetry of our time. While many First World poets have circumnavigated the postwar globe in search of fresh encounters, postcolonial poets, even when staying at home, have long inhabited cultural spaces that are thoroughly multilingual and multicultural.[23]

Before examining the hybrid language and form of postcolonial poetry, we need to remind ourselves of the primary historical cause of this confluence between Third World and Western cultures. Anglophone poetry in the

Third World, like many other culturally hybrid forms, was an indirect consequence of the violent intersection between the British empire and various native cultures—not a mysterious species that spontaneously generated itself in random parts of the world. Postcolonial poetry, as the term itself suggests, is largely unintelligible without some sense of its historical origins. The great scope of postcolonial poetry in English is directly related to the size of the empire that initially wrapped much of the globe in its language and, more recently, to the expanding technological and economic might of the United States. The British empire—the largest, most powerful, best organized of its peers—colonized enormous chunks of the non-Western world, expropriating land, raw materials, and labor from its widely scattered territories overseas. By the beginning of World War I, more than three-quarters of the earth's surface was under direct European dominion, one-quarter of that British, with most of this colonization having occurred during the preceding hundred years. The deep and lasting effects of this colonial expansion still reverberate around the world today, long after the postwar political breakup of most of the British and other European empires. Indeed, the First World and not just the Third would be unrecognizable without its colonial history. Underscoring Europe's dependence on Third World labor for economic advancement, Frantz Fanon remarks starkly: "Europe is literally the creation of the Third World."[24] This material dependence has its psychopolitical corollary in Edward Said's theory of orientalism, according to which "the Orient," and perhaps more broadly the Third World, "has helped to define Europe (or the West) as its contrasting image, idea, personality, experience."[25]

Fanon's *Les damnés de la terre* (*The Wretched of the Earth* [1961]) still stands as the single most vivid reminder of the historical violence of modern European colonialism. According to Fanon, this violence is military (the force by which the settler takes land from the native), cultural ("the violence with which the supremacy of white values is affirmed"), and existential ("a systematic negation of the other person").[26] Fanon famously describes the colonial world as "a Manichean world," "a world cut in two," with the native continually debased and dehumanized.[27] Systematic, efficient, and deeply disruptive, modern colonialism forces "the people it dominates to ask themselves the question constantly: 'In reality, who am I?'"[28] Fanon's vision of the colonial divide remains an indispensable point of departure for interpreting postcolonial culture, even as we have become more aware of nuances of mutual entanglement and historical difference elided by his schematic account. Modern colonial history was not identical, of course, in different European empires, and even British imperialism took on vastly different forms in different regions of the Third World. Crudely put, its most consequential ingredient in the Caribbean was the massive enslavement and deracination of Africans; in Africa, its history was shorter than in the Caribbean, and its implementation more brutally dualistic than in India; and its historical evolution was more incremental in India, its political structure less rigidly Manichean. These broad differences are reflected in the less overtly political tenor of much anglophone Indian writing, the binary structure of much postcolonial African literature, and the agonized quest for an ancestral home in many Caribbean texts.

But none of these propensities is exclusive to a single region. The retrospective quest in Caribbean literature, for example, has its equivalent in other postcolonial literatures. Indeed, this is the first of several broad tendencies that I outline below, hazarding some rough-and-ready generalizations about the bearings of postcolonial poetry before I turn to more particularized readings in subsequent chapters. Fanon's analysis suggests why historical recovery should be such an urgent and pervasive imperative of postcolonial poetry: "By a kind of perverted logic, [colonialism] turns to the past of the oppressed people, and distorts, disfigures, and destroys it. This work of devaluing pre-colonial history takes on a dialectical significance today"—namely, "native intellectuals . . . decided to back further and to delve deeper down; and, let us make no mistake, it was with the greatest delight that they discovered that there was nothing to be ashamed of in the past, but rather dignity, glory, and solemnity."[29] Searching through oral inheritances, written histories, and personal memories, many postcolonial poets seek to give voice to a past that colonialism has degraded, garbled, even gagged. The Nigerian Christopher Okigbo builds poems around the precolonial Igbo river goddess Idoto, as does Soyinka around the Yoruba god Ogun. In the Caribbean, the lesser availability of the ancestral past often spurs a still more intensive quest for its recovery. In *Masks* (1968), the second volume of his epic trilogy *The Arrivants* (1967–69), Brathwaite searches for the occluded sources of many Afro-Caribbean cultural and religious practices. Bennett emphasizes the African provenance of Jamaican words like "nana" and "gungoo." Even Walcott, though suspicious of the longing for ancestral return, makes it a centerpiece of *Omeros:* the sunstruck hero Achille sees himself "mirrored" in his African forefather's features—"the white teeth, the widening hands"—and Ma Kilman conjures the dimly remembered powers of the gods "Erzulie, // Shango, and Ogun."[30] One way of approaching the question "Who am I?" these poets suggest, is to ask "Who were we?"

The recuperative quest in postcolonial poetry is nevertheless qualified by a countervailing skepticism. Even the most "nativist" poets, such as Bennett and Okot, acknowledge that this past has been transformed irrevocably by colonialism and modernity. Fanon again provides insight when he warns against fetishizing and embalming the precolonial past: artists who "turn their backs on foreign culture, deny it, and set out to look for a true national culture . . . forget that the forms of thought and what it feeds on, together with modern techniques of information, language, and dress have dialectically reorganized the people's intelligences and that the constant principles which acted as safeguards during the colonial period are now undergoing extremely radical changes."[31] In postcolonial poetry, this skepticism is often intertwined with the recuperative dynamic it checks. Upon Achille's imaginative arrival in Africa, Walcott's hero—like the poet himself—cannot help but see his ancestral land through the prism of Hollywood rivers, hippopotami, and warriors in "African movies / he had yelped at in childhood."[32] When Brathwaite in *The Arrivants* likewise "come[s] / back a stranger / after three hundred years" to the mother continent, he feels he has a "hacked / face, hollowed eyes, / undrumming heart": he learns that centuries of creolized life in the New World have made it impossible to merge with his African heritage.[33] Brathwaite's and Walcott's skepticism should not be confused with the postmodernist renunciation of all nostalgias, since it is inextricable from the continuing postcolonial drive to rediscover the past.

Postcolonial poets often figure the desire to recuperate the precolonial past as the troubled search for an ancestral home, irreparably damaged by colonialism, as in a poem by the Ghanaian Kofi Awoonor:

The weaver bird built in our house
And laid its eggs on our only tree
. . . .
We look for new homes every day,
For new altars we strive to re-build
The old shrines defiled by the weaver's excrement.[34]

With the departure of the colonizers, this defilement has in many cases continued, now unleashed by the native regimes that replaced the visiting weaver bird. Like the district commissioners and security forces of an earlier era, African dictators, thugs, and thieves have ravaged the native home in many sub-Saharan states. Having "longed for returning," the Gambian Lenrie Peters writes of bitter disillusionment in his poem "Home Coming":

> There at the edge of town
> Just by the burial ground
> Stands the house without a shadow
> Lived in by new skeletons.[35]

To return home is in many cases to reenter mere ruins haunted by the murdered and massacred dead. Often the African poet has returned after a period of solitary confinement or exile. Handcuffed, the Malawian Jack Mapanje watches his mother furiously challenge the police, "How dare you scatter this peaceful house?" Imprisoned for nearly four years without charge or trial, Mapanje is released too late to learn from his now-dead mother "the rites / Of homing in."[36] Fearing for their lives, African poets have often had to leave home: another Malawian, Frank Chipasula, has lived abroad during the long dictatorship of Hastings Banda; Okot p'Bitek spent the years of Idi Amin's brutal rule in exile; and Soyinka secretly left Nigeria when General Sani Abacha's regime confiscated his passport. Other poets have stayed at home and died. At the age of thirty-five, the influential Christopher Okigbo was killed while fighting on the Biafran side in the Nigerian civil war—the first of many civil wars to tear apart postindependence Africa. His prophetic "Come Thunder" compounds frightful details with terrifying abstractions:

> The smell of blood already floats in the lavender-mist of the afternoon.
> The death sentence lies in ambush along the corridors of power;
> And a great fearful thing already tugs at the cables of the open air,
> A nebula immense and immeasurable, a night of deep waters—
> An iron dream unnamed and unprintable, a path of stone.[37]

So too, the charismatic "dub" or performance poet Michael Smith, still in his twenties, was stoned to death by hired thugs in 1983, a day after he spoke out at a political rally during Jamaican elections. The political homelessness lamented with mounting despair in African poetry has, for obvious reasons, no equivalent in anglophone Caribbean or Indian poetry, yet poets from these parts of the world have also accused postcolonial regimes of defacing the native dwelling. Appalled by the damage inflicted by the tourist industry on the landscape of Saint Lucia, Walcott, for example, places in the volcanic hell of *Omeros* "the traitors / / who, in elected office, saw the land as views / for hotels."[38]

Seeking to reclaim the native home despoiled by both European colonialism and the internalized colonialism of more recent governments, some postcolonial poets nevertheless worry that their quest for the past paradoxi-

cally shunts it beyond their grasp. In "Postcard from Kashmir," Agha Shahid
Ali suggests that memory and artifice transform the very past he pursues:

> Kashmir shrinks into my mailbox;
> my home a neat four by six inches.
>
> I always loved neatness. Now I hold
> the half-inch Himalayas in my hand.
>
> This is home. And this the closest
> I'll ever be to home. When I return,
> the colours won't be so brilliant,
> the Jhelum's waters so clean,
> so ultramarine. My love
> so overexposed.[39]

The postcolonial poem, like a postcard, risks miniaturizing, idealizing, and ultimately displacing the remembered native landscape. The Kashmiri Ali dramatizes the postcolonial and diasporic condition that Homi Bhabha, adapting
Freud's *das Unheimliche,* terms "unhomeliness—that is the condition of extraterritorial and cross-cultural initiations."[40] When Okot p'Bitek returned to
Africa to collect "folk" songs of the Acoli and Lango, his British training in
anthropology had irrevocably transformed his relation to his native home.

   Whether going abroad or staying home, postcolonial poets have been
unhoused by modernity and colonialism, by war and politics, by education
and travel, even perhaps by their own artifice, and are thus unable to rest se-
curely in what Bhabha calls the idea of culture "as a homogenizing, unifying
force, authenticated by the originary Past."[41] In Grace Nichols's "Wherever I
Hang," an expatriate speaker affirms "home," but only as a self-conscious
fiction of belonging wherever she finds herself. Playing on Walcott's famous
tortured lines about being "divided to the vein" in "A Far Cry from Africa"
and possibly answering Brathwaite's agonized question, "Where then is the
nigger's / home?" in *The Arrivants,* Nichols writes:[42]

> To tell you de truth
> I don't know really where I belaang
>
>> Yes, divided to de ocean
>> Divided to de bone
>
> Wherever I hang me knickers—that's my home.

The Britishness of "knickers" doesn't deter the poet from transvaluing it as
an ironic marker of "home," any more than the imperial origins of her lan-

guage hinder her from colonizing it in reverse. Housed in houselessness, unified in such ironic self-division, the postcolonial poet knows that cultural identity, as Stuart Hall puts it, "is not a fixed essence. . . . It is not a fixed origin to which we can make some final and absolute Return. Of course, it is not a mere phantasm either. It is *something*—not a mere trick of the imagination. . . . The past continues to speak to us. But it no longer addresses us as a simple, factual 'past,' since our relation to it, like the child's relation to the mother, is always-already 'after the break.' It is always constructed through memory, fantasy, narrative and myth."[43] At once ironic and nostalgic, skeptical like Western postmodernists and recuperative like postconfessionalists and multiculturalists, postcolonial poets recathect the precolonial past as a powerful locus of identity, yet self-consciously probe the multiplicity and constructedness of the home they dislocate in the moment of reinhabiting it.

The richly conflictual relation between postcolonial poets and the English language is another important source of their "unhomeliness." Martin Heidegger famously describes language as the home of being, but what if we experience the language we live in as primary home to another?[44] What if that home was first imposed on us by missionaries and governments that considered us racially and culturally inferior? What if we remain attached to another home even as we try to live in and help to refashion the new one? The result is what Gilles Deleuze and Félix Guattari have (perhaps unfortunately) labeled a "minor literature"—the literature of minorities, immigrants, and others who live in, write in, and are "forced to serve" a "deterritorialized" European "language that is not their own." In this literature, "everything takes on a collective value," in contrast to "major literatures," in which "the individual concern (familial, marital, and so on) joins with other no less individual concerns, the social milieu serving as a mere environment or a background."[45] Reflecting on the mixed European provenance of her name and her poetic language, Eunice de Souza, a poet from a Goan Catholic community in India, comments ruefully on the postcolonial condition of linguistic estrangement:

No matter that
my name is Greek
my surname Portuguese
my language alien

There are ways
of belonging.

I belong with the lame ducks.[46]

Sometimes seen as an "alien" and unassimilable intrusion, the English language is experienced, at its worst, as a tool of oppression: "My tongue in English chains," laments the Indian poet R. Parthasarathy.[47] More often the imposed language is seen as both a liability and a treasure—a "radiant affliction" in Walcott's splendid oxymoron.[48] In "Missing Person" by the Bombay poet Adil Jussawalla, the colonial letter *A* is said to be—in contrast to the Hindi alphabet it has displaced—

> here to stay.
> On it St. Pancras station,
> the Indian and African railways.
>
> That's why you learn it today.
>
> Look out the school at the garden:
> how the letter will happen
> the rest of your life:
> bright as a butterfly's wing
> or a piece of tin
> aimed at your throat.[49]

As a schoolboy, the South Asian child sees the letter *A*—inextricable from British colonial expansion in India and Africa—as potentially dangerous ("aimed at your throat") and potentially beautiful ("a butterfly's wing"). Traveling to the seat of empire, Jussawalla's speaker is made to feel, like many former colonial subjects, as if he is stealing and corrupting someone else's language: "'You're polluting our sounds. You're so rude. / / Get back to your language,' they say."[50] Having been forced into an "unhomely" language but assimilating it as their own, postcolonial poets ironically risk being seen— by both Western and indigenous detractors—as occupying a language to which they have no rightful claim.

One postcolonial response to this dilemma is to abandon English and revert to a native language, a strategy that the Kenyan novelist Ngugi wa Thiong'o famously urged for "decolonizing the mind."[51] But many postcolonial writers reject the assumption—traceable to European romanticism—that the English language has an inherent relationship to only one kind of national or ethnic experience. "The English language is nobody's special property," asserts Walcott.[52] Commenting on the postcolonial appropriation and transformation of English, Salman Rushdie observes, "Those peoples who were once colonized by the language are now rapidly remaking it, domesticating it, becoming more and more relaxed about the way they use it—assisted by the English language's enormous flexibility and size, they are carving out large territories for themselves within its frontiers."[53] In "Listen Mr. Oxford don," the Guyanese poet John Agard speaks of "mugging de Queen's English" and "inciting rhyme to riot."[54] He playfully represents his use of West Indian creole as political rebellion by poetic means. However defiant he may be, the speaker recognizes that his relation to Standard English is complex:

> I slashing suffix in self-defence
> I bashing future wit present tense
> and if necessary
>
> I making de Queen's English accessory
> to my offence

As it turns out, the Queen's English is not only the object of the poet's revolt but also, potentially, an instrument and ally. Sometimes critics reduce postcolonial literatures to a comic-book simplicity, in which the colonized Caliban wages a heroic textual war on the colonizing Prospero. But the resistance is seldom unambivalent. In "A Far Cry from Africa," Walcott can refer to "this English tongue I love" even as he recalls having "cursed / The drunken officer of British rule"; so too, Yeats concedes that "everything I love has come to me through English; my hatred tortures me with love, my love with hate."[55] Because their relation to the English language is mediated by a vexed political history, by other languages, and by non-Standard forms, postcolonial poets transform literary English—both angrily and affectionately—in an astonishing variety of ways.

Anglophone poets write in response to different linguistic contexts in different parts of the Third World. In postcolonial Africa, they grow up speaking not only English but one or more indigenous languages as well. In India, a small minority of the population (perhaps 3 percent) speaks English fluently, and English-language poetry is only a small subset of the many bodies of poetry in different Indian languages, native literatures that have themselves been hybridized by global influences. By contrast to India and Africa, almost everyone in the West Indies is from elsewhere ancestrally, so that an Ngugi would find it hard to return to a native language, in the wake of the destruction of most Arawaks, Caribs, and other indigenous populations. Caribbean poets can avail themselves of an English creole formed centuries ago out of the confluence of English with African and European languages and now heard everyday on the street. In the wake of the pioneering creole verse of Claude McKay, Una Marson, and others, Louise Bennett was the first poet to master completely West Indian English as a language for poetry, and many dub poets, such as Michael Smith and Linton Kwesi Johnson, have fol-

lowed her example. To the charge that Jamaican English is a "corruption of
the English language," she makes this spirited response: "If dat be de case,
den dem shoulda call English Language corruption of Norman French an
Latin and all dem tarra [other] language what dem seh [say] dat English is
derived from."[56] Sharing this suspicion of linguistic hierarchy, many West
Indian poets splice together their Standard English with local creoles—even
a poet as different from Bennett as Walcott, whose "code-switching" *Omeros*
and "Sainte Lucie," for example, leap from Standard English to English creole to French patois. In a related strategy, an African poet like Okot p'Bitek
leaves untranslated many Acoli words for native plants, animals, and religious beliefs, forcing the English-language reader to puzzle them out by context. By their macaronic language, postcolonial poets thus challenge the
Standard as the exclusive norm for poetry.

Even when they write in neither an overt English creole nor a native language, postcolonial poets can subtly creolize Standard English. Schooled in
the colonizer's landscape, they pepper Standard English with local place
names like Lughnagall, Jejuri, and Ibadan and intently name flora like the
mango and red champac tree, fauna like the paradise flycatcher and colobus
monkey. Sometimes all the words are the same as those of a Standard English
dictionary, but the postcolonial poet has still other ways of indigenizing English and English poetic forms. Agha Shahid Ali comments on his attempt at
the "biryanization . . . of English," specifically his desire to bring "the music
of Urdu" into English-language poetry.[57] Before Brathwaite adapted a variety
of Afro-Caribbean musical traditions, their propulsive force had not been
much felt in English poetry: "And / Ban / Ban / Cal- / iban / like to play / pan
/ at the Car- / nival."[58] Straddling languages, Okot p'Bitek inserts literally
rendered Acoli idioms and tropes into English (e.g., the earlier cited metaphor, a tongue is "hot like the penis of the bee"). The astonishingly elastic
syntax of Soyinka's poetry, particularly in the poet's earliest volumes, "yoru-
bizes" English-language poetry. The difficulty of the poem "Dawn" instances
the intercultural effect of hybridizing two syntactic systems:

> Breaking earth upon
> A spring-haired elbow, lone
> A palm beyond head-grains, spikes
> A guard of prim fronds, piercing
> High hairs of the wind[59]

What is the subject? Is the word "spikes" a noun in apposition to the palm or
is it a verb? Delaying the introduction of finite verb and subject for another

four and five lines ("steals / The lone intruder" or sun), Soyinka is forcing English syntax to stretch well beyond its normal breaking point. Yoking English to a local syntax—or vocabulary, rhythm, and idiom—he and other postcolonial writers significantly extend the verbal range of contemporary poetry.

Postcolonial poetry is thus hybrid not only in language but also in form. We might think of the poem "On Becoming a Mermaid," by the gifted Jamaican poet Lorna Goodison, as a dramatization of this process: fish and flesh combine to become what she wonderfully calls—in a line appropriately rife with compounds—"a green-tinged fish/fleshed woman/thing."[60] Because of its stylization, poetry formally embeds a long memory of its diverse cultural inheritances. Brathwaite concludes *The Arrivants* with the hope that Afro-Caribbean peoples, weaving together the disparate sounds and myths deposited in their history, will make, much as he has in his polyphonic poem,

> with their
>
> rhythms some-
> thing torn
>
> and new[61]

But this new composite form, made of a union of disparate fragments of postcolonial inheritance, is seldom a matter of seamless intercultural fusion. Many of these examples of postcolonial poetry more nearly approximate Bakhtin's "intentional hybrids"—strife-riven and dialogic—than his "organic hybrids," but in either case, perhaps the term "hybridity" itself suggests too neat and complete a union of disparate parts. As a "mulatto of style," Walcott encodes in his Greco-African characters and intercontinental genres his cultural "schizophrenia," as either "nobody" or "a nation."[62] At the level of the image, Ramanujan suggests the dizzying gap that separates, even while visual similarities connect, the Indian and the Western parts of his life:

> The traffic light turns orange
> on 57th and Dorchester, and you stumble,
>
> you fall into a vision of forest fires,
> enter a frothing Himalayan river,
>
> rapid, silent.
>
>   On the 14th floor,
> Lake Michigan crawls and crawls
>
> in the window.[63]

In a hallucinatory switch, orange traffic lights flare into forest fires, and a memory of a Himalayan river—leaping across hemispheres—drops into Lake Michigan. The postcolonial poem often mediates between Western and non-Western forms of perception, experience, and language to reveal not only their integration but ultimately the chasm that divides them.

Perhaps the clearest example of formal interculturation in postcolonial poetry is the hybridization of Western literary models and non-Western oral traditions. Because Caribbean poets grow up hearing vibrant English creoles on the street and in the "yard," they draw more heavily on oral traditions than do most Indian poets, whose English tends to be more literary, recalling an ancient written inheritance in indigenous languages. A poet like Kofi Awoonor anglicizes the Ewe dirge tradition in a poem such as "The Weaver Bird." For him, as for many African poets, the most powerful indigenous models are typically oral poems in native languages, so that we can trace images, rhetorical strategies, and whole lines from his "Songs of Sorrow" to traditional Ewe songs. The generic titles of Okot's *Song of Lawino* and *Song of Ocol* indicate their oral provenance, but these hybrid poems are irreducible to either oral African song or Western literary poem.[64] Similarly, to read a poem of Louise Bennett's is to feel plunged in the oral strategies of Jamaican "labrish" or gossip, the wit, puns, and insults of West Indian "broad talk" or performance rhetoric. Yet in the rumshops and in the yard, Jamaican men and women do not typically frame their utterances in the ballad stanza, as Bennett almost always does. To do justice to the formal hybridity of postcolonial poetry, we need to track closely the dazzling interplay between indigenous and Western forms. The postcolonial poem sometimes melds ("an organic hybrid"), at other times sets these resources against each other ("an intentional hybrid"). It may ironize one, both, or neither of its intertexts. In the most successful examples, the result of this intercultural dynamic is transformative—a poem that would have been unimaginable within the confines of one or another culture.

In exploring the complex hybridity of postcolonial poetry, I focus each chapter on the work of an individual poet who has had an especially significant impact on the possibilities of postcolonial poetry in English. Delving into each author's work, I also pursue a theoretical or formal issue that bears more broadly on the poetics of postcoloniality. "Is Yeats a postcolonial poet?" I ask, examining not only the Irishman's eligibility for recanonization but also the field's definitional boundaries. Walcott, one of Yeats's avowed postcolonial inheritors, represents the colonial history of Afro-Caribbean suffering through the emblem of the wound, but this trope turns out to have astonishingly diverse cultural origins, problematizing overly determinate national or ethnic genealogies of postcolonial literature. In the ensuing chapter, I probe Ramanujan's use of metaphor as a rhetorical locus for double vision, making use of the surprising intersections between theories of metaphor and of postcoloniality. Likewise, I argue that Bennett and other postcolonial writers, hybridizing often contradictory cultural perspectives, find in irony, too, a potent linguistic correlative for their biculturalism. Finally, to reexamine assumptions about the relation between anthropology and postcolonial literatures, I study dramatic monologues by the "native anthropologist" Okot p'Bitek to reveal their hybridization not only of Western and African poetics but also of ethnographic and antiethnographic discourses. Engaging the critical literature on individual postcolonial poets, poetic theory, postcolonial studies, and anthropology, I hope that these essays may be of some help in both internationalizing the field of contemporary poetry in English and strengthening the position of poetry within postcolonial studies.

This book began when my personal experience of hybridity came together with a professional devotion to poetry. My interest in postcoloniality is inseparable from having grown up between Western and Third World cultures. Since I am neither Indian, nor African, nor Caribbean, my relation to the cultures explored in this volume is oblique, but it includes the hyphenated experience of someone with attachments to both Western and non-Western cultures and societies. To "declare" my geopolitical "baggage" at the outset, I am a secular Anglo-Persian American, born to a father of Iranian Muslim origin and a mother with a Zoroastrian Iranian father and a Protestant English mother. Growing up with parents naturalized as U.S. citizens, I have had the economic and academic advantages of the First World and have absorbed cultural codes and perspectives from my extended Persian family. While my personal background obviously bears on my interest in the Third World, I suspect that my preoccupation with the defamiliarizing language of poetry may also be rooted in the intercultural experience of a life seen partly from the estranging perspective of the "Orient." Early on, my fascination with the "poetic" texture of language was likely piqued, as it is for many bicultural children, by hearing a non-Western language at home. Shared by more and more readers of English-language poetry, this interstitial background is no longer unusual. Whatever our personal histories, I believe that postcolonial poetry has a great deal to teach us about our relation to an increasingly intercultural and interlocking globe. From the hybrid muse, perhaps we can begin to gain some measure of understanding of the aesthetics, language, and experience of the contemporary world.

CHAPTER TWO

☙ W. B. Yeats:

A Postcolonial Poet?

In life, Yeats was notoriously a member of many literary and hermetic clubs, such as the Rhymer's Club, the Irish Literary Society, and the Golden Dawn. Since his death, he has often been defined by association with a more general company, be it liberals or fascists, the romantics or the moderns. The multifarious Yeats is ripe for reconsideration yet again, now as a candidate for posthumous admission to yet another assembly: the recently institutionalized society of postcolonial writers. Sponsors for his membership could easily find in his curriculum vitae reasons enough to argue on his behalf. They could start by placing Yeats in the first nation to emerge from British colonial rule in the twentieth century, before the decolonization of Africa, the Indian subcontinent, and the Caribbean. They could adduce Yeats's anticolonial resistance to British cultural domination and his nationalist effort to transform the degraded colonial present by recuperating the precolonial past. Yet another angle might be to draw comparisons between Yeats's writing and that of the group's principal members, showing his poetry to be similarly preoccupied with issues of hybridity, cultural identity, and national formation. In valuable testimonials, Edward Said, David Lloyd, and Declan Kiberd have begun to sketch such arguments for Yeats's postcoloniality, though the case has yet to be laid out systematically.[1] Opponents, too, would find in Yeats's profile plenty of grist for their mill. Ridiculing the notion of Yeats as decolonizing rebel, they would cite his long-time membership in the colonizer's club, along with other withered white males. They would bar the canonical poet on account of his Eurocentrism, his whiteness, and his affiliation with the centuries-old settler community of Anglo-Irish Protestants. Opponents on the left would find allies on the right in arguing that Yeats's writing flows within the mainstream of English letters.

Amplifying the rhetoric of "inclusion" and "exclusion," the conceit of a postcolonial club, like the more naturalized idea of a traditional canon, implies a consensus and stability that need to be qualified in the ensuing discussion, which parses multiple definitions of postcoloniality in relation to Yeats. Moreover, the issue of Yeats's "eligibility" for postcolonial status depends not merely on questions of definition; it inevitably gets entangled in institutional interests as well. For the constituencies of Yeats studies, modern studies, and poetry studies, the claiming of Yeats as postcolonial can help renew attention to a poet who, often charged with antifeminism and reactionary politics, has been losing ground to postmodernism, antiformalism, and ethnic writing. Even so, some scholars in these fields will demur at sacrificing emergent writers for a monolith, while others will rush to protect Yeats from a critical fad, and still others worry about obscuring Yeats's affiliations with established writers such as Shelley, Blake, and Pound. Yeats's "postcolonization" can strengthen the claim of Irish studies to be a player in the vibrant field of postcolonial studies, though some critics in this area will balk at recanonizing an Anglo-Irish writer, and others will deny the postcoloniality of all Irish writers, dissociating Ireland from the Third World or viewing Ireland as having been integrated within Britain by the 1800 Act of Union. For postcolonial literary criticism, to adopt Yeats is to fend off ethnic and racial essentialism, to enhance dialogue between modernists and postcolonialists, and to make visible Yeats's global affinities and his influences on writers as diverse as Derek Walcott and Lorna Goodison from the West Indies, Raja Rao and A. K. Ramanujan from India, and Chinua Achebe and Christopher Okigbo from Africa. But for some postcolonialists, to cede Yeats a curricular place within a field cleared for once-subjugated peoples of different colors and ethnicities would be to allow a form of colonial reoccupation. By virtue of his initial position, Yeats's appearance on the postcolonial syllabus risks making him look like the great white male father to a multicolored progeny. It would be naive to suppose that such dangers can be defused, such turf struggles resolved by my hermeneutic study of Yeats within the contexts of postcoloniality.[2] My aim is to determine whether the necessary, not the sufficient, conditions exist for redescribing Yeats as "postcolonial." Influenced probably as much by my institutional identifications as by Yeats's c.v., I answer—as postcolonialist, modernist, and Yeatsian—with a qualified yes.

If Yeats is to be put under the postcolonial microscope, the many different shapes and sizes of postcoloniality need to be distinguished. The introduction of the alien element "Yeats" into these conceptual spheres can help to catalyze a rethinking not only of his poetry but of postcoloniality itself. The primary construal of the prefix is "after" colonialism—that is, after the withdrawal of occupying forces and the establishment of a self-determining nation.[3] Notwithstanding the technicalities of the Act of Union, Ireland was colonized militarily, politically, economically, educationally, and religiously until it emerged from British rule in Yeats's lifetime. But this apparently straightforward criterion snares the taxonomist in various critical traps, raising questions such as whether only Yeats's later poetry is "postcolonial" and his early work "colonial." Since much of Yeats's postindependence poetry is either politically skeptical or Ascendancy-identified, while some of his preindependence poetry is explicitly nationalist, this definition produces the seeming absurdities of Yeats the postcolonial colonialist and Yeats the colonial anticolonialist. There is also the question of which date should be cited as the moment of Ireland's emergence into postcoloniality. As Stuart Hall asks, "When was 'the post-colonial?'"[4] If the Easter Rising of 1916 is the crucial moment, "Easter, 1916" would qualify as postcolonial. But this poem and others begin to disappear from the syllabus if the originary moment is the 1919 drafting of the Declaration of Independence, or the Government of Ireland Act of 1920, or the 1922 establishment of the Irish Free State, or De Valera's 1937 Constitution. Yeats is completely out of luck if the postcolonial era dawned when the Republic of Ireland was officially founded in 1949 or— for that matter—when the partition might one day be dissolved between the six counties of the North and the lower twenty-six. The question of the threshold of postcoloniality bears as much on writers whose postcolonial status is unquestioned as on Yeats, such as V. S. Naipaul (Trinidad), Léopold Sédar Senghor (Senegal), or R. K. Narayan (India), who were publishing now-established postcolonial works long before independence. To shift the criterion from political to cultural independence is unlikely to be helpful, since if "post" means being free from the colonizer's cultural marks and deposits, no anglophone writing is entirely *post*colonial. If postcoloniality is construed not as after decolonization but as since colonization, then Yeats is more easily swept whole into the postcolonial canon, but so too would be all kinds of Irish literature since the twelfth century, perhaps stretching the term "postcolonial" beyond use.

For these and other reasons, many literary critics now prefer anticolonialism over postindependence or postcolonization as the defining criterion for postcoloniality.[5] This concept of postcoloniality as resistance to the discourses of colonization has the advantage of recognizing the continuity of oppositional writing before and after independence and of granting political efficacy to postcolonial literatures (in what may now seem noncontroversial struggles). Does any of Yeats's poetry make the grade of explicit anticolonialism? There is the impressively bitter and satiric "Ghost of Roger Casement," whose titular hero was hanged by the British for attempting to transport arms from Germany into Ireland. Summoning the vengeful ghost of Roger Casement, Yeats personifies Britain as the detested John Bull, mocks popular electoral support for British imperialism, and ridicules the racial grounds for oppressing Indians and other colonized peoples:

> John Bull has stood for Parliament,
> A dog must have his day,
> The country thinks no end of him
> For he knows how to say
> At a beanfeast or a banquet,
> That all must hang their trust
> Upon the British Empire,
> Upon the Church of Christ.
>
> *The Ghost of Roger Casement*
> *Is beating on the door.*
>
> John Bull has gone to India
> And all must pay him heed
> For histories are there to prove
> That none of another breed
> Has had a like inheritance,
> Or sucked such milk as he,
> And there's no luck about a house
> If it lack honesty.[6]

If overtly anticolonial expression is required of the postcolonial writer, such late poetry is Yeats's least ambiguous credential. As Conor Cruise O'Brien observes, "Anti-English feeling, long dormant in Yeats, became increasingly pronounced in the period 1937–38."[7] Yeats's anti-British rage was so intense that it colored and perhaps even determined his views on world events, such as the Spanish Civil War: "I am an old Fenian," he declares in a 1937 letter, "and I think the old Fenian in me would rejoice if a Fascist nation or government controlled Spain because that would weaken the British Empire, force England to be civil to India and loosen the hand of English finance in the far East of which I hear occasionally."[8] Though he goes on to qualify this view as "mere instinct" and "a thing I would never act on," Yeats's late applause for right-wing dictatorship could be seen as arising in part from the ferocity of his anticolonialism.

But the British imperial devastation of Ireland also haunts Yeats's early and middle poetry. At twenty-one, Yeats allegorizes Ireland as a bleeding, rock-enchained youth in "The Two Titans" (1886), and in *The Wanderings of Oisin* (1889) a still enchained, if now feminized, Ireland is possessed by a "demon dull and unsubduable" (*Poems*, 373). Closing an early volume with "To Ireland in the Coming Times" (1892), the young Fenian refers with moral certitude to "*Ireland's wrong*" and declares his ambition to help "*sweeten*" it (*Poems*, 50). And he opens *In the Seven Woods* (1904) with a poem that laments "Tara uprooted, and new commonness / Upon the throne"—namely, Edward VII (*Poems*, 77). Granted, anti-imperial fervor abates in the poems written between 1903 and the Easter Rising, reflecting Yeats's increasingly bitter quarrels with hard-line nationalists, his equivocal reconciliation with Protestant Ireland, and his optimism about Home Rule.[9] Even so, when Yeats in later life introduces his work as a whole, he highlights, among its most important contexts, Britain's genocidal wreckage of Ireland:

> The "Irishry" have preserved their ancient "deposit" through wars which, during the sixteenth and seventeenth centuries, became wars of extermination; no people, Lecky said at the opening of his *Ireland in the Eighteenth Century*, have undergone greater persecution, nor did that persecution altogether cease up to our own day. No people hate as we do in whom that past is always alive; there are moments when hatred poisons my life and I accuse myself of effeminacy because I have not given it adequate expression.[10]

Despite a silence and complicity that he genders feminine and despite long periods of quiescence, Yeats gives powerful expression to this collective grief and rage. In Yeats's middle age, the executions of the Easter rebels and the Black and Tan brutalities spurred him to anti-imperial verses, such as his elegiac ballads "Sixteen Dead Men" and "The Rose Tree" and bitter poems about the Troubles like "Reprisals" and "Nineteen Hundred and Nineteen." In "Sixteen Dead Men," such expression reaches "treasonable lengths," notes Elizabeth Cullingford.[11] Memorializing a brutal episode in the British suppression of Ireland, he decolonizes the *ubi sunt* tradition in the late poem "The Curse of Cromwell" (1937):

> You ask what I have found and far and wide I go,
> Nothing but Cromwell's house and Cromwell's murderous crew,
> The lovers and the dancers are beaten into the clay,
> And the tall men and the swordsmen and the horsemen where are they?
>   (*Poems*, 304)

"Three Marching Songs" issues a call to remember Ireland's centuries of freedom fighters, executed or slaughtered, sent into exile or life-long hiding because they defended "Ireland's soul":

> Remember all those renowned generations,
> Remember all that have sunk in their blood,
> Remember all that have died on the scaffold,
> Remember all that have fled, that have stood,
> Stood, took death like a tune
> On an old tambourine.
> (*Poems*, 333)

In his anticolonial denunciations of Britain's efforts to exterminate the Irish and to obliterate its indigenous culture, to quash heroic resistance and to lay waste to Ireland's churches and houses, Yeats is no less "postcolonial" than Achebe, who in *Things Fall Apart* fictively recalls England's *Pacification of the Primitive Tribes of the Lower Niger* (the ironized title of the District Commissioner's projected book), or Kamau Brathwaite, who in *The Arrivants* chronicles the survival of African gods in the New World despite colonial efforts to wipe them out, or Salman Rushdie, who renders in *Midnight's Children* the horrifying absurdity of the British massacre at Amritsar. When Yeats, speaking at a political gathering in 1898, declared that the English empire "has been built on the rapine of the world," he anticipated Fanon's claim that the "well-being and the progress of Europe have been built up with the sweat and the dead bodies of Negroes, Arabs, Indians, and the yellow races," as well as, Yeats would have added, the Irish.[12]

But to "postcolonize" Yeats along these lines would be to tell only part of the story, for Yeats was also anti-anti-English. He condemned what he called Ireland's "lunatic faculty of going against everything which it believes England to affirm."[13] Yeats's two explicit mentions of England in his poetry encapsulate his anti-English and his anti-anti-English views—a double negative that it is a mistake to resolve as "procolonial." He praises Parnell for having "fought the might of England" in "Come Gather Round Me Parnellites" (*Poems*, 309); but he also wants to give England the benefit of the doubt in his great elegy for the executed leaders of the Easter Rising, asking courageously,

> Was it needless death after all?
> For England may keep faith
> For all that is done and said.
> (*Poems*, 181–82)

England, the poet concedes, might finally have carried out its promise of
granting Home Rule to Ireland. In his *Reveries over Childhood and Youth*
(1916), Yeats reflects ironically on the anti-English stereotypes he grew up
with:

> I did not think English people intelligent or well-behaved unless they were
> artists. Every one I knew well in Sligo despised Nationalists and Catholics,
> but all disliked England with a prejudice that had come down perhaps from
> the days of the Irish Parliament. I knew stories to the discredit of England,
> and took them all seriously. . . . People would tell [a story] to prove that
> Englishmen were always grumbling. "They grumble about their dinners and
> everything—there was an Englishman who wanted to pull down Knock-
> narea," and so on. My mother had shown them to me kissing at railway sta-
> tions, and taught me to feel disgust at their lack of reserve. . . . My Sligo
> nurses, who had in all likelihood the Irish Catholic political hatred, had never
> spoken well of any Englishman . . . and everybody had told me that English
> people ate skates and even dog-fish.[14]

In a familiar subaltern strategy, these stories and images turn the tables on
English stereotypes of the Irish. It is not the Irish but the English who speak
strangely, eat barbaric food, and fail to restrain sexual appetite. Anticipating
a critique of anticolonial nationalism, from Fanon to Seamus Deane, Yeats
worries that anti-English prejudices invert but ultimately preserve the colonizer's terms.[15] Colonizer and colonized remain trapped within their "other-
izing" preconceptions.

But Yeats's dialectical suspicion of such cultural biases, instead of ex-
cluding him from consideration as a postcolonial writer, makes him typical.
In works like Soyinka's *Death and the King's Horseman,* Naipaul's "One Out of
Many," and Louise Bennett's poems about Jamaican racism and classism, cultural prejudices not only of the colonizer but also of the subaltern come under scrutiny. Indeed, Yeats's anti-anti-Englishness highlights the failure of
"anticolonialism" itself to account for the complex ambivalences of much
postcolonial literature. Yeats became an important precursor for poets like
Walcott and Ramanujan less because of his anticolonial rancor than because
he was able to write into verse his ambivalence toward his own emergent nation—what he called "this blind bitter land" ("Words," *Poems,* 90).

Nationalism, typically the positive obverse of anticolonialism, is yet another widely postulated criterion for postcoloniality. A writer qualifies by
rediscovering and reasserting national identity in the wake of colonial suppression.[16] Theorists of postcoloniality, including Yeats's critics, often cite
Benedict Anderson's concept of "imagined community" to indicate the ulti-

mate creative ambition of the cultural nationalist.[17] For Declan Kiberd, Yeats is the Irish Whitman, the writer most responsible for "inventing Ireland." But R. F. Foster, arguing as a historian against the view that "Yeats made history," would show that "history made him"; Foster wants to distinguish Yeats's cultural nationalism from the political nationalism that effected real change in Ireland.[18] Similarly, Seamus Deane, refocusing attention on the particulars of sociohistorical reality, would undo Yeats's aestheticist mystifications of Irish history.[19] But Yeats's view of the constitutive power of art to create national history and desire, though often mocked as aestheticist fantasy, could be seen as powerfully anticipating the vanguard constructivist trend in cultural studies, poststructuralism, anthropology, metahistory, and other modes of inquiry. "We call certain minds creative because they are among the moulders of their nation and are not made upon its mould," wrote Yeats.[20] Expounding on the idea that the poets "built Nineveh with their sighing," he suggests that wars, religious enthusiasms, and industries often owe their existence to "something that a boy piped in Thessaly."[21] Indeed, "the whole ancient world of Erin," he speculates, "may well have been sung out of the void by the harps of the great bardic order."[22] Far from being a dead, passive reflector, culture gives birth to nations and refashions their histories.

It was easiest for Yeats to trace the historical effects of his own cultural productions at times of national crisis and violence. Having accompanied Maud Gonne in a night-time protest of Queen Victoria's 1897 Diamond Jubilee visit to Ireland, including a procession with a coffin that symbolized the British Empire, Yeats "read in the morning papers that many have been wounded; some two hundred heads have been dressed at the hospitals; an old woman killed by baton blows, or perhaps trampled under the feet of the crowd; and that two thousand pounds' worth of decorated plate-glass windows have been broken. I count the links in the chain of responsibility, run them across my fingers, and wonder if any link there is from my workshop" (*Autobiographies*, 277).[23] Similarly, in "Man and the Echo" Yeats writes of being tormented at night by the question, "Did that play of mine send out / Certain men the English shot?" (*Poems*, 345). Since *Cathleen ni Houlihan* helped to inspire the Easter rebels to martyrdom and his early nationalist poetry and activism helped to foment rioting and resistance to British imperialism, Yeats's art should be credited with being partly formative of the postcolonial nation. Looking at the portraits of national figures in the Municipal Gallery, Yeats hears himself moved to speak:

"This is not" I say
"The dead Ireland of my youth, but an Ireland
The poets have imagined, terrible and gay."
(*Poems*, 320)

Through their "Revival," the poets have turned a corpselike Ireland into a living, vibrant, even awe-inspiring "imagined community." Artistic form, not only military might or political movements, defines and defends the national imaginary. Similarly, the telepathic or perhaps novelistic powers of the titular heroes in Rushdie's *Midnight's Children* forge the nation's collective consciousness. Yeats vaunts the transformative and defensive power of the aesthetic in his late poem "The Statues." Artists, working with "mallet or chisel," were responsible for the Greek triumph at Salamis: "Europe put off that foam when Phidias / Gave women dreams and dreams their looking-glass" (*Poems*, 337). Like Phidias, Michaelangelo in "Under Ben Bulben" awakens and shapes the desires of "globe-trotting Madam": erotic dream is bound to the determinations of culture. Desire is the basic unit of the communal imaginary, without which there can be no national aspiration or hope. Without the constitutive force of culture giving form to dreams, "the indomitable Irishry" would fall under domination once again (*Poems*, 327).

Yeats is thus a nationalist and perhaps postcolonial writer in the strong sense of nation-maker. In the weak sense of nationalism as reflecting the majoritarian views of the nation, or as supporting the state, Yeats is less creditably "nationalist." This and not merely a shift in his ideas helps to explain why Yeats could write late in life, "I am no Nationalist, except in Ireland for passing reasons" (*Later Essays*, 216). Much earlier he decried the view that "nothing about a man [is] important except his utility to the State" (*Essays*, 102). Since writers widely recognized as postcolonial, from Fanon and Naipaul to the Nigerian playwright Femi Osofisan, have written vehemently against the postcolonial state or have stood outside the mainstream of indigenous opinion, nationalism in this sense cannot serve as a criterion for postcoloniality.[24] Yeats, like many later postcolonial writers, was told repeatedly that he and other playwrights of the Abbey Theatre "have no right to the name" of a "National literature . . . because we do not plead the National cause in our plays."[25] For much of his career, Yeats's general attitude can be described as an "ironic nationalism": to prepare the way for an imagined Irish community but to remain aware of the fictiveness of this ideal, of the disparity between his fiction and others, and of the continual imaginative acts necessary to perpetuate the nation. "Nationality was like religion," he wryly recounts, "few could be saved, and meditation had but one theme— the perfect nation and its perfect service" (*Autobiographies, 272*). With an amusing anecdote, Yeats deflates nationalist obeisance and orthodoxy, which extended even to a kind of dress code: "I believed myself dressed according to public opinion, until a letter of apology from my tailor informed me that 'It takes such a long time getting Connemara cloth as it has to come all the way from Scotland'" (*Autobiographies, 272*). Illusions of national purity paradoxically depend on foreign imports, made possible in the first place by empire. Yeats believed that the literature of Young Ireland undermined its nationalist pretensions by its reliance on English models. Under this movement's influence, "All the past had been turned into a melodrama with Ireland for blameless hero and poet; novelist and historian had but one object, that we should hiss the villain, and only a minority doubted that the greater the talent the greater the hiss" (*Autobiographies, 173*). While acknowledging that "there really had been, however different in their form, villain and victim," Yeats nevertheless wanted to supplant this monolithic melodrama with a more complex vision of Ireland, to prepare the way ultimately for a "master of irony" like John Synge—perhaps even for a Sean O'Casey or Paul Muldoon (*Autobiographies, 173, 174*).

Yeats's nationalism ironizes itself in the knowledge that fulfillment would come at great cost to a poetry built on melancholic desire. Conceiving his work as a preparation for something that never happens, Yeats looked back in "The Bounty of Sweden" (1924) at the work of his colleagues and himself in the Irish Literary Revival and saw it as "seeking foundations for an Ireland that can only come into existence in a Europe that is still but a dream" (*Autobiographies, 406*). Also longing equivocally after erotic fulfillment, Yeats defers the postcolonial no less than the postcoital in much of his poetry, needing always a "*little space for the rose-breath to fill*" (*Poems, 31*). Even his poems of passionate national yearning reflect his ironic nationalism, since they, like many of his love poems, expose and explore the gap between desire and achievement, knowing this space to be the basis of their own existence.[26] Sometimes this gap is between the real and the fantasized object, as Yeats surmises in "The Circus Animals' Desertion": disillusion with the actual beloved "brought forth a dream and soon enough / This dream itself had all my thought and love" (*Poems, 347*). In "The Fisherman," Yeats delivers out of the bowels of his disappointment with the real Ireland an imagined community, as typified by the poem's titular hero:

Maybe a twelvemonth since
Suddenly I began,
In scorn of this audience,
Imagining a man,
And his sun-freckled face,
And grey Connemara cloth,
Climbing up to a place
Where stone is dark under froth,
And the down-turn of his wrist
When the flies drop in the stream;
A man who does not exist,
A man who is but a dream;
And cried, "Before I am old
I shall have written him one
Poem maybe as cold
And passionate as the dawn."
            (*Poems*, 148–49)

Yeats's fisherman has many of the essentialist trappings of Irishness—rugged
and independent, simple yet skilled, white and freckled. But Yeats could
scarcely be more deliberate about the fictiveness of his Irish ideal, "imagining" such a man but emphasizing that he "does not exist" and "is but a
dream." The fisherman's Connemara cloth, after all, may well have come all
the way from Scotland. Self-reliant, his wrist down-turned, the ideal Irishman resembles the ideal poet. Poet and audience blend in an imagined community that, if ever achieved, would mean the collapse of the poem's own
basis in imaginative desire. Paradoxically, poem and the realization of the nationalist ideal are incompatible.

Yeats explores the close interrelation between the imaginative constructedness of poem and nation through an insistent imagery of measurement and boundaries in "To Ireland in the Coming Times" (1924 revision).
In "*measured*" verses that offer the poet's heart to future readers, Yeats plays
on the word "*measure*" until it means the original rhythmic pulse that created the nation, the musical and artistic works that sustain the nation, and
the future peace that is the nation's ultimate ambition:

When Time began to rant and rage
The measure of her flying feet
Made Ireland's heart begin to beat;
And Time bade all his candles flare

> To light a measure here and there;
> And may the thoughts of Ireland brood
> Upon a measured quietude.
> (Poems, 50)

The desirous and beating "*heart*" the poet delivers to the future is both his own and Ireland's. The rhyme of "*feet*" and "*beat*" accentuates the mirror relation between the formally molded and metered poem and the nation's "*red-rose-bordered-hem*." In these ways, Yeats resembles earlier nationalist poets and would be, to continue the measurement trope, "*counted*" among them and "*accounted*" their brother. But Yeats's poetic relation to the ideal nation is different from theirs because his "*rhymes more than their rhyming tell*," more than the accountable and measurable: secret knowledge "*from unmeasured mind.*" Beyond the hemmed-in form of the imagined nation and the metered poem is a supranational, extrapoetic wisdom that ironizes forms and boundaries of any kind. True, these uncontainable mysteries find expression only through measure, but they exceed it, delimit it, and point the way to postnationalist, postformalist ways of thinking and feeling.

Resembling postcolonial writers because of his nationalism and antinationalism, his anticolonialism and anti-anti-colonialism, Yeats may still fall short of postcoloniality, for "postcolonial" is often understood to be synonymous with "Third World." Even critics who associate Yeats with Third World writers concede the distinctions between Ireland and other former British colonies in Africa, South Asia, and the Caribbean. As Luke Gibbons comments astutely, "Ireland is a First World country, but with a Third World memory."[27] Comparing Ireland with these countries, Said notes the closer "geographical connections" between Ireland and England, and Kiberd emphasizes the longer duration of British colonialism in Ireland and the resultant thoroughness of its cultural penetration.[28] Nevertheless, Said and Kiberd suggestively group Yeats with what Said calls other "poets and men of letters of decolonization—Tagore, Senghor, Césaire." Said argues that Yeats can be seen "as an exacerbated example of the 'nativist' phenomenon that flourished elsewhere (e.g., *négritude*) as a result of the colonial encounter."[29] Building on Fanon's distinctions, he sees Yeats's nativism as belonging to an early phase of anti-imperialist writing that seeks nationalist independence, in contrast to the "liberation" phase that Yeats only glimpsed.[30] Kiberd, in contrast, identifies Yeats less with the nativist than the liberationist model— "the reconstruction of a national identity, beginning from first principles all over again."[31] Because Yeats's nationalism and anticolonialism are often con-

flicted and skeptical, he could also be seen as anticipating the postlibera-
tionist ironism toward new states and cultures that pervades much Third
World writing, especially since the 1960s, from Okot p'Bitek's *Song of Ocol* to
Naipaul's *A Bend in the River* and Soyinka's *A Play of Giants.* And he could
even be seen as a writer of the phase that Fanon identifies as prior to nativism
and nationalism—namely, assimilation, since his writing is closely tied to
the colonizer's literary language, style, and history.[32]

In my view, we have not understood Yeats's multifaceted postcoloniality
until we grasp that he is a man of all these masks, with varying emphases
across his lifetime: an assimilationist, drawn to the romantic poets and their
precursors in English literary tradition; a nativist, dedicated to reviving the
myths, place names, and consciousness of the precolonial past; a liberationist, committed to the creation of a new national imaginary; and an ironist, skeptical of rigid nationalisms and invested in transnational modes of
thinking, feeling, and writing. Indeed, the elusiveness and multiplicity of
Yeats's position should help to remind us that the evolutionary phases attributed to postcolonial writing often converge simultaneously in a single period, career, or even work.

For Declan Kiberd, Yeats's life-long contacts with Eastern writers,
philosophers, and artists suggest postcoloniality by association.[33] Long before such contacts became commonplace, they indicate, at the very least, the
complexity of his relation to the Western cultural mainstream. Dazzled at
the age of twenty-one by his first meeting with the "Brahmin philosopher"
Mohini Chatterjee, Yeats sought confirmation in Indian thought for his early
convictions about the primacy of consciousness and the illusory nature of
the external world (*Autobiographies*, 98). In Rabindranath Tagore, Yeats
found a fellow poet, mystic, and leader of a national literary revival. After be-
friending Tagore in 1912, he chanted the Bengali poet's work at soirées, introduced and touched up the English-language version of the *Gitanjali*
(1912), and in 1913 directed the play *The Post Office* at the Abbey Theatre.
Still later, Yeats collaborated with an Indian yogi he met in 1931, Shri Purohit Swami, working with him to help introduce, publish, and translate Indian spiritual texts.[34] In introductions to English-language translations of
Tagore's *Gitanjali*, the swami's spiritual autobiography, *An Indian Monk*, and
the autobiography of the swami's master, *The Holy Mountain*, as well as *The
Mandukya Upanishad*, *The Ten Principal Upanishads*, and *Aphorisms of Yôga*,
it becomes clear that Yeats is attracted to India largely because it represents
the Unity of Culture he wished for Ireland. In Tagore's Bengal, Yeats speculates, civilization is shared by a "common mind" instead of being "broken

into a dozen minds that know nothing of each other," so that Tagore's verses eventually will be known not just by leisured ladies or university students, as in the West, "but as the generations pass, travellers will hum them on the highway and men rowing upon rivers" (*Later Essays,* 167, 168). In the East, Unity of Culture overrides divisions of class or labor. "Indifferent to history," India has not only synchronic Unity of Culture across social differences but also diachronic unity across time (*Later Essays,* 154). Yeats also projects onto India Unity of Being or individual consciousness. Drawing on the Upanishads, Yeats lauds the Indian "'unbroken consciousness of the Self,' the Self that never sleeps, that is never divided, but even when our thought transforms it, is still the same," as opposed to Western fragmentation of consciousness in time and the body (*Later Essays,* 160). Closely familiar with the intricacies of Hindu meditation, Yeats becomes rhapsodic in evoking the fourth stage or *Samādhi,* when "the mind can enter all or any of the previous states at will; joyous, unobstructed, it can transform itself, dissolve itself, create itself" (*Later Essays,* 158). Yeats often seeks to evoke this state in his poetry, perhaps most memorably at the end of "A Dialogue of Self and Soul."

In the first group of lyric poems in *The Collected Poems,* there is almost as much attention given to India as to Ireland; the poems in *Crossways* evoke cross-cultural ways of love, belief, and disillusionment.[35] Indian wisdom makes a resurgence in such late poems as "Mohini Chatterjee" and "Meru"—the one poem about the cycles of reincarnation, the other about the natural cycles that remain once all such beliefs have been stripped away. In "Meru" the Irish poet's cross-cultural appeal to the Indian hermits' unillusioned wisdom could be seen as representing a postcolonial understanding of "Civilisation" as "rule" and "manifold illusion," repression and deception. Postcolonial poet and postcolonial hermit look into the "desolation of reality" after imaginatively delivering themselves from the cultural fraud imposed by such imperial civilizations as Egypt, Greece, Rome, and no doubt Great Britain (*Poems,* 289). That Yeats makes this appeal in the highly "civilized" poetic form of the sonnet heightens the irony of the poet's quest to think in but beyond the boundaries of colonially imposed language, artistic structure, and intercultural connection.

The depth and duration of Yeats's interest in Indian and other so-called Third World cultures, are not, however, enough to warrant recanonizing him as Third World poet, side by side with the Bengali Tagore and Martinican Césaire, the Senegalese Senghor and Barbadian Brathwaite. Indeed, his idealization of India as site of Unity of Culture may be read as just the opposite—an indication of Yeats's orientalism, his conceptualizing of the East as site of ideal fulfillment and yet as impossibly alien, regressive, and potentially hostile. When Yeats claims a national affinity between Ireland and India, it is typically between modern India and early Christian Ireland; he romanticizes yet infantilizes India, repeating the notion that "in the nursery" all humans are "Asiatic."[36] India seems frozen in an archaic prehistory; as such, it gives Westerners access to both their personal and their cultural infancy, in relation to which they can construct their narratives of "development." Comparing Indian with ancient Irish philosophy in his introduction to *The Ten Principal Upanishads,* Yeats writes that "our genuflections discover in the East something ancestral in ourselves" (*Later Essays,* 173–74). Introducing another Indian mystical text, he hesitates: "whenever I have been tempted to go to Japan, China or India for my philosophy, Balzac has brought me back, reminded me of my preoccupation with national, social, personal problems, convinced me that I cannot escape from our *Comédie humaine*" (*Later Essays,* 139). The alluring Unity that Yeats projects onto the East is exactly what makes it inaccessible to the Western mind, inassimilable to its reasoned distinctions and earthly attachments. In a diary entry Yeats associates the West with "efficient rule," "the body," and "thaumaturgy," as opposed to the East's "indifference to rule, scorn of the flesh, contemplation of the formless. Western minds who follow the Eastern way become weak and vapoury, because unfit for the work forced upon them by Western life" (*Autobiographies,* 356).

Nevertheless, in the same paragraph, which begins in orientalist preconceptions, Yeats arrives at the potentially anticolonial insight versified in "Meru": "Civilisation is held together . . . by artificially created illusions." Yeats's intellectual relation to the Third World is not entirely assimilable to a paradigm of affiliation, but neither is it reducible to orientalist oppression. On the one hand, there is the obvious Eurocentrism of a poem like "The Statues," which celebrates the victory of European measurement and art over the formless foam of the Persians at Salamis—a victory that the Irish should aspire to live up to. There can be little question of Third World affiliation here. On the other hand, Yeats is more open than many of his contemporaries to the thought and culture of the Third World. Compare him with his friend Ezra Pound, who, despite his initial enthusiasm for Tagore and prolonged fascination with East Asia, sneered: "I loathe and always have loathed Indian art. . . . Obnubilated, short curves, muddle, jungle, etc. Waaal, we find the hin-goddam-do is a bloody and voracious usurer . . . life as of herd of wild animals in Africa: no main structure to the country, *nothing* to satisfy European, Rodam, J. Adams sense of the state."[37] Set side by side with such dis-

dain, Yeats's statements about India overflow with honeyed good will. The
Indian indifference to the state that appalls Pound harmonizes with Yeats's
postcolonial skepticism.

The early poem "The Indian upon God," originally published as section
5 of "From the Book of Kauri the Indian" (1886), offers a first glimpse into
the complexity of Yeats's relationship to the East.[38] In this charming poem
about religious perspectivism, each being, whether moorfowl, lotus, roe-
buck, or peacock, projects its own form onto the divine, which mutates
according to the identity of the believer. The most powerful if buried imaginative connection in the poem is between its understanding of religion as
projection of oneself onto the divine other and its own attribution of this
perspectivist concept to the cultural other. At some level the poem acknowledges that, by its own logic, the poet's effort to imagine cultural otherness inevitably imposes a cultural self-image onto the other. In its passage to India,
the poem crosses cultures to uncover a shared truth (it is often said to draw
on the *Bhagavat Gita*); yet it also suggests that no such crossing can ever be
authentic and must always mask to some extent the cultural other toward
whom it reaches.

A last framework for understanding the nature of Yeats's postcoloniality
is that of hybridity. Supplementing historical or political models of postcoloniality, this concept highlights the cultural in-betweenness of writers who
inhabit, explore, and articulate the *after*-colonial interrelationships between
the imposed culture of the colonizer and the native culture of the colonized.
The concept of hybridity has often been attacked for depoliticizing postcoloniality, for flattening out the inequalities between the two sides of the colonial divide, and for presupposing a false antithesis of purity.[39] While these
dangers are real and need to be guarded against, the advantages of the notion
also deserve recognition. Unlike baldly political conceptualizations of postcoloniality as anticolonialism, nationalism, and Third-Worldism, hybridity
is potentially more responsive to the aesthetic complexity of literary texts.
Whereas an idea like anticolonialism or nationalism can barely account for
the intricate texture of a literary work, an idea like hybridity or creolization
invites the exegete to attend to the intercultural tensions and fusions at the
level of language, style, concept, and genre.

Not that the formal hybridity of Yeats's work is separable from the politics of his "in-betweenness." Yeats's right to the claim of representativeness
as national writer has long been questioned because of his roots in Ireland's
Protestant middle class, his anti-Catholic identification with the Anglo-Irish
Ascendancy, and his many years of residence in England. In effect, he is ac-

cused of belonging to the settler population responsible for oppressing the Catholic majority population for centuries. But while it is true that Yeats was alienated from the Catholic middle classes, he was often no less infuriating to Protestant—particularly Unionist—opinion. He attacked Irish Protestants for selling out their own country to the English and upbraided the "Irish upper classes for putting everything in a money measure."[40] He was antipathetic toward central institutions of Protestant culture, such as Trinity College, and politics, such as the Castle (*Autobiographies,* 191–92).[41]

Too anglicized to be Irish and too "gaelicized" to be English, the Anglo-Irish Yeats typifies the intersticial writer of the postcolonial world. Walcott emerged from the small Methodist minority in predominantly Catholic Saint Lucia and belonged to the "brown bourgeoisie," between the poor blacks descended from slaves and their white overlords.[42] Ramanujan came from the tiny educated Brahman minority in South India and, because of his long residency in the West, has sometimes been shunned as a less than truly "Indian" writer. The in-between position of writers like the Indo-Trinidadian-turned-Englishman Naipaul and the Indo-Afro-Guyanese emigrant David Dabydeen, the Anglo-Dominican Jean Rhys, and the white South African J. M. Coetzee scarcely needs elaboration. Seamus Deane has persuasively defended a de-essentialized concept of Irishness, but his influential attack on Yeats's representativeness could be seen, ironically, as tied to an essentialist notion of Irishness as Catholic and middle class. Yeats's awareness that Irishness only existed as reflected back through the lens of England should help to defuse such essentialisms. He credits the founding of modern Irish literature to work by the Protestant Standish O'Grady and his cousin Hayes, which was heavily dependent, strange to say, on the British Museum, as was much of Yeats's own early "nativist" research (*Later Essays,* 206). In a similar vein, the Indologist and poet Ramanujan reflects with bemusement that, like Irish studies, "Indology is an invention and gift of Western scholarship."[43]

Championing a new Irish literature in English, Yeats sparred with the proponents of Gaelic in terms that anticipate the postcolonial debate over language.[44] "In order to de-anglicise ourselves," Douglas Hyde argued, "we must at once arrest the decay of the language"; similarly, the Kenyan novelist Ngugi wa Thiong'o claimed that to decolonize the mind, African writers had to embrace native languages like his own Gikuyu, since colonial "language was the most important vehicle" of imperial "subjugation."[45] English had more deeply saturated 1890s Ireland than 1960s Africa or India. Two weeks after Hyde delivered his seminal lecture of 1892, "The Necessity for De-Anglicising Ireland," Yeats responded that by writing new literature in En-

glish and translating old Irish stories, "we will do more to de-Anglicise Ireland than by longing to recall the Gaelic tongue and the snows of yester
year." Irish writers should work to "build up a national tradition, a national
literature, which shall be none the less Irish in spirit from being English in
language."[46] Author of poems that lend a greener shade to English, Yeats
hailed the hybrid concept of an English-language literature with "an indefin-
able Irish quality of rythm [sic] and style."[47] While Yeats helped to pave the
way for later postcolonial poets who "yorubize" English (Soyinka), or "ur-
duize" it (Agha Shahid Ali), or "caribbeanize" it (Bennett), he ironically did
not foresee their achievement. The older Yeats asserted, after recalling a
speech to Indian writers in which he "denounced the oppression of the people of India," "I could no more have written in Gaelic than can those Indians
write in English; Gaelic is my national language, but it is not my mother
tongue" (*Later Essays*, 211, 212). When he grew disenchanted with Tagore,
he blamed the Bengali poet's declining reputation on his English-language
poetry: "Tagore does not know English, no Indian knows English. Nobody
can write with music and style in a language not learned in childhood and
ever since the language of his thought."[48] Yeats underestimated the potential
of multilingual Indian poets like Ramanujan and Ali, Adil Jussawalla and Eunice de Souza to make powerful contributions to English-language literature.

Notwithstanding fears that the concept of hybridity depoliticizes postcoloniality by suppressing asymmetries of power, Yeats understood the shap-
ing political circumstances behind his creolization of an English-language
literature with an Irish spirit and style. Introducing his collected works, he
places his ambivalent feelings about writing in English within the context of
a long history of "wars of extermination" and unparalleled "persecution" of
the Irish by the English, though this "hatred" of the English is counterbalanced with sympathy and even "love":

> Then I remind myself that, though mine is the first English marriage I know
> of in the direct line, all my family names are English and that I owe my soul to
> Shakespeare, to Spenser and to Blake, perhaps to William Morris, and to the
> English language in which I think, speak and write, that everything I love has
> come to me through English; my hatred tortures me with love, my love with
> hate. I am like the Tibetan monk who dreams at his initiation that he is eaten
> by a wild beast and learns on waking that he himself is eater and eaten. (*Later
> Essays*, 211)

In these extraordinary lines, hatred of English colonial rule is set on the scales
with personal affection for an Englishwoman, familial and literary inheritances, and the mother tongue. The poet's love and hatred, far from being sus-

pended in a comfortable balance, are locked in perpetual strife. Yeats's simile powerfully figures his cultural ambivalences: he feels that he is both devoured by and devourer of the English language and other cultural inheritances.

Yeats's literary hybridity, as the above passage suggests, is as much a matter of literary history as of language. The colonizer's language, while the poet's medium of expression, is also the medium through which a colonial literary history is imposed, transmitted, and transformed. Yeats everywhere acknowledges his apprenticeship to the English literary masters. But his appreciation of his English forebears is, as he himself suggests, complicated by politics. Writing angrily about "Wordsworth, that typical Englishman," Yeats contrasts the poet's homage to one anticolonial rebel, Toussaint L'Ouverture of Haiti, with his perturbing silence in the same year about the hanged Irish rebel, Robert Emmet, as well as the abortive 1798 rebellion of the United Irishmen, led by Wolfe Tone (*Later Essays*, 211).

Still, Yeats can easily dismiss Wordsworth because he liked neither his poetry nor his politics, whereas Spenser, whose work Yeats edited, introduced, and even openly imitated in *The Island of the Statues* and "Shepherd and Goatherd," presents a more complicated problem. For all his appreciation of Spenser's poetics, Yeats at times rereads the Englishman's work from the perspective of the Iron Man's victims: "Like an hysterical patient he drew a complicated web of inhuman logic out of the bowels of an insufficient premise—there was no right, no law, but that of Elizabeth, and all that opposed her opposed themselves to God, to civilisation, and to all inherited wisdom and courtesy, and should be put to death" (*Essays*, 361). Calling the Queen "the image of the State which had taken possession of his conscience," Yeats indignantly deconstructs Spenser's idolatry of Elizabeth and, by implication, the imperial state she headed: "She was over sixty years old, ugly and, historians will have it, selfish, but in his poetry she is 'Fair Cynthia,' 'a crown of lilies,' 'the image of the heavens,'" and thus Yeats continues to quote, using the poet's own words to choke Spenser's colonial lie (*Essays*, 371). The lengthy passages he cites from Spenser's *View of the Present State of Ireland* are even more chilling, the English poet praising the terrible wars that burned and starved the Irish, and left a once populous landscape "voyde of man or beast" (*Essays*, 374). In Yeats's view, Spenser is not only a worse person because a colonial administrator, enthralled with "efficient" brutality on behalf of his beloved imperial state, but also a worse poet, blind to the Irish landscape he lived in and deaf to the Irish people around him. In a brilliant speculative maneuver, Yeats laments what a better poet Spenser might have been had he opened his mind to the great indigenous oral poets of Ireland, whose "wonderful imaginations" were more abundant and powerful than Spenser's own intellectualized fancy (*Essays*, 372). In his skeptical reading of Spenser, Yeats anticipates by more than half a century the decentering postcolonial readings by writers like Achebe of *Heart of Darkness* or the Barbadian George Lamming of *The Tempest*.

Yeats transmutes Shakespeare, by contrast, into an avatar of his own antipathies toward "the State" and Celtic interest in the expression of personality (*Essays*, 103). "At a moment of imperialistic enthusiasm" late in the nineteenth century, as Yeats acutely observes, the celebration of a victorious, state-identified Henry V reached its apotheosis, whereas Yeats would show that Shakespeare preferred instead the failed, dreamy, poetic sensibility of Richard II (*Essays*, 104). Anticipating African and Caribbean transvaluations of Shakespeare, Yeats lays claim to the deposed Richard II and spurns the martial valor of a Henry IV or V, much as Fanon, Césaire, Lamming, and others will recuperate Caliban at the expense of Prospero.[49]

Shakespeare's other doomed heroes are at the core of Yeats's late poetics of tragic joy. In "Lapis Lazuli" (*Poems*, 294–95), the lyric culmination of this idea, Shakespeare's heroes teach how to respond with gaiety to the recurring catastrophes of death and destruction, often driven by imperial wars, like that of "King Billy" of Orange. If Shakespeare's plays had been used to legitimize the British empire, Yeats harnesses them in the service of postcolonial skepticism toward imperial "civilisations," which inevitably go to ruin and "wrack." To the extent that this poem's tragic gaiety was a response to the fears of Edmund Dulac, donor of the piece of lapis lazuli, that London would be bombed, Yeats ironically derives from Shakespeare a postcolonial model for how to respond to the potential destruction of the bard's metropolitan center. Similarly, in "An Irish Airman Foresees His Death," the tragic equanimity of the Shakespearean pilot reflects his peculiarly postcolonial status as half-hearted fighter against mutual antagonists of the British empire ("Those that I fight I do not hate") on behalf of the British empire ("Those that I guard I do not love") (*Poems*, 135). In both poems, Yeats summons Shakespeare to the side of the colonized. Indeed, Ireland turns out to be truer than England as inheritor of Shakespeare: "Ireland had preserved longer than England," for example, "the rhythmical utterance of the Shakespearean stage" (*Essays*, 528). Yeats hoped to dissolve the apparent contradiction of creating a fully Irish literature schooled in the English canon. Already in the lecture "Nationality and Literature" (1893), he argues that "we can learn from English and other literatures without loss of national individuality" and that imperial literatures could even help lead newer national literatures to maturity.[50]

Like other postcolonial writers, Yeats developed a poetry that is also hybrid at the level of form. But while it is customary to understand postcolonial literatures as complex intercultural fusions—Rushdie's digressive plots, for example, merge traditional Indian oral storytelling and European postmodernism—Yeats's poetry has seldom been conceptualized in like terms. Let us start with the seemingly simple question of place names. In Yeats's poetry they are often obvious signifiers of native ground—Drumahair, Scanavin, Lugnagall, and Mocharabuiee. Through acts of poetic imagination, Yeats seeks—as emphasized by Deane, Said, Kiberd, and George Bornstein—to reclaim a land violently possessed by the British.[51] The recitation of place names represents a double decolonization: of the geographical place long under the physical occupation of an imperial power and of the literary space of poetry in English. "There is no river or mountain that is not associated in the memory with some event or legend," Yeats avers, summoning Irish writers to "fix upon their memory the appearance of mountains and rivers and make it all visible again in their arts" (*Essays*, 205). At his most mimetic, Yeats is convinced that "one's verses should hold, as in a mirror, the colours of one's own climate and scenery in their right proportion" (*Essays*, 5). "Might I not," he asks, "with health and good luck to aid me, create some new *Prometheus Unbound*; Patrick or Columcille, Oisin or Finn, in Prometheus' stead; and, instead of Caucasus, Cro-Patrick or Ben Bulben? Have not all races had their first unity from a mythology that marries them to rock and hill?" (*Autobiographies*, 166–67). As these passages indicate, the poet's task of reclaiming the land is manifold and difficult, since to indigenize the Irish landscape, increasingly cut off from the myths of native peoples, the poet must also indigenize the English romantic tradition of Shelley and others, adapting it to native ground, and must also indigenize heroism, wresting it from imperial Greco-English types like Prometheus and returning it to Hibernians like Oisin. To rename the land is, thus, not just to recover its essential Irishness; the poet grafts Irish myths, heroes, names, and poems onto colonial paradigms. The project of literary deanglicization is inevitably inscribed by the alien place holders—*Prometheus Unbound,* Prometheus, Caucasus—that it would displace.

If Yeats's local place names deanglicize the land, they nevertheless anglicize Irish words, which sometimes become nearly unrecognizable in their hybrid form (Drumcliff for *Drom Cliabh,* Ben Bulben for *Benn Gulban,* according to Brendan O Hehir).[52] Grumbling that Christianity had displaced holiness from Ireland to a Holy Land elsewhere, Yeats indicates that decolonization of the native land involves not only its partial deanglicization but also its partial dechristianization (*Later Essays,* 156–57). To be nativized, the land must be remythologized—made readable in terms of sanctifying Irish myths and legends. Above all, it must be renamed in memorable poems: not only Innisfree and Ben Bulben, Coole and Ballylee, but Drumahair, Lissadell, Scanavin, and Lugnagall in "The Man Who Dreamed of Faeryland," Dooney, Kilvarnet, and Mocharabuiee in "The Fiddler of Dooney." Imaginatively recovering the land through names, later postcolonial poets reveal this "native" space to be ineluctably intercultural: the Jamaican poet Lorna Goodison playfully invokes Accompong, Alps, Lapland, and Armagh in "To Us, All Flowers Are Roses," and Walcott begins "Sainte Lucie" with the villages "Laborie, Choiseul, Vieuxfort, Dennery."[53]

Moreover, Yeats's poetry is far from being unambiguously Irish in topography. True, a student at the Yeats International Summer School can, through sited readings, performatively reconnect Yeats's poetry to the appropriate Irish places—Innisfree, Ben Bulben, Thoor Ballylee, Coole, and Cashel. But the field trips would become fabulously expensive if students tried to follow out all the cartographic indications of the poetry, from Ireland to Greece and Rome, and from Turkey to Egypt, India, China, Japan, and elsewhere. In one of his best-known poems, to "sail the seas" is Yeats's figure for his poetic impulse to move imaginatively beyond the boundaries of Ireland. Even so, the geography of Yeats's poetry is hardly unbounded: he seldom takes us, for example, to England, the United States, or Africa. But our exact imaginative location is often difficult to secure. Already in the lyrics eventually gathered as *Crossways,* we may find ourselves by Sleuth Wood, Rosses, or Glen-Car in one poem, only to be dislocated by another to an Indian temple or the Himalayan mountains, returning in another to Knocknarea and Inishmurray. The geographical coordinates of many later poems are still less determinate. Does "Lapis Lazuli" *take place* in 1690s Ireland ("King Billy") or Great War Europe ("Zeppelin"), in Elizabethan England, Attic Greece, or China in the Ch'ien Lung period? Such historio-geographic bounds over boundaries indicate the inadequacy of our novelistic sense that Yeats's poetry is "Irish" because firmly situated within the native island's borders. Still, Yeats's hybridization of geographies should not be seen as idle cosmopolitanism: it represents, at least in part, a reverse colonization, the world-gathering gesture of a poet whose country has been occupied for centuries and whose culture has been threatened with extinction. It finds its "antiself" in the shrunken and deflative poetics of a postimperial English writer like Philip Larkin. "Out of Ireland" Yeats comes, imaginatively repossessing the island

and annexing vast territories beyond ("Remorse for Intemperate Speech,"
Poems, 255).

Like his intermappings of the globe, Yeats's mythic bricolage is also
based in Ireland but expands beyond it. Under his leadership, the Celtic
movement opened "the fountain of Gaelic legends," which he considered "a
more abundant fountain than any in Europe" (*Essays,* 186–87). To "bring
the halves together," Yeats hoped to found a new nonsectarian Irish literature
on pre-Christian myths (*Autobiographies,* 105). Reading Yeats's early poetry
for the first time, the neophyte, non-Irish reader must learn the legends of
Fergus, Cuchulain, Deirdre, Grania, the Sidhe, Oisin, Niamh, the Danaan,
Cumhal, Maeve, and Aengus. Countless postcolonial writers recover native
myths, disseminating them to both local and outside populations. But no
sooner has Yeats indigenized the mythic base of lyric poetry than he returns,
by midcareer, to the classical and Judeo-Christian stories that are the mythic
substructure of the Western lyric: he summons Helen, Proteus, Leda, Solomon, Sheba, Dionysus, Christ, Attis, Hector, and Antaeus. Yeats's mythic al-
lusions and retellings, like his cartographic imaginings, demand both Irish
and extraterritorial cultural literacies. Even the native names of Yeats's characters are, like his local place names, hardly pure Irish; they, too, hybridize
Gaelic with English orthography and phonetics.[54] Having just described in a
late essay the Irish syncretism of Christianity and Druidism, Yeats instances
this quality of his own mind in extraordinary leaps from Saint Patrick and
Christ to the Upanishads to Neoplatonism, the Kabbalah, and Gaelicism
(*Later Essays,* 208). Yeats's mythic syncretism, which explodes in *A Vision,*
foreshadows the intercultural possibilities that such later postcolonial poets
as Walcott, Soyinka, and Christopher Okigbo would explore. The occult
fascinated Yeats not only because of his Irish Protestant background but
also because of its cosmopolitanism, fusing mysticisms of widely diverse origins—Christian, Jewish, Persian, Indian, Arab, Scandanavian, Chinese, and
so forth. His *Spiritus* or *Anima Mundi* sometimes looks like a pretechnologi-
cal form of the Internet. Its fluidity proves that national, psychic, and historical boundaries are permeable, that "the borders of our memories" and "the
borders of our mind are ever shifting" (*Essays,* 28).

The mixed geographies and mythologies of Yeats's poetry would count
for little in poetry unless they were expressed through similarly melded
tropes, genres, syntax, diction, and prosody. Yeats emphasized the necessity
of some disidentification from the metropolitan center, lest its influence
overwhelm any native elements of style. Like other postcolonial writers, he

often describes his own stylistic maturation as a process of indigenization; but given his predominantly English influences, even this developmental trajectory needs to be seen not as a purification but as a hybridization. As if at first infantilized by the overwhelming British colonial legacy of Shelley and Spenser, Yeats sought to "make a style which would not be an English style and yet would be musical and full of colour" (*Essays*, 3). Poetic ontogeny resembles national self-determination. Yeats genders his stylistic development as an evolution away from feminine dependency and toward masculine self-reliance.[55] In contrast to his early "unmanly" poetry of "sentiment and sentimental sadness," heavily indebted to British decadence and late romanticism, he wants to make a new "more masculine" style with "everything hard and clear":

> When I found my verses too full of the reds and yellows Shelley gathered in Italy, I thought for two days of setting things right, not as I should now by making my rhythms faint and nervous and filling my images with a certain coldness, a certain wintry wildness, but by eating little and sleeping upon a board. (*Essays*, 5)

> Years afterwards when I had finished *The Wanderings of Oisin,* dissatisfied with its yellow and its dull green, with all that overcharged colour inherited from the romantic movement, I deliberately reshaped my style, deliberately sought out an impression as of cold light and tumbling clouds. I cast off traditional metaphors and loosened my rhythm, and recognising that all the criticism of life known to me was alien and English, became as emotional as possible but with an emotion which I described to myself as cold. (*Autobiographies,* 86)

He reconceives his earlier style as being too warm, as if cloyingly close to its parental origins, too colorful, as if overpowered by a parent's choices, and too regular in its meters, as if controlled by the rhythms of the maternal body. Even so, the poet's developmental aim of a cold, hard, masculine self-reliance depends for definitional contrast and for initial formation upon the mother Britannia from which it would be weaned.

The comparative rhythmic freedom of "The Lake Isle of Innisfree," which Yeats called "my first lyric with anything in its rhythm of my own music," stylistically incarnates cultural and national freedom, of the sort that the poem implicitly yearns for (*Autobiographies,* 139). Not that national or formal independence can ever be complete. The island's name, Gaelic for Heather Island, not accidentally embeds the English word "free," in a bilingual pun. Its vision of self-reliance, as figured by an economy of subsistence farming and as encoded in nonpentameter lines of six and four stresses, nevertheless relies on removal to the metropolitan center for its conception: a fountain in a London shop window was the poem's inspiration. Writing about his prosody, Yeats suggests that his Irish subject matter did not easily fit into colonially inherited forms: "There was something in what I felt about Deirdre, about Cuchulain, that rejected the Renaissance and its characteristic metres" (*Later Essays*, 214).[56] But Yeats's response is not to abandon but to open up traditional prosody. In meter for Yeats is community, history, collective memory: "The contrapuntal structure of the verse, to employ a term adopted by Robert Bridges, combines the past and present." The strict pentameter line is, as Yeats describes it, "a ghostly voice, an unvariable possibility, an unconscious norm. What moves me and my hearer is a vivid speech that has no laws except that it must not exorcise the ghostly voice" (*Later Essays*, 214). The interplay between Yeats's vigorous, varied rhythms and inherited meters is emblematic of his cultural hybridity: he knows he cannot spring free from the collective cultural inheritance of colonialism but neither must he allow himself to be tyrannized by it. The "ghostly voice" of inherited English form lives within his Anglo-Irish verse, heard but not permitted to dominate, absent but insistent in its presence.

Yeats himself prepares the way for a conceptualization of the elements of his style as hybrid forms. Yeats's complex negotiations with English and European genres have been read by critics (myself included) as a modern poet's resistant transactions with his literary past; they should also be seen as a postcolonial or Irish poet's ambivalent responses to his English literary inheritances. Yeats's major genre is, of course, lyric poetry, and although he acknowledges his debt to English lyric tradition, he sees his passion for lyric brevity as Irish. "Contemporary lyric poems . . . seemed too long," given his "Irish preference for a swift current" (*Later Essays*, 212). Extending this topographical metaphor, Yeats suggestively connects poetic space with national geography. "The English mind is meditative, rich, deliberate; it may remember the Thames valley. I planned to write short lyrics or poetic drama where every speech [would] be short and concentrated, knit by dramatic tension" (*Later Essays*, 212). Coming from an island with "Great hatred, little room," he favors lyric poems that are compact and tense, in contrast to the expansive languor of English poetry ("Remorse for Intemperate Speech," *Poems*, 255).

Moreover, Yeats inherits and partly indigenizes various English lyric subgenres. In poems such as "The Fish" and "My Descendents," he adapts the curse—a subgenre with a strong Irish pedigree but also used by English writers. The interfusion of love and death in much of his love poetry draws on a European tradition descended from Petrarch and intensified by late nineteenth-century decadence; but it also recalls the Irish tradition of love poetry: "Love was held to be a fatal sickness in ancient Ireland," he writes in "The Celtic Element in Literature," "and there is a love-poem in the *Love Songs of Connacht* that is like a death-cry: 'My love, O she is my love, the woman who is most for destroying me, dearer is she for making me ill than the woman who would be for making me well. . . . She is my love, O she is my love, the woman who left no strength in me; a woman who would not breathe a sigh after me, a woman who would not raise a stone at my tomb'" (*Essays*, 180). Helen Vendler has described Yeats's breaking of the sonnet form in "Leda and the Swan," "Meru," and elsewhere as an Irish poet's forceful remaking of an inherited English form.[57] Similarly, Yeats absorbs but refashions the English elegy in poems like "Upon a Dying Lady," "In Memory of Alfred Pollexfen," and "Easter, 1916": an "Irish" astringent joy in the face of death mutes the characteristic sorrow of the English elegy; Yeats's de-idealizing quarrels with the dead supplant England's typically unblemished portraits. Further, the group form that Yeats prefers in his elegies is traceable to a large body of Irish laments for the collective dead, such as the elegies he gathered in his anthology *A Book of Irish Verse*. In these and many other subgenres, Yeats can be seen appropriating major forms through the English poetic tradition but either transforming their dominant codes or hybridizing them with indigenous traditions.

To make "a language to my liking," Yeats sought, "not as Wordsworth thought words in common use, but a powerful and passionate syntax, and a complete coincidence between period and stanza" (*Later Essays*, 212). Yeats's Anglo-Irish syntax helped to reverse the current of influence from metropolitan center to postcolony: "Then, and in this English poetry has followed my lead, I tried to make the language of poetry coincide with that of passionate, normal speech" (*Later Essays*, 212). Like many poets of the postcolonial world, especially such West Indian poets as Bennett, Brathwaite, and Michael Smith, Yeats sought to create a poetry that resembles in its syntactic patterns and vivid style the immediacy, spontaneity, and urgency of speech. Like U.S. minority and postcolonial poets of strong oral cultures, Yeats remembers in his poetic style, as in his performative chanting, that "Ireland has a still living folk tradition," in contrast to what he thought of as the writtenness of England's "impersonal philosophical poetry" (*Later Essays*, 100). For Hugh Kenner, Yeats's "feel for the aspective" and his "layering" of clauses are what make for an "Irish" syntax.[58] Much as Yeats's syntax influenced metropolitan writers, so too his diction also helped to reverse the current; Auden praised it as "the diction of a just man" and incorporated favorite Yeatsian words into his own lyrics.[59]

In his characteristic images and symbols—the rose, the tree, the moon, the gyre, the eagle, the country house—Yeats sometimes indigenizes Anglo-European figures, sometimes engrafts tropes with distinctive Irish genealogies onto an English base. He submits symbols in English poetry to intercultural translation: Shelley's wolf and deer "remind" Yeats "of the hound and deer that Oisin saw in the Gaelic poem chasing one another on the water . . . and of a Galway tale that tells how Niamh, whose name means brightness or beauty, came to Oisin as a deer" (*Essays*, 90). Yeats believed nations to be "unified by an image, or bundle of related images," which he, in turn, sought to deepen and enrich (*Autobiographies*, 167). Yet he is under no illusion that the nation's storehouse of images can be ethnically cleansed of foreign influences, and he gladly raids the world's other imaginative repositories. In the example cited above, Yeats filters Shelley's images through an indigenous symbolic prism, but his intercultural translations also sometimes reverse the lens, and at other times Yeats uses English and European figures to "make sense" of Eastern ideas, as when he explains *Samādhi* in the Upanishads: "The initiate, all old Karma exhausted, is 'the Human Form Divine' of Blake, that Unity of Being Dante compared to a perfectly proportioned human body; henceforth he is self-creating" (*Later Essays*, 162).

In his outward- and inward-looking style, Yeats anticipates the dual emphasis of many later postcolonial writers, eager at once to explore, expand, and promote the poetic resources of their own cultures and at the same time to ransack the international literary trove of the *Spiritus Mundi*. Instead of representing Yeats as either Irish master of indigenous traditions or as British heir of the English literary canon, we would do well to attend to the interplay between these different modalities in his poetry. Not that Yeats was a rootless cosmopolitan. Like other postcolonial writers whose nations have been threatened with erasure, he affirmed his indigenous identity. As a teenager he might have been convinced "that art is tribeless, nationless, a blossom gathered in No Man's Land," but soon he "could not endure," as he puts it, "an international art, picking stories and symbols where it pleased" (*Essays*, 205; *Autobiographies*, 166).[60] Yet neither was Yeats a provincialist. Attacked like such later writers as Walcott, Rushdie, Soyinka, Naipaul, and Amitav Ghosh for insufficient nativism, Yeats proclaims, "A writer is no less National because he shows the influence of other countries and of the great writers of the world," as instanced by the cross-cultural influences of French meters and Italian forms on great English poets. "No nation," he retorts to his identitarian accusers, "since the beginning of history, has ever drawn all its life out of itself."[61] Yeats skillfully navigates between the Scylla of blinkered provincialism and the Charybdis of shallow internationalism. Indeed, perhaps his weightiest credential in earning admittance to the postcolonial literary society is the *cosmopolitan nativism* he shares with many of its most esteemed members. Though white and canonical, though non–Third World and Anglo-Irish, Yeats has at least enough in common with the present members to make for some animated conversation.

CHAPTER THREE

❧ The Wound of Postcolonial History: Derek Walcott's *Omeros*

From an early age Derek Walcott felt a special "intimacy with the Irish poets" as "colonials with the same kind of problems that existed in the Caribbean. They were the niggers of Britain."[1] Passionately identifying with Yeats, Joyce, Synge, and other Irish writers, Walcott shared especially in their conflicted response to the cultural inheritances of the British empire— its literature, religion, and language. At school, Walcott recalls, Joyce's Stephen Dedalus was his "hero": "Like him, I was a knot of paradoxes," among other things "learning to hate England as I worshipped her language."[2] His best known lyric, "A Far Cry from Africa" (1956), elaborates the poem of ambivalence toward imperial and anti-imperial bloodshed, building on Yeats's simultaneously anticolonial and anti-anti-colonial stance in works such as "Easter, 1916" and "Nineteen Hundred and Nineteen."[3] As Yeats used a series of counterbalanced questions to dramatize his inner divisions after the Easter Rising, Walcott forty years later responds to the Mau Mau rebellion with a spiral of questions that "turn" on each other with ever stronger torque:

> I who am poisoned with the blood of both,
> Where shall I turn, divided to the vein?
> I who have cursed
> The drunken officer of British rule, how choose
> Between this Africa and the English tongue I love?
> Betray them both, or give back what they give?
> How can I face such slaughter and be cool?
> How can I turn from Africa and live?

Another thirty-four years later, in his Caribbean epic, *Omeros* (1990), Walcott is still puzzling out what it means to love the English language yet hate English imperialism. As a character within his own narrative, Walcott travels to Ireland, literalizing his revisitation of Joyce and Yeats as precursors, and there—struck anew by the shared postcolonial problem of linguistic and literary inheritance—he memorably declares Ireland "a nation / split by a glottal scream."[4]

An epic divided to the vein, a poem split by a glottal scream, *Omeros* asks how the postcolonial poet can both grieve the agonizing harm of British colonialism and celebrate the empire's literary bequest. Walcott's pervasive figure of the wound can help us to understand his answer to this question, as the figurative site where concerns with imperial injury, literary archetype, and linguistic heritage most graphically intersect. "This wound I have stitched into Plunkett's character," ventures the poet early in *Omeros*. Conflating wound and suture, Walcott suggests that the odd surgery of poetry may have to disfigure a character with wounds to repair historical injuries. "He has to be wounded," continues the poet defensively. Why must the poet stitch some kind of wound into all of his major characters, from Philoctete, the emblematic black descendant of slaves, to Plunkett, the representative white colonial; from the lovelorn Achille to Hector, Helen, even himself? Because, the poet explains, "affliction is one theme / of this work, this fiction," as indeed of Afro-Caribbean literature and much Third World literature in general (28). That the wound trope is central to *Omeros* suits preconceptions of postcolonial writing as either "victim's literature" or "resistance literature." But Walcott's use of the figure—for example, attaching it here to the white colonial Plunkett—frustrates the assumptions it elicits. Indeed, this seemingly unsurprising motif continually turns strange and unpredictable in Walcott's hands; this strangeness starts with his willingness to embrace the motif after having denounced the literature of Third World suffering for decades.

In examining Walcott's elaboration of the wound in *Omeros,* I trace the complex genealogy of its primary bearer, the black fisherman Philoctete. Appropriating the classical type of the wound-tormented Philoctetes paradoxically enables Walcott to give new voice to the suffering of Afro-Caribbean peoples under European colonialism and slavery.[5] In this character, Walcott fuses still other literary prototypes of North and South, Old World and New. The astonishing hybridity of Walcott's black victim exemplifies the cross-cultural fabric of postcolonial poetry and contravenes the widespread assumption that postcolonial literature develops by sloughing off Eurocentrism for indigeneity. Repudiating a separatist aesthetic of affliction, Walcott turns the wound into a resonant site of interethnic connection within *Omeros,* vivifying the black Caribbean inheritance of colonial injury and at the same time deconstructing the uniqueness of suffering. Hybrid, polyvalent, and unpredictable in its knitting together of different histories of affliction, Walcott's radiant metaphor of the wound helps to dramatize poetry's promise as one of the richest and most vibrant genres of postcolonial writing.

Perhaps the most ambitious English-language poem of the decolonized Third World, Walcott's massive *Omeros* is written in long rolling lines—typically of twelve syllables—grouped in loose terza rima stanzas; alludes abundantly to Homer, Joyce, and Aimé Césaire; and ranges from precolonial Africa to eighteenth-century Saint Lucia, from the nineteenth-century United States to contemporary Ireland. Interwoven with its story of Philoctete's wound are plots of a Saint Lucian Achille and Hector struggling over a beautiful Helen, of an English Plunkett and Irish Maud seeking peace in the Caribbean, and of a composite poet—part Walcott, part blind pensioner—striving to tell the history of his island. Of Afro-Caribbean poems in English, only Kamau Brathwaite's *The Arrivants* (1967–69) is a work of comparable scope, size, and aspiration. Brathwaite's fragmentary trilogy also revisits the trauma of the Middle Passage and looks back to Africa, bases characters on inherited literary types and intermingles West Indian creole with literary English. But whereas an epic poem of Caribbean "wounds" or "hurts of history" might be expected of Brathwaite, professional historian and poet of New World African dispossession and survival, Walcott in the 1960s and 1970s declared his hostility to Afro-Caribbean literature about "the suffering of the victim."[6] While many Caribbean writers of this period chronicled the inherited devastation of European slavery and colonialism, Walcott, accusing Brathwaite among others of being absorbed in "self-pity," "rage," and "masochistic recollection," called instead for an artistic celebration of the Adamic potential of the New World African: perpetual exile was, in his view, the condition for a new creativity.[7]

In Walcott's poetry of this period, the wound or scar is often the figurative locus of such criticisms. Toward the end of his grand autobiographical poem *Another Life* (1973), Walcott blasts Caribbean artists for their "masochistic veneration of / chains," for revering "the festering roses made from their fathers' manacles."[8] He casts into the volcanic pit of his Antillean hell "the syntactical apologists of the Third World":

> Those who peel, from their own leprous flesh, their names,
> who chafe and nurture the scars of rusted chains,
> like primates favouring scabs, those who charge tickets
> for another free ride on the middle passage. . . .
> . . . .

they measure each other's sores
to boast who has suffered most,
and their artists keep dying,
they are the saints of self-torture,
their stars are pimples of pus
on the night of our grandfathers,
they are hired like dogs to lick the sores of their people. . . .[9]

Pitching his voice in a willfully intemperate tone, Walcott attributes the scars, scabs, and sores of his damned not only to slavery but to recent masochistic indulgences. Grimly yet gleefully analogizing, Walcott maps onto Africanist returns to the trauma of slavery the Dantean figuration of hell as compulsive repetition of the past.

But in writing an epic poem of his native Saint Lucia, Walcott takes up the postcolonial poetics of affliction he once condemned, anatomizing the wounded body of Caribbean history through Philoctete,[10] injured by a rusted anchor:

He believed the swelling came from the chained ankles
of his grandfathers. Or else why was there no cure?
That the cross he carried was not only the anchor's

but that of his race, for a village black and poor
as the pigs that rooted in its burning garbage,
then were hooked on the anchors of the abattoir.
    (19)

Walcott makes an oblique reference to colonialism, comparing the wound to the "puffed blister of Portuguese man-o'-war" (19); and he also evokes "a wounded race" (299) and "the tribal / sorrow that Philoctete could not drown in alcohol" (129). Even after he is supposedly healed, Philoctete joins Achille in a Boxing Day rite that, like the Caribbean limbo dance, recapitulates the trauma of the Middle Passage, including the primordial deracination that Philoctete reenacts when he slaughters the yams:

All the pain

re-entered Philoctete, of the hacked yams, the hold
closing over their heads, the bolt-closing iron. . . .
    (277)

In using the wound motif to signify slavery and colonialism, Omeros resembles countless other texts of African diaspora literature, and the reason for this prominence and pervasiveness is far from obscure. As C. L. R. James recalls in his discussion of the vicious treatment of Caribbean slaves, wounds were inflicted in many gruesome ways, and even "salt, pepper, citron, cinders, aloes, and hot ashes were poured on the bleeding wounds."[11] Early on in *Omeros,* Walcott uses one of Philoctete's seizures to suggest that the inexpressible physical suffering of enslaved Africans is retained in the bodies of their descendants and that the pain still presses urgently for an impossible verbal release:

> His knee was radiant iron,
> his chest was a sack of ice, and behind the bars
>
> of his rusted teeth, like a mongoose in a cage,
> a scream was mad to come out; his tongue tickled its claws
> on the roof of his mouth, rattling its bars in rage.
> (21)

Naming conditions of black enslavement with the words "iron," "bars," "rusted," and "cage," Walcott portrays the pain of the wound as colonizing Philoctete's entire body. More than any of Walcott's previous works, *Omeros* memorializes the institutionalized atrocity of New World African slavery. Though as late as the 1980s Walcott continued to castigate West Indian literature for sulking—"Look what the slave-owner did"[12]—at the beginning of *Omeros,* Philoctete rolls up his trouser leg and "shows" his punctured shin to paying tourists, figuring, by extension, the poem's large-scale exhibition of Afro-Caribbean pain to the touristic reader (4). And whereas Walcott once locked in hell "those who peel, from their own leprous flesh, their names," Philoctete refers to the colonially imposed name as one source of the ancestral wound:

> What did it mean,
>
> this name that felt like a fever? Well, one good heft
> of his garden-cutlass would slice the damned name clean
> from its rotting yam.
> (20)

Nursed and inspected, magnified and proliferated, the metaphor of the wound forms the vivid nucleus of Walcott's magnum opus. In an interview, Walcott indicates that the figure was the germ of *Omeros:* "A very good friend of mine had died," he recounts, "an actor, and I was thinking about that. And where this poem started was with the figure of Philoctetes, the man with the wound, alone on the beach: Philoctetes from the Greek legend and Timon of Athens as well."[13] How can we reconcile Walcott's earlier and later positions? Part of the answer is that they are less antithetical than my juxtapositions make them appear to be. In spite of his pronouncements, Walcott was already mourning early on what he memorably called the "wound," the "deep, amnesiac blow" of slavery and colonialism.[14] He was deeply aware of the central trauma of Afro-Caribbean history and drawn to bodily figurations of it. Even so, he remained hesitant about fully sounding this theme before *Omeros,* so what made it possible for him to shift from one self-defined stance on the literature of Third World suffering to its apparent opposite? The classical figure of Philoctetes is an important part of the answer, the bridge by which Walcott crosses his own divide. His Afro-Greek Philoctete is a compromise formation, the venerable vehicle legitimizing the tenor of black rage and suffering. While still granting cultural authority to Europe, Walcott also reclaims it for Caribbean blacks more vigorously than before, tropicalizing and twisting an ancient Greek hero into a vibrant new figure for Afro-Caribbean pain. One of the oldest dead white European males is reborn in a wounded black body; a member of the colonizing tribe resigns his part to limp among the colonized.

Walcott's appropriation of the wounded Philoctete broadly resembles other well-known indigenizations of canonical Western characters. To dramatize Caribbean suffering and anticolonialism, Aimé Césaire remakes the doltish Caliban in his play *Une tempête,* Kamau Brathwaite the submissive Uncle Tom in *The Arrivants,* and Jean Rhys the raving Bertha Rochester in *Wide Sargasso Sea.* Racked by an unhealing wound, Philoctete's body literalizes the anguish and anger of his celebrated West Indian counterparts. Like these writers, Walcott poetically inverts the material transfers of colonization, abducting a major character from the Western canon to dramatize the legacy of the West's atrocities. Just as "empires are smart enough to steal from the people they conquer," Walcott has remarked, "the people who have been conquered should have enough sense to steal back."[15]

But whereas Césaire, Brathwaite, and Rhys appropriate characters already oppressed by virtue of their gender, class, or race, Walcott strangely blacks up the classical white male war hero responsible for victory in the Trojan War. Like Walcott's seemingly perverse use of Crusoe instead of Friday to personify the Caribbean condition, the metamorphosis of this wounded Greek castaway is more violent and tangled than that of Caliban, Tom, or Bertha—white to black, colonizer to colonized, classic to contemporary.[16] These dislocations are not merely subversive or "exotic" but emphatically defamiliarizing.[17] Keeping the ironies acute, Walcott presents his Philoctete as even less a self-standing character, even more a signifier of the work of postcolonial reinscription—a Mona Lisa with a distinctively Caribbean mustache.[18] With only minimal credibility as a naturalistic Caribbean fisherman, Walcott's Philoctete seems to have wandered out of Greek literature and stumbled into a textual universe where he suddenly embodies the colonial horrors perpetrated by the West. To highlight his reliance on a culture of slavery to indict the practice of slavery, Walcott pointedly refers to the institution as "Greek" (177) and ironically adduces "the Attic ideal of the first slave-settlement" (63), even as he turns a Greek hero into his synecdoche for all the damage wrought by slavery and colonialism. He repeatedly signals the seeming oddity of Philoctete's name in the Saint Lucian context (greater than that of the simpler Achille or Hector or Helen), as if to make of the name a foreign-language sign hung around his neck. "Pheeloh! Pheelosophee!" scream boys on their way to school (19), and sheep bleat "Beeeeeh, Philoctete!" (20); only at the moment of his apparent cure, "The yoke of the wrong name lifted from his shoulders" (247). Instead of naturalizing the name, Walcott turns it into a trope for violent colonial imposition, a partial cause of the wound to which it is metonymically linked.

Most familiar from Sophocles' eponymous play but also portrayed in countless other retellings from Homer to Seamus Heaney and in the visual arts from Attic vase painting to neoclassical sculpture, Philoctetes, with his exquisitely elaborated pain, has long served as the classical alternative to Christ in the Western iconography of pathos and innocent victimhood. Bitten by a venomous snake and abandoned on the isle of Lemnos by his Greek compatriots, the groaning, shrieking Philoctetes languishes for nine years, his wound stinking, his body convulsed with pain, his flesh covered only with rags.[19] If Philoctetes enabled Lessing to affirm his neoclassical faith in the "moral greatness" of heroic endurance and helped Edmund Wilson to advance a psychological conception of artistic genius as "inextricably bound up" with "disability" and "disease," he becomes for Walcott, as for Heaney in *The Cure at Troy* (1991), an allegorical figure for the postcolonial condition.[20] As agent of Troy's defeat, Philoctetes might seem a dubious choice to represent the colonial victim, yet it is also true that the Greeks exploit him to conquer Troy, that he is transported to an island and abandoned there, and that he lives in poverty, hunger, and pain. Unintelligible stammerings—literally the discourse of the *barbaric*—interrupt his Greek when he suffers spasms of pain. And his wound suggests not only affliction but also colonial penetration, evacuation, and forgetting. Faithful to the classical Philoctetes in remembering his stinking wound, island fate, physical misery, and eventual cure, Walcott nevertheless transports him to a different archipelago, darkens his skin, trades his bow for a fisherman's net, transcribes his pained ejaculations in creole, and effects his cure through an obeah woman. While it might be a tempting, if pedantic, exercise to dissect each of these modifications, the risk would lie in trapping Walcott's Philoctete in an exclusive relation to his Greek namesake; but his affinities are more culturally polyphonous than such a narrowly typological analysis could allow.

Despite the apparently obvious line of descent signaled by his name, from Philoctetes to Philoctete, Walcott has spliced a variety of literary genes and even antithetical cultures to create a surprisingly motley character. Like a composite character in one of Freud's dreams, the wound-bearing Philoctete encompasses a strange array of penumbral literary figures. Rei Terada discerns the "variegated" and even "confusingly overdetermined" models behind characters in *Omeros,* but critics have tended to see Philoctete as a character with a simple pedigree.[21] If even the character in *Omeros* who appears to be simplest in his cultural inheritance turns out to have a multiple and contradictory parentage, then perhaps the postcolonial poet's seeming capitulation to or seeming subversion of Western influences needs to be rethought as a more ambiguous and ambivalent synthesis than is usually acknowledged.

Philoctete represents Walcott's absorption and refiguration not only of Philoctetes but also, strangely enough, of Caliban. Caliban? Doesn't Walcott scorn the postcolonial transvaluation of Caliban as West Indian hero? Doesn't this poet, who saw himself in youth as "legitimately prolonging the mighty line of Marlowe, of Milton," belong, unlike George Lamming, Aimé Césaire, and Kamau Brathwaite, among the adherents of Prospero, whose Caribbean makeover as "white imperialist" he debunks as "fashionable, Marxist-evolved" revisionism?[22] Walcott's seemingly shameless mimicry of a character out of the classical tradition distracts us, I believe, from his covert refashioning of the Caribbean paradigm of anticolonial defiance. Philoctete, when we first meet him, describes the cutting down of trees, though for making canoes rather than firewood. Closely associated with the land, he mirrors, as if by magical sympathy, his natural island environment in the Caribbean. He personifies his entire race's grievance against the colonizers. He launches an abortive revolution by demolishing the garden that sustains him. He "curse[s]" because never "*black people go get rest / from God,*" much as Caliban curses and rues his compulsory hard labor (21). At the moment of Philoctete's cursing, "a fierce cluster of arrows / targeted the sore, and he

screamed"; similarly, Caliban's curses prompt his master to promise, "I'll
rack thee with old cramps, / Fill all thy bones with aches, make thee roar."[23]
Seized by the unpredictable onset of physical torment, Walcott's Philoctete
fuses a classical paradigm with the Third World's transvaluation of Shakespeare's wretch. But whereas the new Caliban was already becoming a West
Indian cliché a couple of decades earlier, Walcott paradoxically refreshes the
symbol of postcolonial agony and anger by reaching for a still more wizened
prototype. His career-long resistance to Caliban, as to the wound trope, helps
him to flush these literary inheritances with new power and complexity.

As figures of Caribbean oppression, Philoctetes and Caliban complement each other: one of them, tormented on an island that is rightly his, is
especially well-suited to allegorizing colonization, while the other, transported to an alien island, easily figures the displacement and deracination of
West Indian slavery. But whereas Philoctetes has remained the cultural property of the West, Caliban's postcolonial indigenization has been so vigorous
that, at least regionally, he is as much a Caribbean as a Shakespearean figure.
Walcott's closet Caliban bears the impress of postcolonial revisionism or
what he concedes are the often "brilliant re-creations" by fellow Caribbean
authors.[24] Unlike Shakespeare's but like Césaire's Caliban, for example, Walcott's Philoctete is suspicious of his cumbersome name and even wants, as
we have seen, to slice it from his body. In Césaire's *Une tempête,* Caliban de-
cides he doesn't "want to be called Caliban any longer" because Caliban
"isn't [his] name" and his real "name has been *stolen.*"[25] To perpetuate Caliban, Walcott paradoxically de-indigenizes him, reroutes the figure back
through colonial culture, and thus makes him new. Exemplifying the twists
and turns of intercultural inheritance, this literary maneuver belies the narrative of postcolonial literary development as progression from alien metropolitan influence to complete incorporation within the native cultural body.
The culturally alien and native, outside and inside can, it seems, stage a poly-
rhythmic dance.

Nevertheless, to see Walcott's wounded character as a combination of
the classical Philoctetes and the Caribbean Caliban still oversimplifies his
genesis. When Walcott yanked Philoctetes out of antiquity to recast him,
still other figures from other cultures stuck to the prototype. Philoctete, as
Walcott remarks of Crusoe, "changes shape . . . with Protean cunning."[26]
Drawing on Western classicism for his character's base, veering homeward
for a Caribbean admixture, Walcott spins the globe again and picks up other
traces from Western modernism. Caliban may seem fishlike, but a Euromodernist text that also interpolates *The Tempest* provides a closer antecedent for

Walcott's wounded fisherman, who, with his "unhealed" wound, "limp[s]" and languishes at the waterside, feeling his "sore twitch / its wires up to his groin"—a mysteriously unhealed wound that reflects the wounded condition of the land and indeed the entire region (9, 10). Like the Fisher King in Eliot's *Waste Land,* Philoctete is a synecdochic figure for a general loss, injury, and impotence that must be healed for the (is)lands to be set in order. If Philoctete is a kind of Caribbean Fisher King, Achille plays the role of questing knight who must journey to the Chapel Perilous—in *Omeros,* Africa, site of ancestral enslavement—to rejuvenate the wounded fisherman, the land, and its people.

Remembering the modernist metamyth of the wounded vegetation god, Walcott places *Omeros* in a line that stems not only from Eliot but from a throng of Western artists and anthropologists as well. The animistic opening scene of *Omeros* recalls, for example, Sir James Frazer and Robert Graves in its description of the sacrificial felling of godlike trees for the making of canoes. Philoctete narrates how he and his companions steeled themselves "to turn into murderers," "to wound" the trees they depend on for their livelihood (3). As a tree fell, the sun rose, "blood splashed on the cedars, / / and the grove flooded with the light of sacrifice" (5). Achille "hacked the limbs from the dead god, knot after knot, / wrenching the severed veins from the trunk" (6), but once the tree is reborn on the water as a canoe, it and Hector's canoe "agreed with the waves to forget their lives as trees" (8). Alluding to the annihilation of the Arawaks, Walcott adapts the vegetation myths of the aboriginal inhabitants of the island, as mediated through archetypalist modernism: "The first god was a gommier." He metaphorically reenacts a sacrificial rite to open the way for his own tale: much as the fishermen must kill trees to remake them as canoes, so the poet must hew the linguistic timber of his forebears to remake it as his own vehicle. Introducing the character Philoctete before anyone else, the poem insists on the analogy between his representative wound and what it repeatedly calls the "wound" suffered by the trees. Thus it makes of him the poem's spirit of life, of nature, and of the island, and his wounded body the synecdoche for all the wounds suffered by the island's natives, slaves, and natural beings, possibly even its epic poet.

Like Osiris and other vegetation deities in the modernist metamyth, Philoctete requires the ministrations of a female counterpart to be healed, in his case the obeah woman or sibyl Ma Kilman. Paralleling Achille's magical return to Africa, Ma Kilman discovers an herbal antidote of African origins, transplanted by a sea swift, and she brews the remedy in an old sugar cauldron, allegorized as "the basin / of the rusted Caribbean" (247). His "knuckled spine like islands," Philoctete emerges from his healing bath "like a boy . . . with the first clay's / innocent prick"—the new Caribbean "Adam" (248). But whereas the concept of the New World Adam resonates throughout Walcott's earlier work, he is now an aspiration, a potential achievement in the New World; the wounded, impotent Adonis, Parsifal, Fisher King, or Philoctetes more nearly represents the New World condition, overcome provisionally and strenuously. Philoctete becomes Adamic because an African flower rejoins him to the African past, not, as in the earlier Walcott, because of his "amnesia." Indeed, at the risk of crowding the field of prototypes still further, we can gauge Walcott's change in the difference between his earlier tendency to imagine the West Indian as healthy castaway and Crusoe's replacement in *Omeros* by another sort of castaway—this one harboring a stinking, ulcerous wound, his body tormented by the persistence of the past, ameliorated only by the retrieval of a precolonial inheritance.[27]

For all Philoctete's links with the Euromodernist figure of the vegetation god, we must spin the globe again to appreciate why the wound-healing quest in *Omeros* turns to Africa. Responsible not only for the postcolonial reappraisal of Caliban but also, of course, for the Caribbean recuperation of African aesthetics and values, negritude might seem an unlikely influence on Walcott, given his testy assessment of it in essays like the grudgingly titled "Necessity of Negritude" (1964).[28] While granting that negritude helped to restore "a purpose and dignity to the descendants of slaves," Walcott suggests that "nostalgia" and uniquely French pressures of "assimilation" produced the movement's "artificial" reconstruction of a black identity rooted in Africa. "Return," Walcott later writes, is "impossible, for we cannot return to what we have never been."[29] Yet in *Omeros* the return to Africa is key to healing the torn black body and racial memory of the Caribbean, as personified by Philoctete. Walcott describes in loving detail how "centuries ago" an African swift managed, in bringing a special seed across the ocean, "to carry the cure / that precedes every wound" (238, 239). This curative plot of return to a precolonial Africa would have been unimaginable without negritude, however long past its heyday and however often resisted by Walcott. Moreover, Ma Kilman commits what would seem to be another cardinal Walcottian sin in reviving the African gods "Erzulie, / / Shango, and Ogun" to find the African flower that will cure Philoctete (242). For "the new magnifiers of Africa," Walcott had tartly stated, the "deepest loss is of the old gods," and poets who look "to a catalogue of forgotten gods . . . engage in masochistic recollection."[30] True, the narrator of *Omeros* emphasizes that the gods, "their features obscured" and "thinned," "had lost their names / / and, therefore, considerable presence" (242). Nevertheless, he assures us, "They were there" (243). In one of the most memorable scenes of *Omeros,* the gods, having earlier "rushed / across an ocean" in "loud migration," swarm like bats in Ma Kilman's grove, their wings forming "crisscrossing stitches" that presage the closing of Philoctete's wound (242). Walcott even flirts momentarily with the concept of race-based blood inheritance of African belief: the old gods sprout through Ma Kilman's body, "as if her veins were their roots" and her arms their branches (242).[31]

While negritude overcomes Walcott's resistances in his mythologizing of Africa as site of wholeness and cure, it also plays a part in engendering the wound figure itself. Since Walcott is seldom thought to owe much to negritude poetry, it might be worth pausing on this seemingly improbable point of connection, for all the obvious differences. In *Cahier d'un retour au pays natal* (1947), called by Walcott "the most powerful expression of Negritude," Césaire repeatedly personifies his West Indian homeland as a wounded body.[32] The speaker reconciles himself to returning to and even embracing a land disfigured by its forgotten wounds ("je reviens vers la hideur désertée de vos plaies"; "je dénombre les plaies avec une sorte d'allégresse").[33] Even as he celebrates and idealizes the black body, he also remembers its wounds cut by the slavemaster's whip and brand, wounds that still sound like tom-toms ("tam-tams inanes de plaies sonores").[34] One year after the first French edition of the *Cahier* was published, another crucial text of negritude followed hard on its heels in 1948, an anthology of francophone African and West Indian poets, prefaced by Jean-Paul Sartre's influential essay "Orphée Noir." The black poet, according to Sartre, writes great collective poetry when, in part, "exhibiting his wounds."[35] The black poet's capacity for articulation is so fused with a historical condition of pain and injury that, in one of the poems Sartre cites, the Haitian writer Jacques Roumain pleads in an apostrophe to Africa, "make . . . / of my mouth the lips of your wound [*plaie*]."[36] The collective memory that unites black poets of different languages and regions, according to Sartre, is one of untold, massive suffering. Slavery, despite its abolition half a century before the negritude poets were born, "lingers on as a very real memory," a point that he supports by quoting first Léon Damas of French Guyana:

Still real is my stunned condition of the past
of
blows from knotted cords of bodies calcinated
from toe to calcinated back

of dead flesh of red iron firebrands of arms
broken under the whip which is breaking loose . . .

and, second, the Haitian poet Jean-François Brierre:

. . . Often like me you feel stiffnesses
Awaken after murderous centuries
And old wounds bleed in your flesh . . .
[Et saigner dans ta chair les anciennes blessures . . .][37]

The vividness of the trope of the wounded black body in these influential
negritude texts should prompt us to reconsider the assumption that in
Omeros Walcott has simply transported the classical Philoctetes among other
Homeric types to the Caribbean, reincarnating him in a black body, encasing
him in African skin. It may be equally plausible to argue that Walcott places
a Greek mask on the wounded black body of negritude.

Yet neither of these paradigms offers the definitive solution to the implicit question I have sought to complicate by oscillating between North and
South, West and East, Europe, Africa, and the Caribbean: simply put, where
does Philoctete's wound come from? Literally, from a rusty anchor, and alle-
gorically, from slavery; but once the question is shifted from the mimetic to
the literary historical register, the puzzle of origins multiplies. Does it come
from the wounded black body of Afro-Caribbean negritude or the Euromodernist fertility god? From the Caribbean Caliban or the Greek Philoctetes?
Yet even these regional designations are reductive: the Caribbean Caliban
evolved from a Western canonical figure; many vegetation gods appropriated
by Western modernists were originally Eastern; and negritude developed in
part as a dialectical reversal of Western colonialist stereotypes. In intermingling Caribbean and European literary paradigms, Walcott thickens the
cultural hybridity of each. Rather than purify what might be called the "di-
alectic" of the tribe, Walcott accelerates, complicates, and widens it.

One of Walcott's recurrent metaphors for cultural hybridity may seem,
at this point, unsurprising: the scar. Comparing the cultural heterogeneity of
the Antilles to a shattered but reassembled vase, Walcott said in his Nobel address that the "restoration shows its white scars" and that "if the pieces are
disparate, ill-fitting, they contain more pain than their original sculpture."[38]
More somber than Walcott's tropes of webbing and weaving, let alone popular metaphors like melting pot, salad bowl, or callaloo, the scar signifies cultural convergence in the Americas without effacing its violent genesis. At the
end of "The Muse of History," Walcott movingly recalls the violent past deposited in his body, apostrophizing a white forefather, "slave seller and slave

buyer," and a black forefather "in the filth-ridden gut of the slave ship." But the scars left by the slavemaster's "whip" are metamorphosed in Walcott's magnificent image for his and the Caribbean's fusion of black and white skins, of Northern and Southern Hemispheres: "the monumental groaning and soldering of two great worlds, like the halves of a fruit seamed by its own bitter juice."[39] Even though the wound has scarified in these descriptions, Walcott never reduces the bitterness or pain to a condition that can be repaired completely; rather, it is constitutive of the new synthesis. Walcott returns to this figure near the end of *Omeros*, when he represents the intercultural labor of his poem as having

> followed a sea-swift to both sides of this text;
> her hyphen stitched its seam, like the interlocking
> basins of a globe in which one half fits the next. . . .
>   (319)

In Yeats's words, Walcott suggests that "nothing can be sole or whole / That has not been rent."[40]

Seaming black skin and white masks, white skin and black masks, Walcott's Philoctete stands in a long line of Walcottian personifications of cultural and racial hybridity. His name taken from the culture of colonizer and slaver, yet his wounded black body allegorizing their cruelty, Philoctete recalls the "divided" speaker of "A Far Cry from Africa," cursing the brutality of the colonizers yet cursing them in the language they have given him. Greco-Caribbean, Euro-African, Anglo-Hebraic, Philoctete is a boldly intercultural amalgamation, like the self-defined Shabine of "The Schooner *Flight*":

> I have Dutch, nigger, and English in me,
> and either I'm nobody, or I'm a nation.[41]

Although Philoctete seems at first to represent but one cultural and racial pole of the Caribbean and thus to differ from Shabine and from Walcott's other early hybrids, Walcott suggests that even in constructing a seemingly monocultural character, in this case to allegorize black pain, the Caribbean poet builds into his aesthetic construct inevitably mixed cultural inheritances. Even Philoctete's cure, like his wound, turns out to be transcultural. Ma Kilman relies, as we have seen, on a specifically African plant and on African gods to heal Philoctete's wound. But she attends five o'clock Mass on the day she delivers Philoctete of gangrene. When she finds the curative African flower, she still wears her Sunday clothes. Vacillating between

Greece and the Caribbean, the poem calls Ma Kilman "the sibyl, the obeah-woman." This apposition reverses the presumably literal and metaphoric, and succeeding lines perpetuate the whirligig in naming her "the spidery sibyl / / hanging in a sack from the cave at Cumae, the obeah / . . . possessed" woman (245).

Decades before the academic dissemination of such concepts as hybridity, creolization, cross-culturality, postethnicity, postnationalism, *métissage,* and *mestizaje,* Walcott argued vehemently for an intercultural model of postcolonial literature.[42] Against a "separatist" black literature that "belligerently asserts its isolation, its difference," he counterposes a vision of the Caribbean writer as inevitably "mixed": New World blacks must use what Walcott ironically calls "the white man's words" as well as "his God, his dress, his machinery, his food. And, of course, his literature."[43] But Walcott also attacks pervasive assumptions about so-called white American literature—a more powerful if less visible identitarian counterpart to negritude and nativism: "To talk about the contribution of the black man to American culture or civilization is absurd, because it is the black who energized that culture, who styles it, just as it is the black who preserved and energized its faith."[44] For Walcott, as for other Caribbean writers such as Wilson Harris and Edouard Glissant, tribalist views from either extreme disfigure the mixed reality of New World culture, repressing it in favor of simplistic narratives of cultural origin.

The twisted skein of intercultural influences in Philoctete reveals the distortion involved in conceiving of postcolonial literature as a progression from colonial dominance to indigeneity, European subordination to nativist freedom.[45] According to this standard narrative, Walcott's use of the Philoctetes type would seem to be a regression to an earlier phase of Eurocentric indebtedness; yet the same linear narrative would also have to note in the figure a progressive step toward indigenous articulation of West Indian suffering. Is Walcott recolonizing Caribbean literature for Europeans by using this and other Greek types? Or is he decolonizing it by representing Caribbean agony? Does the poet reenslave the descendant of slaves by shackling him with a European name and prototype? Or does he liberate the Afro-Caribbean by stealing a literary type from former slavers and making it signify their brutality? Too simplistic for the cultural entanglements of a poem like *Omeros,* the evolutionary model of postcolonial literature is rooted in a discredited model of national development. We need a more flexible language to describe how a poet like Walcott can put into dialectical interrelation literary and cultural influences that may seem incompatible. Critics

have seen an evolution in Walcott's work from literary Eurocentrism to Afrocentrism, from denying to embracing African influences on his and others'
Caribbean art. Yet Philoctete's wound and cure show Walcott not shedding
but deepening his European interests as he explores his African commit-
ments, becoming neither a Eurocentric nor an Afrocentric poet but an ever
more multicentric poet of the contemporary world.

Having traced the cross-cultural literary genealogies of the wound and its
bearer in *Omeros,* I would like to turn from the vertical axis and questions
of literary sedimentation to the horizontal and the wound's intratextual res-
onances, and here too the profoundly intercultural character of Walcott's
trope emerges. Once again this hybridity may be surprising, since the
wound in *Omeros* at first seems to encode unambiguously the painful Afro-
Caribbean legacy of slavery and colonialism. While using the wound motif
to honor the uniqueness of this black experience, Walcott nevertheless
cross-fertilizes the trope, extending it to other peoples as well. Hybrid in its
intertextual ancestry, the wound is also a trope of polymorphous diversity
within the text. No sooner has Walcott identified the wound motif with the
black experience than he introduces his principal white character, who also
happens to be wounded. "He has to be wounded," because of the poem's
cross-racial thematics: "affliction is one theme / of this work" (28). What
caused Plunkett's wound, other than Walcott's desire to create a cross-
cultural echo? Like Philoctete's wound, Plunkett's has only the bare outlines
of a literal pathogenesis. Major Plunkett, wounded in the head by an explosion during the North African campaign of World War II (27), also seems to
bear the inherited wound of European colonialism. He even discovers that a
midshipman with his name suffered a "fatal wound" in the Battle of the
Saints, the famed eighteenth-century battle for Saint Lucia (86). Certainly,
Plunkett's wound differs suggestively from Philoctete's: it is to his head, not
his body, and it never induces spasms of uncontrollable physical pain. These
and other differences point up the more cerebral nature of white suffering in
the aftermath of colonialism. Even so, Walcott insists by emblem and analogy that both colonizer and colonized inherit a legacy of affliction in the
Caribbean.

As if repeated application of the word "wound" to a Euro-Caribbean and
an Afro-Caribbean were not enough to reveal their commonality, Walcott
rhymes Plunkett and Philoctete in a variety of ways. Their names may not literally rhyme, except perhaps for the final syllable, but they share an initial *p,*

an *l*, and the nearly anagrammatic final letters -*kett* and -*ctete*. Though the men differ predictably in appearance, Plunkett, with "a cloud wrapped around his head" during convalescence, recalls the "foam-haired Philoctete" (28, 9). The stoic Philoctete resolves to "endure" his affliction with the patience of an "old horse" (22), even as Plunkett, true to his own stiff-lipped heritage, rejects the "easy excuse" of blaming his temper on his injury (22, 56). Philoctete's wound apparently renders him impotent, and the great sorrow of Plunkett's life is his inability to father a son (29). Like Ma Kilman, the female anointer of Philoctete's wound, Plunkett's wife, Maud, his nurse in the war, looks after his head injury.[46] After Maud dies, Ma Kilman acts as a medium in Plunkett's effort to contact her. Whether these links are instances of "Homeric repetition," "coincidence," or Joycean counterpoint (96), they make inescapable the connections between one affliction and the other. As early as "Ruins of a Great House" (1962), Walcott tries to hold in a single work the bitter knowledge that "some slave is rotting in this manorial lake" and "that Albion too was once / A colony like ours," that both slave and master inherit histories of excruciating pain, cruelty, and abuse.[47] As Walcott says of "doubt," the wound "isn't the privilege of one complexion" (182).

Walcott's use of the wound at first seems to satisfy Fredric Jameson's well-known generalization: "All third-world texts are necessarily . . . allegorical, and in a very specific way: they are to be read as what I will call *national allegories*."[48] Read thus, the Walcottian wound would be a trope of unproblematic referentiality and stand for the particular historical experience of a particular race in a particular part of the world. Long codified as a dominant trope for black enslavement and mimetic of real wounds perpetrated on real black bodies for hundreds of years, the wound would seem to be the perfect, unambiguous allegory of Afro-Caribbean history. But Walcott plays energetically on the instabilities of the trope. For the wound also has, as Elaine Scarry observes, "a nonreferentiality that rather than eliminating all referential activity instead gives it a frightening freedom of referential activity."[49] Discourses of realist fiction and of nationalist politics might seek to control and even defeat the "referential instability" of the wound, affixing it to a particular people, motive, or cause. But by attaching the wound trope to the name Philoctete and to a black body, Walcott already contaminates and disrupts the specificities demanded by "national allegory." Moreover, the lancet wound that Philoctete suffers from confounds inside and outside; it is the point at which racially unmarked interiority erupts as exteriority and the world within breaks through the epidermal surface. While much contemporary criticism views postcolonial texts, more than their metropolitan

counterparts, as preeminent examples of the literature of national and ethnographic specificity, Walcott devises a transnational allegory about both the
wound of black Saint Lucian history and a larger subject—what he calls "the
incurable // wound of time" (319).

To write about pain and mortality as transcultural experiences may seem
to risk an easy humanism or discredited universalism. Walcott keeps this
tendency in check by reserving for the wound an interpretive opacity.
Philoctete's wound is a piece of body language that, like many literary
wounds, signifies its status as polyvalent sign by resembling a "mouth" (18).
But it is a dumb mouth, a sign that also signifies its inarticulateness. Although it is an external mark that tourists, associated elsewhere in the poem
with neocolonialism, pay "extra silver" to see, it remains mysterious, turned
inward, folded and guarded. Walcott describes it as "puckered like the
corolla / of a sea-urchin," in contrast to "a garrulous waterfall" that tourists
hear "pour out its secret." Philoctete "does not explain [the wound's] cure. /
'It have some things'—he smiles—'worth more than a dollar'" (4). Hovering
between dumbness and communication, the wound offers touristic readers
an entryway into Afro-Caribbean experience even as it reminds them that
they can never fully comprehend the local burden of historical pain, that
they must remain voyeurs peering from without. Philoctete's wound elicits
from him a scream that is "mad to come out" but that is held back "behind
the bars // of his rusted teeth" (21). Inducing yet disabling speech, the
wound figures both the promise and the limits of language as vehicle of interpersonal and intercultural understanding.

Walcott can thematize Philoctete's wound as language without betray-
ing the Afro-Caribbean experience because Caribbean blacks also suffered
the wound of colonially imposed languages, such as French and English,
which are interwoven (sometimes in creole) throughout the poem. Just as
Philoctete experiences his alien and inscrutable name as a festering wound
he wishes he could cut from his body, Achille realizes that he does not share
his forebears' belief in an essential connection between names and things,
that he does "not know" what his name means: "Trees, men, we yearn for a
sound that is missing" (137). If Philoctete's wound is a language—partly
readable, partly opaque—his language is also a kind of painful wound
haunted by the memory of an Adamic language it has displaced. But this
woundlike language is also potentially its own cure: as the narrator remarks
near the end of *Omeros,* "Like Philoctete's wound, this language carries its
cure, / Its radiant affliction" (323). The line break, in a pregnant syntactic
ambiguity, hovers between an elided conjunction (which would make the

cure and affliction opposites) and a relation of apposition (in which the cure would be the affliction). The metaphor of light, repeated from earlier descriptions of the wound as "radiant" (9, 21), tips the seeming antithesis toward identity, much as the poet has done earlier in punningly mistranslating Philoctete's complaint in French creole that he is wounded, "*Moin blessé*," as "I am blest" (18). The poet's discovery of likeness between the words *blessé* and "blest," like his monolingual play on "affliction" and "fiction" (28), demonstrates how the European languages inflicted on West Indians can be turned from curses into blessings. Like Yeats, who could never give up his "love," in spite of his "hatred," for the English language, the poet of *Omeros* refers to "the wound of a language I'd no wish to remove," even after the poet character and Plunkett mimic upper-class accents in a linguistic charade (270).

Philoctete's wound, no less than the colonial language it partly figures, carries its cure dialectically within itself. Indeed, wound, weapon, and cure belong to a metonymic family that Walcott strengthens by metaphoric substitutions throughout the poem. When Walcott compares a "running wound" to "the rusty anchor / that scabbed Philoctete's shin," for example, he identifies the shape and color of the wound with the weapon, and the word "scabbed" suggests both the injury and its cure (178). As if to close the gap between a punctured leg and the healing agent, Walcott chants their prepositional coalescence: "the flower on his shin," "the flower on his shin-blade," "the foul flower / on his shin" (235, 244, 247). The tropological binding up of seeming antitheses also works in the opposite direction. In writing that the "pronged flower / / sprang like a buried anchor," Walcott identifies the curative African plant with the weapon whose injury it reverses, as later with the wound it heals: "The wound of the flower, its gangrene, its rage / festering for centuries, reeked with corrupted blood, / / seeped the pustular drops instead of sunlit dew" (237, 244). Using metaphor to leap the gap between destruction and healing, Walcott's language performatively converts injury into remedy. The only flower that can heal Philoctete's wound must match, perhaps even exceed, the wound's "bitterness," "reek," and "stench" (237); thus Walcott suggests that the poem cannot contribute to healing the wounds of Afro-Caribbean history without reproducing their pain. Like the Boxing Day rite in which "all the pain / / reentered Philoctete," the poet's language carries a cure that must continually reopen and expose the wound (277). In fashioning a mirror relation between injury and remedy, Walcott represents within *Omeros* the poem's homeopathic relation to the traumatic history of the West Indies. Joining black and

white, Old World and New, the wound's cross-cultural metaphoricity ex-
hibits the structural doubleness that is fundamental to the poem's logic.

The wound motif exemplifies the slipperiness and polyvalence of poetic
discourse that circulates between races, crossing lines of class and community, bridging differences between West Indian fisherman and Greek warrior.
With its resonance and punning, imagistic doubling and metaphoric webbing, Walcott's poetry demonstrates the kinds of imaginative connections and
transgressions that have ironically made poetry a minor field in postcolonial
literary studies. For poetry, at least in Walcott's hands, is less respectful than
prose fiction of racial, regional, national, and gender loyalties.[50]

The lancet wound migrates from Philoctete to a white American
woman, when Walcott attributes to Catherine Weldon "the wound of her
son's / / death from a rusty nail" (176). By means of the wound trope and others, Walcott crosses and recrosses lines of race, nation, and gender. Moreover, Walcott rides the trope across the line between narrative and lyric
poetry as he compares his personal loss in a failed marriage to Philoctete's
historical and communal injury: "There was no difference / between me and
Philoctete" (245), he says, later coupling himself and Philoctete in a mirror
image when they wave in greeting: "We shared the one wound, the same
cure" (295). Although postuniversalist sensibilities might bridle at such assertions of identity, Walcott signals the distances he traverses by trope. The
poet stays at a hotel; the fisherman lives in a poor village. The estranged poet
looks "down" from a "height" at his island, "not like Philoctete / / limping
among his yams and the yam flowers" (250). Philoctete is a contemporary
black man; Catherine Weldon is a nineteenth-century white woman. But
Walcott refuses to accept the identitarian fear that shuttling across these
enormous differences erases them; he shoots the gulf (in Emerson's phrase),
suggesting that the greater danger lies in becoming captivated by the narcis-
sism of differences. As the poem's primary wound-bearer, Philoctete embodies the principle of metaphorical coupling, mediating not only between
Greece and Africa, white and black, wound and cure but also between
Achille and Hector ("Philoctete tried to make peace between them" [47]),
between capitalist and Marxist parties (he campaigns for "United Love"
[107]), and between the living and the dead (he names drowned fishermen
[128]), as well as between male and female (he and Achille become "androgynous / warriors" during their Boxing Day dance [276]).

The wound joins the major characters of *Omeros* in a large metaphorical
company. The pervasive love wound is one example of this effect: Hector's
transport or minivan is like a "flaming wound" because he fears Helen still

loves Achille (118); Achille "believed he smelt as badly as Philoctete / from the rotting loneliness" (116); Helen so misses Achille that it seems the nightingale's "monodic moan / / came from the hole in her heart" (152); Plunkett is afflicted with another wound on the death of his wife (309); and Saint Lucia's fishermen suffer "that obvious wound / made from loving the sea over their own country" (302). Promiscuously linking various characters in amorous anguish, the wound trope also comes to signify the love that poets like Shelley have long associated with metaphor. A metaphor for metaphor, the wound even circulates through various parts of the nonhuman world, from the volcano whose "wound closed in smoke" (59) to the French colonial ship *Ville de Paris* "wallowing in her wounded pride" (85), and from a field (170), a bay (238), a cauldron (246), and a hut (272), to shacks (178), coves (249), the entire island (249), the sky (313), even the whole Caribbean basin (247). Unleashing the pathetic fallacy, Walcott sees the region's brutal history reflected throughout its natural and human landscape. While a prodigious passion for likeness is characteristic of Walcott's poetry, this passion also typifies a much older and larger propensity of poetry, harnessing the metaphorical play of resemblance within language to amplify and free it. Acknowledging this legacy, he presents the phantasmagoria of the poet, Omeros, as the ideal embodiment of metaphorical conjuncture. Omeros's language is a "Greek calypso," and his images flicker between black and white, the living and the dead, the real and the fantastic (286).

From the perspective of the identity politics that sometimes underwrites the study of Third World literatures, metaphor and postcoloniality might seem to be strange bedfellows, but they should be regarded as reciprocal, interwoven, and mutually enlarging. The movement of metaphor across ethnic, regional, and gender boundaries is well suited to the openly hybrid and intercultural character of postcolonial literature and finds perhaps its fullest articulation in poetry, from Walcott to Ramanujan, Soyinka, and Agha Shahid Ali. Forced and voluntary migration, crossings of one people with another, linguistic creolization, and racial miscegenation—these are the sorts of displacements, wanderings, and interminglings that poetic metaphor can powerfully encode in the fabric of a postcolonial text. To trace the spiralings of the wound motif in *Omeros* is to begin to understand how a poetic imagination as fecund as Walcott's can, in its restless work of discovering and creating resemblance, confound tribal, ethnic, or national limits.

"Trauma" is, of course, Greek for wound, and Walcott's *Omeros* could be said—extending a psychological analogy of Glissant's—to remember, repeat, and work through the trauma of Afro-Caribbean history.[51] But this ameliorative work should not be confused with a definitive healing. Although both the character Philoctete and the "phantom narrator" are represented as being cured, Walcott so proliferates and disperses the trope that, even after the climactic scene of healing, the wounds of history and language are shown to persist. As early as the opening of *Omeros,* to which I return by way of conclusion, we can already see that Walcott turns the trope with such vigor that no fictive cure will ever put a stop to its motion. Even in this first canto, the wound bounces from trees to earth to blacks to native people. In the poem's scene of origination, Walcott wants to show victimizer and victimized to be ambiguous, shifting positions.[52] Philoctete starts out as neocolonial victim: he "smiles for the tourists, who try taking / his soul with their cameras." Walcott suggests that the neocolonial tourist and, by implication, the touristic reader perpetuate the colonial trauma in trying to penetrate the interior of the Caribbean descendant of slaves ("trauma" derives from a word for "to pierce" [*tetrainein*]). But soon enough Philoctete is telling how he and the other fishermen had "axes" in their "eyes," as the tourists have piercing gazes. Indeed, he and his comrades, like latter-day colonizers, become "murderers": "'I lift up the axe and pray for strength in my hands / to wound the first cedar'" (3). Suddenly reader, tourist, and colonizer become vulnerable to the wounding they at first seemed accused of committing. If metaphor turns Philoctete's wounds into weapons, it also inverts his black victimization as soon as that status is established. But neither is the alternative role stable, for Philoctete now reveals his own painful scar, which identifies him with the wounds that he will perpetrate on the trees. And as Walcott alludes to the annihilation of the Arawaks and their language, he recalls a still-earlier trauma from which there can be no question of recovery. Sharing a fate of island suffering yet surviving it to replace the native population, Philoctete and the other black fishermen soon resume the role of inflicting, not receiving, wounds: they turn off the chain saw and then, ripping "the wound clear" of vines, "examine the wound it / had made," as the blood of a Saint Lucian sunrise "trickled" and "splashed" on the trees (5).

Is Walcott, as poet of cross-cultural affliction, a "fortunate traveller" of transnational trope? Because he sets this most politically loaded of metaphors spinning, does he irresponsibly confound distinctions between colonizer and colonized, oppressor and oppressed? How can this cross-racializing of the wound be reconciled with the asymmetrical suffering that marks colonialism and postcoloniality, let alone slavery? These are the undeniable risks of Walcott's free riding of the wound trope across moral and historical divisions, but his wager is that they are risks worth taking.

If exclusive fidelity to a single history of affliction is required of the Third World poet, then Walcott certainly fails this test. But Walcott conceives the Antilles as a site of multiple and inextricable histories of victimization and cruelty, histories deposited not only in its landscape and its languages but even in his body. From an identitarian perspective, poets like Walcott who metaphorically enact interethnic connections falsify the historical specificity of their people's experience. But for Walcott, the greater falsification would lie in an aesthetic separatism blind to the culturally webbed history of the Caribbean, of his ancestors, and of his imagination, in a viewpoint hostile to the cross-racial and cross-historical identifications the New World offers.

As graphic emblem of convulsive, bodily pain, the wound in *Omeros* memorializes the untold suffering of Afro-Caribbeans, yet as trope, it inevitably poeticizes pain, compares this particular experience with others, and thus must either mar or deconstruct experiential uniqueness by plunging it into the whirlpool of metaphorical resemblance and difference. Anchor-like in shape and origins, the wound trope in *Omeros* drifts from the ground of a particular people's experience to the afflictions of native peoples, Greeks, Jews, colonial Americans, even the English. Because Walcott's intermappings of suffering never occlude Philoctete's primacy and never sugarcoat the trauma of slavery, they keep in view differences between oppressor and oppressed, even as they open up and reveal the connections between the experiences of Afro-Caribbeans and others. Appropriating a Western icon of suffering and refashioning a polysemous and multiparented trope, Walcott's *Omeros* champions a postcolonial poetics of affliction that unravels the distinction between "victim's literature" and its supposed opposite.

CHAPTER FOUR

🌿 Metaphor and

Postcoloniality:

A. K. Ramanujan's Poetry

Long associated with universalist philosophy and formalist poetics, with Aristotle and the New Criticism, the analysis of metaphor may seem to have little bearing on postcolonial studies. But, improbable though it may seem, the two areas remarkably intersect even at the level of theory, and their unnoticed convergence might help us to rethink not only their relation but also each of the fields. The relative metaphoric density of poetry, which helps to make it less ethnographically transparent than other genres, has contributed to its marginalization in postcolonial studies, but if metaphor and postcoloniality are affiliated as structures of experience, and if metaphor is indeed a principal discursive site of postcoloniality, then perhaps anglophone poets of the Third World deserve a more prominent place in postcolonial studies, from Walcott and Brathwaite to Okot and Okigbo. Having considered the interculturalism of Walcott's polyvalent use of metaphor, I examine the revealing overlap between theories of postcoloniality and metaphor before turning to A. K. Ramanujan as exemplar of the potentially fruitful convergences between the two discourses.

"Displacement," "transfer," "migration"—these terms belong to the standard lexicon of postcolonial studies, but they also appear in well-known discussions of metaphor. Etymology begins to help explain this strange intersection of vocabularies. Basic to the word "metaphor," Greek for "transference," is the metaphor of movement in space; that is, "metaphor" metaphorizes semantic and hermeneutic change as spatial movement from one place to another, one "realm" or "context" to another. "*Phora,*" as Paul Ricoeur points out, "is a kind of change, namely change with respect to location"; "the *epiphora* of a word is described as a sort of displacement, a movement 'from . . . to. . . .'" Further, "*metaphor is the transposition* of a name that Aristotle calls 'alien' (*allotrios*)"—a word that implies "borrowing," since "the displaced meaning comes from somewhere else."[1] Found scrawled on the wall of a university bathroom, "Transference, Displacement, Alienation, Borrowing, Movement between Realms, Change of Location" would probably seem to echo lectures on postcoloniality, not metaphor. But this conclusion would be overhasty, since the study of metaphor and of the postcolonial are both concerned with what has been called "the location of culture" or, perhaps even more crucially, its dislocation. Metaphor and postcoloniality are both conceived of in terms of the movement, transference, or alienation of discourse from one place to another, a movement that involves not only a one-way shift but inevitably a bidirectional hybridization. While postcolonial studies articulates the cultural convergence of places known as East and West, North and South, metropole and colony, metaphor is, according to I. A. Richards, a "transaction between contexts."[2] "Things or ideas which were remote appear now as close," Paul Ricoeur writes of metaphor, describing the "rapprochement," "epiphora," or "transfer" of metaphor as "nothing else than this move or shift in the logical distance, from the far to the near."[3]

Lest these analogies seem merely the product of etymological play on Aristotle's terminology, let us look at a more recent analysis of metaphor that trades heavily in the geographic language usually associated with postcolonial studies. In his influential *Languages of Art,* Nelson Goodman conceives of metaphor as the bringing together of two different "realms."[4] Notably described as "disjoint" or "native and foreign," these realms are the aggregate associations between one idea, word, or sense and many others. In metaphor, "a set of terms . . . is transported" or "detached from the home realm" and "applied for the sorting and organizing of an alien realm."[5] Interestingly enough for our purposes, after this transfer, the terms are not blandly assimilated to the new realm but bring along their associations: "The organization they effect in the alien realm is guided by their habitual use in the home realm." What happens as a consequence of this "expedition abroad," after a label or idea or schema "is transported" to or more aggressively "takes over new territory," after its "invasion" or "migration"?[6] A "reorientation": the convergence transforms each of the realms.[7] Describing metaphor, Goodman sometimes sounds like a bizarre cross between Aristotle and V. S. Naipaul:

> The home realm of a schema is the country of naturalization rather than of birth; and the returning expatriate is an alien despite his quickening memories.
>
> Its travels result in some displacement on its return (otherwise we shouldn't even know it had been away); but the displacement is far from total.

Sometimes a schema may take a longer round trip, with more stopovers, and be more drastically displaced on its return.[8]

Does it matter that one can talk metaphorically about metaphors in ways that recall postcolonial displacement, relocation, and transfer? Exile, expatriation, diaspora, and migration? Alienation and hybridization? Or is it merely a coincidence? It pays, of course, to reflect on why one can describe sex in terms borrowed from death, argument in the language of construction, and wars as if they were games.[9] In none of these cases is the metaphorical traffic between realms essential, but neither is it negligible. So too, I would suggest, the analogies between metaphor and postcoloniality should awaken us to our oddly geographical understanding of metaphor and, conversely, to the prominent role that metaphor ought to play in our understanding of the postcolonial. Although metaphor has often been deconstructed as a totalizing trope of identity and organicity, a postcolonial perspective can help to renew our awareness that displacement, difference, and alienation are no less inherent than equivalence in the structure of metaphor.[10]

Perhaps I could spell out further some implications of these analogies between metaphor and postcoloniality. Dislocations of discourse, meaning, or culture from one context to another are fundamental to both the metaphorical sentence and the postcolonial text. Moreover, complete integration within the new discursive or cultural field produces dead metaphors and overassimilated art. In order for the newly hybridized discourse to reorient perception, a tension must remain between the native and foreign, tenor and vehicle, focus and frame. Metaphorical or poetic discourse, as Victor Shklovsky famously argued, renews perception by "defamiliarizing" the world. It disrupts the "habitualization" that "devours" objects, slowing down perception and making the world "unfamiliar" again.[11] Similarly, in Third World literatures, juxtapositions caused by colonization and migration throw into relief what habit normally conceals, defamiliarizing the cultures of colonizer and colonized. Split vision is characteristic of postcolonial literatures, a seeing of cultures in terms of one another. Phrases like "split reference" and "stereoscopic vision" have also served to describe how metaphor produces and maintains a tension between two modes of perception or reference.[12] Further, the rhetoric of "sameness" and "difference," with an emphasis on "the tension between *same* and *other*," is basic to analyses of both postcolonial texts and of metaphor.[13] "The meeting of two distant realities" is how one poet, as if writing about the postcolonial experience, describes the foundation of metaphor.[14]

Admittedly, to emphasize the location of postcoloniality, like metaphor, within discourse, culture, or rhetoric is to risk diminishing its sociopolitical basis. The postcolonial aesthetics of intercultural hybridity and metaphoric tension arose out of a historical matrix of violence, occupation, and resistance. Opening up the metaphorical resemblances between metaphor and postcoloniality, one personifies metaphor, as if tenor and vehicle were like peoples brought together by geopolitics, and depersonalizes postcoloniality, as if colonizer and colonized were less peoples than linguistic, discursive, or rhetorical units. Like any comparison, this one inevitably highlights some aspects of each term and shuts others into darkness. Yet such an emphasis might be salutary at a time when political and sociological analysis often overshadows the figurative dimension of postcolonial aesthetics. By teasing out the homologies between metaphoric and postcolonial hybridity, displacement, and split perception, I hope to make visible an underlying reason for the dramatic ascendancy of postcolonial literatures in the second half of the twentieth century. To explain why the postcolonial experience is especially amenable to aesthetic expression, in particular to highly figurative modes such as poetry and magical realism, it helps to consider that dislocations of meaning, unexpected conjunctions of discourse, stereoscopic vision, defamiliarizing incongruities, linguistic hybridity, and consciousness of sameness in difference are integral to both postcoloniality and the very structure of metaphor. Hoping to suggest the crucial importance of metaphor in postcolonial literatures as a rhetorical locus of stereoscopia, hybridity, and dislocation, I explore the postcoloniality of metaphor and the metaphoricity of the postcolonial as exemplified in the work of one writer, the most distinguished anglophone Indian poet before his death in 1993, Attipat Krishnaswami Ramanujan.

Long underestimated and therefore perhaps still in need of introduction, Ramanujan's poetry now seems poised on the brink of worldwide recognition. In 1995 Oxford University Press published *The Collected Poems of A. K. Ramanujan,* gathering together *The Striders* (1966), *Relations* (1971), and *Second Sight* (1986), as well as material for an incomplete fourth volume, *The Black Hen.* In 1999 it published *The Collected Essays of A. K. Ramanujan,* with *The Uncollected Poetry and Prose* still to come. Since the 1960s, Indian contemporaries such as Nissim Ezekiel and R. Parthasarathy have hailed Ramanujan as the best Indian English poet. If Ramanujan's earlier poetry is sometimes overwhelmed by the satiric ferocities of Pound and Eliot, anglo-modernist influences nevertheless helped Ramanujan fend off the sentimentality and abstraction that often clouded Indian English verse. His later volumes, above all *Second Sight,* ever more successfully absorb and remake the forms, tonalities, and tropes inherited from English-language poets such as Williams, Stevens, and Yeats, brilliantly fusing them with the traditions of ancient and medieval Dravidian poetry. A MacArthur Award–winning professor of linguistics at the University of Chicago, Ramanujan translated and studied South Indian literatures, garnering Western and Eastern recognition for these and other neglected, non-Sanskrit traditions of India. Resisting the "monism" and even "cultural imperialism" of proponents of a single "pan-Indian Sanskritic Great Tradition," Ramanujan reaffirmed that "cultural traditions in India are indissolubly plural and often conflicting." "India does not have one past," he emphasized, "but many pasts."[15] Best known in the West for his crystalline translations of classical and medieval Tamil and Kannada verse, Ramanujan draws on many features of these older literatures in his own anglophone poetry: the strikingly vivid and structural use of metaphor, the intensification of one image by another, "montage" and "dissolve" effects, streams of association, flowing syntax, spare diction, avoidance of heavily stressed rhythms, delight in irony and paradox, precise observation of both interior (*akam*) and exterior (*puṟam*) worlds, and reliance not on metaphysical abstraction but physical detail for complex thinking.[16]

As translator of classical Dravidian poetry, Ramanujan renders its forceful metaphors into contemporary English, using them in turn as models for his own anglophone poetics. His indigenous models complement anglo-modernist principles of concision, economy, and nondecorative use of metaphor, as seen in an example of ancient Tamil poetry that almost seems proto-Imagist:

> The bare root of the bean is pink
> like the leg of a jungle hen,
> and herds of deer attack its overripe pods.[17]

In Ramanujan's translation, the metaphor of the exposed root—emphatically visible and vulnerable—superimposes hen leg on bean root, hybridizing vegetable and animal, color and taste, autochthony and mobility. Considering the broad contours of Ramanujan's career, one might speculate that this Tamil metaphor of a root that mutates into a mode of transportation may have held Ramanujan's interest for other reasons as well. Though rooted in South Indian Brahman culture since his birth in Mysore in 1929, he lived from 1959 onward in the United States, wrote primarily in English, drew on modern Anglo-American poetry, and criticized Sanskrit-based Indology, Hindu zealotry, and Indian revivalism. Conversely, though an English-language poet in the United States, he devoted his life to South Asian studies, wrote primarily about India, drew inspiration from Dravidian literatures, and often seemed clinically detached from the English language he worked in.[18] On this last point, R. Parthasarathy notes that Ramanujan's use of English "has a cold, glass-like quality," as if "to turn language into an artifact."[19] Ramanujan writes from within English yet as if outside it—a recognizably postcolonial practice that recalls Deleuze and Guattari's analysis of "minor literature."[20] Ramanujan remembers that in youth he associated the English language with "colonial India and the West, which also served as a disruptive creative other that both alienated us from and revealed us (in its terms) to ourselves."[21] In keeping with the distinction in Tamil poetics between *akam* (interior) and *puṟam* (exterior), Ramanujan describes himself as split between his "'outer' forms"—"English and my disciplines (linguistics, anthropology)"—and his "'inner' forms"—his lived Indian experience and lifelong study of its cultures.[22] Poet and translator, Ramanujan relies on both metaphor and translation to interweave his outer and inner worlds, while also exploring the gaps between them. Describing the translator's "several double allegiances," Ramanujan suggests that metaphor and translation function for him as closely related forms of mediation between languages, between cultures, perhaps even between halves of the brain.[23]

"The word *translate,* as you know," Ramanujan has commented, "is only Latin for the Greek word *metaphor.* Both mean 'carry across.'"[24] As translator and scholar, Ramanujan labored to carry poetry across differences of language, time, and culture, all the while reflecting in his own English-language poetry on what is lost in translation. At the heart of Ramanujan's poetry are ironic, if plangent, meditations on transfer and loss between East and West, on survivals and disappearances between past and present. As a switchboard through which spatiotemporal differences migrate and meet, metaphor discursively locates and animates this in-betweenness. Metaphor can itself be conceived as a "contact zone" or "third space" that aesthetically embodies postcolonial interculturation.[25] Close analysis of several of Ramanujan's finest lyrics may help to probe in detail the connections between metaphor and the postcolonial. Specifically, I tease out of Ramanujan's poetry the many forms that metaphor takes in mediating postcoloniality: as contact point between one culture and another; as connective tissue of postcolonial memory; as agent of cultural reproduction; as conduit between the postcolonial subject and its origins or endings; and as discursive incarnation of resemblances between the postcolonial self and its private, national, or transnational family.

The opening of "Waterfalls in a Bank" in *Second Sight* reflects Ramanujan's immersion in the work of translation and, more broadly, his understanding of the parallels between metaphor, intercultural translation, and intertemporal connection:

> And then one sometimes sees waterfalls
>   as the ancient Tamils saw them,
> wavering snakeskins,
>
> cascades of muslin.[26]

From Tamil into English, from ancient to contemporary, Ramanujan translates metaphors of snakeskins and muslin, which in turn "translate" waterfalls. His eye a "rainbow bubble," Ramanujan would, as he rhymes in a later poem, "see all things double"—or perhaps even quadruple, as with this waterfall ("Mythologies" 2, 226). Beholding a manmade waterfall in a Chicago bank, Ramanujan's vision is split stereoscopically between waterfall and snakeskin/muslin. This metaphorical juncture straddles, in turn, the "postcolonial" junctures of India and the United States, old Tamil texts and his own writing. To see through the prism of postcoloniality, with its fusion of alien perspectives, is already to possess something akin to the double vision of metaphor. Ramanujan decommodifies and indianizes the confined waterfall in an American bank, putting metaphor to work in a kind of reverse colonization. The ancient Indian vehicles of snakeskin and muslin paradoxically enliven with danger and wonder an image hackneyed in Western poetry.

   Poetic metamorphosis begins in metaphor's activation of memory. The bank's waterfall not only occasions memories of the East but soon becomes itself a metaphor for postcolonial recollection. The poet's rush of memories—children, Biafra, love songs, bomb sites—ends in an image of his personal origins in a "mother's labouring / / thighs." Summoning the multiple relations of resemblance in the family (poet and foremothers), nature (American and Tamil waterfalls), culture (the United States and India), and time (ancient and contemporary), Ramanujan compares such metaphorical "transactions between contexts" to money exchanged in a bank:

> As I transact with the past as with another
>   country with its own customs, currency,
> stock exchange, always
>
> at a loss when I count my change. . . .

In exchanges between past and present as well as one culture and another, the transaction is transformative: the poet is punningly "at a loss" to understand his profound "change," both impoverished and enriched by his submission to an alien economy.[27] In a later essay, Ramanujan again compares the mutually transformative experiences of cross-cultural and cross-temporal encounter: "The past is another country, as the saying goes. With the past, too, one adds oneself to it as one studies it. One is changed by it and the past itself is changed by one's study of it."[28] Postcolonial quester after origins, Ramanujan nevertheless represents the cultural past as irrecuperable and unknowable in and of itself, unlike the static past of the revivalist. The metaphorical links by which the poet helps us to cross into the past inevitably transfigure it, even as it transfigures us. In Ramanujan's as in much postcolonial writing, metaphor is a primary conceptual and linguistic site of both intercultural and intertemporal exchange. As in Ramanujan's not-just-financial bank, it is a place where diverse cultures and temporalities come together to be transacted, transposed, and defamiliarized. The "stereoscopic" structure of metaphor, Ramanujan indicates, is isomorphic with the structure of postcolonial experience.

In the climactic scene of "Waterfalls in a Bank," Ramanujan metaphorically bridges the distances between past and present, East and West. Standing in a Western financial institution, the Brahman poet remembers from his childhood the mirror image of what he might have become—a Brahman mendicant ascetic. Rheumatoid, diseased, spasmodic, the sadhu lifts his loincloth with one finger and "pisses" on two flowers beside the street. The modern West commingles with the ancient East in the metaphorical blending of the bank's waterfall with the sadhu's "stream" of urine. But the most remarkable transfusion of cultural opposites occurs when "a car turns the corner," illuminating the sadhu's urination:

> Headlights make his arc
>
> a trajectory of yellow diamonds,
>   scared instant rainbows, ejecting spurts
> of crystal, shocked
>
> by the commonplace cruelty of headlights.

This startling confluence of Western modernity and an ancient Eastern way of life produces an epiphanic moment, when, to speak a little grandly of an old man's urination, both liquid and light seem transfigured into something beyond themselves—either East or West, precolonial or postcolonial. A luminous "exchange of contexts," this climactic image figures in part Ramanujan's own poetry: a humble world lit up by poetic form, an ancient sensibility startled by its encounter with modernity, a traditional Brahman past metamorphosed by the onset of the Western present—in short, a metaphor-making poesis that hybridizes and transfigures its cultural sources. Having begun in metaphoric transactions between old Tamil metaphors and a waterfall in a Chicago bank, Ramanujan's poem culminates in the creation of a new metaphor for the postcolonial experience of convergent temporalities and cultures.

Prominent in Ramanujan's poetry, memory has, of course, played an important role in postcolonial literature and theory from Césaire and Fanon to Achebe, Rushdie, and Glissant. In Fanon's resonant analysis, the Third World intellectual, confronting the colonial distortions and disfigurations of the precolonial past, remembers, revalues, and reclaims it, though that resurrected past becomes static and exotic unless integrated with the emergent present.[29] Ramanujan lays bare the metaphoric dimension of memory, foregrounding the mutual transformations of past and present by what psychoanalysis terms "condensation." Metaphor affords mnemonic connection but thereby radically dislocates Ramanujan's postcolonial speakers. In "Breaded Fish," a poem in Ramanujan's first volume, *The Striders* (1966), eating a breaded fish triggers an unsettling memory of a sand-grained corpse:

> a dark half-naked
> length of woman, dead
> on the beach in a yard of cloth,
>
> dry, rolled by the ebb, breaded
> by the grained indifference of sand.
> (7)

As in "Waterfalls in a Bank," metaphor is the site of energies exchanged between past and present, but here the energies transferred are overwhelmingly negative. In this and other poems by Ramanujan, the past recuperated by the poet is filled with death, loss, or degradation, not reassuring precolonial plenitude. The speaker's self-possession shattered by the metaphoric condensation of fish and corpse, of psychic and oral incorporation, the poem mimics aurally the resurgence through metaphor of an irrepressible past by repeating the rhyme words "breaded," "headed," "mouth" in the last stanza. The postcolonial experience is one of twin temporalities, seemingly unrelated, surely unintegrated, yet suddenly bridged, breached, and transfused by unpredictable moments of resemblance. Commenting in an interview on the persistence of the individual, historical, and cultural past, Ramanujan remarks, "you cannot entirely live in the past, neither can you entirely live in the present, because we are not like that. We are both these things."[30]

Metaphoric transport across lines of nation and history becomes still more ominous in "Some Indian Uses of History on a Rainy Day," from Ramanujan's second volume of poetry, *Relations* (1971). While Ramanujan often celebrates the power of metaphor to recover the past or engage another culture, he also acknowledges the risks in this poem about a "Professor of Sanskrit / on cultural exchange" who misreads a swastika in the Nazi Berlin of 1935 (75). Lost, bewildered, unable to make out the German signs in the rainy streets, the professor

> suddenly comes home
> in English, gesture, and Sanskrit,
> assimilating
>   the swastika
> on the neighbour's arm
> in that roaring bus from a grey
> nowhere to a green.

Appropriated by the Nazis, the swastika is in turn renaturalized by the Indian professor, nostalgically riding it back to his cultural home. But his *nostos,* or return home, is based on a grotesque misinterpretation of the decontextualized metaphor, which has been violently recontextualized in the service of an ideology and politics antithetical to the professor's projection. Blinded by his nativist and professionalized longing for roots, the Indian professor unconsciously reproduces in reverse the Nazi distortion of the Sanskrit sign. Although Ramanujan is alive, like Walcott, to the splendid intercultural and intertemporal possibilities of metaphor, he nevertheless shines a harsher light throughout his poetry on what metaphor leaps across—gaps in time and place, differences of culture and history.

In his four-part meditation "Drafts," from *Second Sight,* Ramanujan dissects the connections and misconnections in various forms of metaphoric resemblance—between personal past and present, original and copy, earlier and later cultures, parent and child, even among these different kinds of resemblance. That reproduction, refiguration, and inheritance should imagi-

natively engage the postcolonial poet is hardly accidental, concerned as Ramanujan is with recasting precolonial cultures for the contemporary world.
More surprising, perhaps, is Ramanujan's deft articulation of what fails in
translation, what is lost in the gaps crossed by metaphor. Ever alert to these
differences, Ramanujan is especially wary in "Drafts," as in "Some Indian
Uses of History on a Rainy Day," of the metaphor-driven mythologization of
beginnings, despite his knowing complicity in the recuperative quest. Building on Said's critique of myths of beginnings, Rashmi Bhatnagar warns that
"the search for . . . origins" may become "for the colonized people a longing
for an impossible purity and a yearning for the fullness of meaning that is not
only uncritical but also politically suspect in that it can unwittingly serve the
reactionary forces of revivalism. Nowhere is this danger greater than in the
Indian context, where the search for the source of Hindu identity in the
Vedic times has almost invariably led to a loss of commitment to our contemporary plural/secular identity."[31]

Scrutinizing the structure of resemblance, Ramanujan first ponders in
"Drafts" the detective's reconstruction of a paradoxically "well-known // but
half-seen" face (157–58). Police and witnesses attempt to refigure a crimi-
nal's face, "what one thought / one always knew," but must rely on such figurative simulacra as rubber noses and lips. "A rough draft, getting rougher,"
the poem wryly begins: as detective or poet tries to close the gap between
reproduction and original, tenor and vehicle, it yawns more widely. As a
deconstructive poet of *différance* or "aporia" and a reconstructive poet of
transfer and translation, Ramanujan suspects our knowledge of cultural,
temporal, and interpersonal alterity, dependent as it is on such traces, drafts,
fragments, and prostheses, yet he also suggests that for all of us, including
the expatriate bricoleur-poet, these mediating structures of resemblance
may well be our only means of access to that alterity.

Further deconstructing the hierarchized resemblances between memory
and the real, copy and original, the poet turns from detective work to the historian's reconstruction of the ancient Eastern past:

> Itself a copy of lost events,
>   the original is nowhere, of which things,
> even these hands,
>
> seem but copies, garbled by a ciphered
>   script, opaque as the Indus,
> to be refigured

from broken seals, headless bodies,
    mere fingers, of merchants and dancers
in a charred city

with sewers, bath houses, a horned god
    of beasts among real homebodies,
family quarrels,

itches, clogs in the drain, the latter
    too ordinary to be figured
in the classic seals.

Ramanujan questions both the West's orientalist nostalgia for Eastern origins and the East's nativist nostalgia for a precolonial past. Instancing the much theorized, if often qualified, interrelation between postcolonial and postmodern skepticisms, he emphasizes the layers of mediation and slippage between past and present, original and copy. The seal, age-old device for certifying authenticity, is an ironic emblem for such lapses in transmission. Here, the ancient Indian imprint is a "copy" of a lost "original" seal, which was, in turn, "itself a copy of lost events." The prized originals turn out to be copies in an unanchored metaphoric chain of reproductions. The deictic phrase "these hands" momentarily asserts the felt presence of the past; but the bodily immediacy of "hands" quickly melts into scribal copies of copies, as "hand" turns out to be a metonymy for inscription. In words like "hands" and "refigured," Ramanujan chiastically weaves together the scrambled, indecipherable text and the bodily fragments—"headless bodies, / mere fingers." Working with evidence that is already at several removes from lived experience, a historian cannot reach through "opaque" script and "broken" iconography to deliver the past whole into the present. Though dubious of both Western and Third World efforts to render transparent an ideal, unitary, precolonial past, Ramanujan nevertheless suggests that something of the past comes back to life through the co-creative engagement of the imagination. Supplementing the high mimesis of the classic seals with the low mimesis of contemporary poetry, Ramanujan marvelously evokes transhistorical ordinary life in the declining series "real homebodies, / family quarrels, / / itches, clogs in the drain." "The past," as Ramanujan writes elsewhere, "like other cultural constructions, changes as we attend to it."[32] But unlike the unremittingly corrosive ironies of some postmodernisms, Ramanujan's deconstruction playfully reinstates the postcolonial poet as agent of cultural reconstruction.

In the middle of this poem, Ramanujan quickens the dance among resemblances of different kinds, turning each into a metaphor for the metaphorical conjunctions of original and copy, present and past. Ramanujan protests the validity of the concept of the "original," all the while ironically eroding the concept by multiplying the play of mirror on mirror:

> And we have originals, clay tigers
>   that aboriginals drown after each small-
> pox ritual,
>
> or dinosaur smells, that leave no copies. . . .

Dependent "copies" strangely threaten the concept of the "original," since they make possible substitutions between the two terms. Hence Ramanujan humorously conjures an original—"dinosaur smells"—that guarantees its primordialness because it could "leave no copies." Revivalist nostalgia for an origin uncontaminated by the logic of reproduction leads to absurd conjecture about prehistoric odors. Similarly, Ramanujan mocks the reliance on earlier customs and peoples, "originals" and "aboriginals," to ground a variety of narratives about human descent—from an infantilized, Eastern Other, from a pristine, precolonial Other, or from the prehistoric, animal Other. In each case, reversals made possible by the symmetrical structure of metaphoric resemblance put the foundational polarities in jeopardy.

In a sudden twist, the poet rapidly spins out examples of

>   copies with displaced originals
> like these words,
>
> adopted daughters researching parents
>   through maiden names in changing languages,
> telephone books,
>
> and familiar grins in railway stations.

From the oldest originals without copies, Ramanujan turns to the latest copies without originals—"these words," which could mean either printed words in their immediacy on the page or the poet's words at the moment of inscription. In either case, the original—written draft or inspired thought—cannot be found. As "copies with displaced originals," the poet's words instance the broader condition of postcolonial deracination. In a splendid leap, Ramanujan compares these orphaned words to adopted daughters, triply dislocated from their familial origins—by adoption, by the patriarchal displacement of the maternal name, and by dislocation from one region's

language to others. The vexed daughterly quest for origins—indeed, Ramanujan's entire meditation on mutually estranged copies and originals—is,
once again, clearly suggestive of the experience of linguistic and cultural displacement, disinheritance, and expatriation. The poet's words are like children dislocated not only from an original draft text but a cultural and
linguistic context. They have little chance of ever bridging the colonial divide that separates them from their "primary" world, which must itself remain, at least in part, an imaginative fabrication. While mocking the
revivalist desire to reach beyond drafts and copies, Ramanujan nevertheless
foregrounds the inevitable participation of his own verse in the postcolonial
longing for an original home—a stabilizing source beyond the wanderings
of meaning, metaphor, and migration. In its purest form, this longing is
doomed, he suggests, to modes of melancholia and irony, since even if recov-
ered, the original would necessarily metamorphose into something different
and unforeseen.

In this poem the postcolonial ironist's quest for originals has led him
through police evidence, historical relics, aboriginal customs, and maternal
names. In each case, a spatiotemporal chasm separates copy from original,
warping, fracturing, or garbling their relations of resemblance, transforming
copies into originals and originals into copies. Not to attend to these gaps
would lead, in Ramanujan's view, to orientalist and revivalist falsifications of
one's relation to the past. "The past never passes," Ramanujan commented in
an interview; "Either the individual past or historical past or cultural past. It
is *with* us." Yet, he continues, "the disconnection is as much an understanding of the past as making the connection. And people living in the present
have to see both, because to assert continuity where there is none, where
we cannot see any, is to be a revivalist."[33] As a postcolonial poet, Ramanujan
is profoundly aware of the copies and reproductions that enable the
metaphoric imagination to cross multiple barriers, as well as of the estrange-
ments of memory, history, and language that complicate these similitudes.
The "alien" element, the "foreign" admixture continually obtrudes, he
knows, into resemblance. Between revivalism and revisionism, nativism and
postmodernism is the self-conscious metaphoricity of his own and indeed
much of the best postcolonial poetry.

In the last section of "Drafts," Ramanujan pivots to the family transmission of resemblances:

> The DNA leaves copies in me and mine
>   of grandfather's violins, and programmes
> of much older music;

the epilepsies go to an uncle
   to fill him with hymns and twitches,
bypassing me for now;

mother's migraines translate, I guess,
   into allergies, a fear of black cats,
and a daughter's passion

for bitter gourd and Dostoevsky. . . .

The scientific letters "DNA" seem to signal a shift to predictability, away from fallible discourses of reproduction. But the effects of genetic replication can be just as obscure as those of memory or history. To trace his hybrid musical interests back to his grandfather, his allergies and fears back to his mother's migraines, is to "guess," to concoct an imaginative story of personal origins, no less fallible than anthropological or historical narratives of the past. Ramanujan thus likens the transmission of a genetic trait between people to the translation, metaphor-like, of a word from one language to another, in which the new semiotic context and cultural environment result in unpredictable recombinations. Indeed, after all these twisted, fateful reproductions, Ramanujan ends the poem with a glimpse of a future seemingly beyond predestined lines of transmission:

   mother's almond eyes mix with my wife's
ancestral hazel

to give my son green flecks in a painter's eye,
   but the troubled look is all his own.

While self-mockingly disavowing what might well be his influence on his son, the poet also indicates that a kind of "originality"—human or artistic— can suddenly erupt into the world, scrambling the narratives of reproduction and resemblance that we tell ourselves about where we come from—indeed, that he has been telling throughout the poem. Ramanujan's knowing wink at art brings the poem's meditations to bear on its own reality, as a tissue of inheritances from earlier poems, Western and Eastern, which might, however, begin to break free. Writing about Indian literature, Ramanujan comments: "Mirror on mirror. Doubles, shadow worlds, upside-down reflections, are common in Indian myth and story. . . . When Śiva creates, he creates clones of himself. As with DNA, to create is to project one's copies onto the world."[34] Similarly, Ramanujan's poem is one of ceaseless doubling and multiple reflection, ironic reversal and imagistic elaboration, the creator perpetuating himself through lyric self-figuration, a refiguration of the eddying resemblances between himself and his textual, cultural, and genetic past. Both original and copy, creator and clone, the self-begetting poet is in turn begotten in the mirrors of history, language, culture, and genetics.

The question of origins is still more explicitly and urgently pursued in "Elements of Composition," once a long poem drafted in about twenty-five sections.[35] "Where do I come from?" is, of course, a particularly insistent question for the postcolonial subject, rooted in uprootedness, located in dislocation. For the anglophone Indian poet, the analogous question, "Where does this lyric 'I' come from?" is also inherently vexed. In this proem to *Second Sight*, Ramanujan quests for his origins in the material and linguistic "elements" composing his literal and literary "I" (121–23). In doing so, he paradoxically dislocates his identity even as he grounds it, seeing himself metaphorized as congeries of others, as a weave of alterities. The temporal split rehearsed in Ramanujan's poetry—the poet *is* and *is not* his origins—is again inextricable from the cultural split of the postcolonial—the anglicized Indian *is* and *is not* Indian or Anglo-American.[36]

Elaborating Nietzsche, Foucault remarks that the skeptical genealogist finds at the beginning of things not "immobile forms that precede the external world of accident and succession," "not a timeless and essential secret, but the secret that they have no essence or that their essences were fabricated in a piecemeal fashion from alien forms. . . . What is found at the historical beginning of things is not the inviolable identity of their origin; it is the dissension of other things. It is disparity."[37] Ramanujan's poetic quest both recalls and parodies the nativist quest for a unitary source, relocating the self in a past that is radically elemental, yet neither coherent nor homogeneous:

Composed as I am, like others,
    of elements on certain well-known lists,
father's seed and mother's egg

gathering earth, air, fire, mostly
    water, into a mulberry mass
moulding calcium,

carbon, even gold, magnesium and such,
    into a chattering self tangled
in love and work,

scary dreams, capable of eyes that can see,
    only by moving constantly,
the constancy of things

like Stonehenge or cherry trees. . . .

Insofar as this lyric "I" is a literary and grammatical "composition," the "chattering" poem speaks metaphorically of its mixed genesis out of "elements" both textual ("lists") and psychological ("love and work"). Implicitly it also bespeaks its hybrid cultural genesis out of Indian and Western poetics: the poem recalls ancient Tamil poetry in its one-sentence structure, its fluid montage of images, and its interplay of interior (*akam*) and exterior (*puṟam*),[38] while its archaeology of individual consciousness evokes modern descendants of the Greater Romantic Lyric. To recompose imaginatively his identity, the poet must first decompose himself into elemental properties that make him *like*, not unlike, "others." Instead of following the revivalist in privileging a single mythology of beginnings, he rapidly turns from one metaphorical order of self-explanation to another, enumerating a variety of secular creation myths. In the vocabulary of reproductive biology, the self comes from the union of sperm and egg; in older cosmologies, it is composed of the "elements" of "earth, air, fire," and—in a scientific twist—"mostly / water." For the contemporary chemist, it is made up of the more fundamental "elements" of the periodic table. The psychologist tells another story of origins that metaphorizes the self as language ("chattering") and the unconscious ("love and work, / / scary dreams"). As Vinay Dharwadker writes of the poem, "What is particularly paradoxical and ironic about the constitution of the self, in relation to its various 'others,' is that the process which accumulates its defining characteristics becomes indistinguishable from the process which evacuates its identity."[39] Instead of locating a secure ground for self-identity, the poet disperses the authority of each origin and highlights the quest itself.

In "moving constantly," the poem mimics perception, postcolonial dislocation, and even perhaps the continuity-in-change of human identity. Instead of delivering the expected "constancy," the last line of the initial series pauses over the seeming stability of Stonehenge only to blossom into movement with "cherry trees." The postcolonial experience of cultural dislocation and migration forces genuine constancy into view—the constancy of mutability. As Salman Rushdie writes, the "migrant's-eye view of the world," the "experience of uprooting, disjuncture and metamorphosis," can stand as "a metaphor for all humanity."[40] This conception of the individual as its metamorphic elements also reflects what Ramanujan half-ironically characterizes as "an Indian way of thinking": "the body is a meeting-place, a conjunction of elements," as indicated by Indian medical texts, which "have a physiology, but no anatomy." Refuting the stereotype of Indians as "spiritual," Ramanujan insists on the material transformations of the self: each individual is caught up in the "constant flow (the etymology of *saṃsāra!*) of substance from context to object, from non-self to self (if you prefer)—in eating, breathing, sex, sensation, perception, thought, art or religious experience."[41] The poem also instances the "context-sensitivity" by which Ramanujan defines "the Indian way of thinking," in contrast to the "context-free" habits of Western thought. Ramanujan boldly argues that Indian culture generally prefers context-sensitive rules in literature and behavior, as inflected by region (witness the regional differences in *dharma*), the stage of one's life (*āśramadharma*), class or *jāti* (*svadharma*), and emergency (*āpaddharma*).[42] Contrasting these Indian ideals with the universals of the Enlightenment, Ramanujan admits that context-free cultures also produce "counter-movements," and perhaps the contextualism of postmodern thought could be seen as a reactive movement in the West. For this reason, "Elements of Composition" can look at one and the same time like a profoundly traditional Indian depiction of the self—embedded in endlessly fluid, concentrically arranged contexts—yet also like a postmodern vision of the self as decentered and composite, provisional and context-bound.[43]

When Ramanujan turns from physical elements to memories as foundations of the self, these psychic "elements" are likewise jumbled, shifting, and heterogeneous:

> add uncle's eleven fingers
>   making shadow-plays of rajas
> and cats, hissing,
>
> becoming fingers again, the look
>   of panic on sister's face
> an hour before
>
> her wedding, a dated newspaper map
>   of a place one has never seen, maybe
> no longer there
>
> after the riots, downtown Nairobi,
>   that a friend carried in his passport
> as others would
>
> a woman's picture in their wallets. . . .

All of the ingredients are here for a self-portrait of an expatriate pining for his family and place of origin—except that the family is represented in metonymies of deformity and anxiety, not idealized wholeness, the place in metonymies of displacement and disorientation, not secure location. Alluding to the speaker's genesis in the initial scene of artistic representation, the poem's associational logic turns from shadow plays to other disconcerting memories of representation—a wedding that makes a sister panic and the map of an absent, unseen place.

From Kenya to South India, the poem nimbly leaps across distances of space, reiterating its recipe-like direction to "add" memory to memory, in imitation not only of unconscious sedimentation but also of the Indian experience of the new superimposed, time and again, on the old:

> add the lepers of Madurai,
>   male, female, married,
> with children,
>
> lion faces, crabs for claws,
>   clotted on their shadows
> under the stone-eyed
>
> goddesses of dance, mere pillars,
>   moving as nothing on earth
> can move—

The retrospective sequence illustrates the disjunctive structure of the self, which, perhaps especially in the postcolonial world, knows temporality not as logical evolution or natural progression but as accretion and rupture. Here, too, the memory is about both procreation and representation, but far from sentimentalizing familial or cultural origins, Ramanujan continues to insist on the deformity and indifference screened out by postcolonial nostalgia. Unlike the revivalist's, Ramanujan's return is to a place of disease, to a grotesque parody of the loving family unit, to art stonily indifferent to the suffering it shelters.

In both nativist and late romantic lyric, the recapitulation of an idyllic past often enables self-consolidation and self-projection into the future. Here, in contrast, poetic identity disperses itself into its memories even as it enumerates the ingredients composing it:

> I pass through them
>   as they pass through me
> taking and leaving
>
> affections, seeds, skeletons. . . .

This is not a poetic identity that colonizes its earlier selves, rediscovering its preferred "I" in a nugget of the past; rather, present and past selves interpenetrate one another, their boundaries fluid, their relations of dominance am-

biguous and shifting. The self drinking at the well of the past absorbs and is
absorbed by earlier desires, possibilities, incapacities. Recurring to an ar-
chaeological metaphor of the self, Ramanujan compares the permanent impressions left by fleeting experiences to

> millenia of fossil records
> of insects that do not last
> a day,
>
> body-prints of mayflies. . . .

Like the impressions of dead insects on the earth, experiences remain in the
unconscious mind by virtue of their absences and traces—negative imprints
that consciousness in turn seeks to fill. "The past never passes," says Ramanujan in a dictum that makes the psychologist, the geneticist, and the traditional Hindu all compact.

A final memory allegorizes the poet's quest to fill up the "body-prints"
left by past experiences:

> a legend half-heard
> in a train
>
> of the half-man searching
> for an ever-fleeing
> other half. . . .

But complete communion with the past, an identity fused with all it remembers and desires, a complete healing of postcolonial and metaphoric displacements—these Platonic or revivalist dreams of totality are, he knows,
impossible:[44]

> even as I add,
> I lose, decompose
> into my elements,
>
> into other names and forms,
> past, and passing, tenses
> without time,
>
> caterpillar on a leaf, eating,
> being eaten.

"Elements of Decomposition" might have served as well as the title for Ramanujan's meditation on the self-scattering quest for biochemical, psy-
chohistorical origins. To redescribe the self as "other names and forms" from

the past is to metaphorize it as traces and alterities. Incorporating yet truncating the prophetic vision of what is "past, or passing, or to come" at the end of Yeats's "Sailing to Byzantium," Ramanujan's poetic "composition" demonstrates how it feeds on the "elements" of earlier "compositions." "Individual poems," according to Ramanujan, "are created out of all the given 'elements of production,' and all the language of past poems."[45] Having roved from Yeats to the Upanishads, Western science to Eastern spiritualism, physical to psychic discourses, Stonehenge to Nairobi and Madurai, Platonic parable to Islamic festival (Muharram), the poet maps the multifarious geography deposited in his identity and his poem, almost as if he, like Salman Rushdie's Indian Everyman, Saleem Sinai in *Midnight's Children,* personified the diverse and uncontainable cultural origins of modern India. As Ramanujan writes in his allegorical portrait of India as a great house through which everything circulates:

> Things come in every day
>
> to lose themselves among other things
> lost long ago among
> other things lost long ago. . . .
>   ("Small-Scale Reflections on a Great House," 96)[46]

Concluding "Elements of Composition" with an allusion to the Upanishads, Ramanujan suggests that what he translates elsewhere as "Food Chain, Sanskrit Style" is a logic that holds for both body and mind, both poem and nation:

> And what eats is eaten,
> and what's eaten, eats
> in turn.[47]

In the decolonizing Third World, the boundaries between selves, between poems, and between nations are more obviously permeable and blurred than they may be elsewhere. To recompose them into discrete identities is to falsify their complex filiations and mixed origins. Better to adopt a poetic that rides the shuttle of metaphor between past and present, here and there, representing whatever lines it draws and totalities it arranges as composite, provisional, and open-ended. Better to locate the postcolonial self and poem in the dislocations of time, metaphor, and culture, to move with the movements of the eye and the word.

Like beginnings, endings also enable self, poem, and nation to define themselves in relation to a horizon that delivers the contours of identity.

"Where do I go to?"—like "Where do I come from?"—is a pressing and problematic question for a postcolonial poet. If the elements of composition are key to understanding identity, so too are the elements of decomposition—death and dispersal, bodily and spiritual afterlives, national and literary destinies. In "Death and the Good Citizen," Ramanujan reverses "Elements of Composition." Meditating on endings, he metaphorizes the self not as its bodily and psychic origins but as the imaginary possibilities of its future (135–36). Whether viewing the human life cycle from the vantage point of its start or its finish, Ramanujan indulges but critically revises the genealogical and eschatological impulses of much postcolonial literature and theory. For him, neither the beginnings nor the endpoints of the self are singular and fixed; they are fluid, manifold, and indeterminate. Exuberant ironist of origins, Ramanujan is revealed by "Death and the Good Citizen" to be a no less playful, no less poignant ironist of endings.

In "Death and the Good Citizen," the Hindu themes of reincarnation (*saṃsāra*) and of the world as food (*annamayan jagat*) shape Ramanujan's fascination with the recirculation of human beings into food, vegetation, and other human bodies. "All forms arise out of food and return to it," says Ramanujan in summarizing "one of the descriptions of brahman, the ground of being. In the transformations of food, inorganic becomes organic, one form is metamorphosed into another; the eater is eaten, big fish eat little fish, and if you wait long enough, little fish eat big fish."[48] Ramanujan also alludes in "Death and the Good Citizen" to "Hindu notions of death and the Vedic chant recited during the death ritual . . . : '[*To the dead man:*] May your eye go to the sun, your life's breath to the wind. Go to the sky or to earth, as is your nature; or to the waters, if that is your fate. Take root in the plants with your limbs. [*Ṛgveda,* 10.6].'"[49] Even so, Ramanujan recirculates these traditional ideas of the life-and-death cycle through postcolonial themes of cultural displacement, translation, and metamorphosis. Addressing an Audenesque "good citizen" with mock admiration, the poet begins by recounting the citizen's daily transformation of his bodily waste into grass for the consumption of cows and rhinos, into oranges for humans. Although facing the opposite temporal horizon from the speaker of "Elements of Composition," this citizen also conceives of himself in terms of his elements, in metaphors of bodily dispersal, translation, and displacement. The citizen's life is a daily diaspora, a scattering of himself into other lives and places.

Implicitly compared with the Sanskrit food chain, the citizen's recirculation of his donated organs in the ensuing verse paragraph is a decidedly non-Sanskrit, non-Hindu form of reincarnation:

                                you will
      your body to the nearest
           hospital, changing death into small
      change and spare parts;
           dismantling, not de-
      composing like the rest
           of us. Eyes in an eye bank
      to blink some day for a stranger's
           brain, wait like mummy wheat
      in the singular company
           of single eyes, pickled,
      absolute.

In this modern, scientific version of reincarnation, human organs are exchanged like money or refitted like car parts. Disembodied, they are deposited in "banks"—isolated, decontextualized. Yet there they form an
amusingly anonymous company of sorts, before being reincorporated within
an utterly unknown body. Ramanujan shows that projections into the future,
like metaphorical exchanges with the past, are imaginative transactions that
can transform identity. By conceiving of the self as an assembly of discrete
parts that might function within other human structures, the citizen erodes
the finality of the boundary against which the self normally constitutes its
uniqueness. Ramanujan humorously refigures postcolonial displacement
and hybridization in his depiction of eyes displaced from one body to another, of formerly discrete bodies unpredictably recombined with one
another. Within its own language, his poem enacts a literary version of postcolonial reincarnation, incorporating not only Vedic death chant and romantic organicism but also Yeats's trope of "mummy wheat" into its textual
body—a figure, appropriately enough, for wisdom that ripens after apparent
death.[50]

      The postcolonial impetus behind Ramanujan's multilayered meditation
on the recirculation of nutrients, organs, and texts becomes explicit when he
figures organ donation as cultural displacement and integration:

      Hearts,
                with your kind of temper,
           may even take, make connection
      with alien veins, and continue
           your struggle to be naturalized:
      beat, and learn to miss a beat
           in a foreign body.

Disorienting and incongruous, the postcolonial or diasporic experience resembles an ultimate crossing of boundaries—between one body and another. Ramanujan's exhilarating metaphoric leap from interbodily to intercultural transplantation suggests how precarious, violent, and strange it is to be refitted into a new national and social organization. Like the postcolonial or migrant subject, torn out of one cultural context and inserted into a new one, the eye that blinks in a new head and the heart that beats in a new chest cannot always adapt with ease to its new surroundings. At the same time, the poem implicitly invites our hearts to "take, make connection / with alien veins," with the individual sensibility and cultural experience inscribed within its lines. So too, the poem enacts its own connections and naturalizations. It reinscribes the English lyric metaphor of the heart within its textual corpus, even beating with the word "beat" at the beginning and end of a line, as well as the internal rhyme "take, make."

Having explored how waste, food, and organs—along with peoples, texts, and tropes—circulate through different kinds of bodies, Ramanujan closes his poem with a skeptical yet playful meditation on Eastern and Western rites of ultimate closure, efforts through Hindu cremation and American embalming to defeat physical recirculation. Ironically identifying his "tribe" as "incarnate / unbelievers in bodies," the poet imagines his own death in India:

> they'll cremate
> me in Sanskrit and sandalwood,
>   have me sterilized
> to a scatter of ash.

Unlike the citizen who decays into food for other organisms or is disassembled into organs for other bodies, the Hindu believer in reincarnation defeats these other forms of reincarnation. From Ramanujan's ironically naturalistic perspective, Western rites for disposing of the body seem no less perverse:

> Or abroad,
> they'll lay me out in a funeral
>   parlour, embalm me in pesticide,
> bury me in a steel trap, lock
>   me out of nature
> till I'm oxidized by left-
>   over air, withered by my own
> vapours into grin and bone.

Far from arresting the processes of natural metamorphosis, the modern funeral director merely condemns the body to transformative decay by its own gaseous emissions. Having defamiliarized the crematory practices of his Indian readers, Ramanujan makes the burial practices of his Western readers look even more absurd. Again incorporating a phrase from Yeats's "Sailing to Byzantium" ("once out of nature"), Ramanujan remembers Yeats's mildly ironized hope of transcending nature through art, counterpointing it with humanity's pathetic attempts at escape through burial and crematory practices. Opening the body of his poem to Yeats's words, Ramanujan links the closed poem, supposedly pure and autonomous, to a corpse, narcissistically trapped in its own putrid gasses. Further recycling a trope from the poem's beginning, the last lines return to the image of bodily waste recycled as oranges. The histories of embalming, a practice recycled from ancient Egypt by Civil War America, and of cremation, similarly appropriated from the East by the modern West, paradoxically demonstrate at the level of culture the kind of recirculation they are designed to arrest at the level of nature. As if to suggest that these rites for disposing of the body aim for a purity translatable into xenophobia, the poet punningly says that embalming is aimed at ensuring that his body "will never know newsprint, / never grow in a culture." But in metamorphosing the English language, Western lyric tropes, the Anglo-Irish Yeats, Hindu ritual, even his own words in this poem, Ramanujan indicates that the recirculation of print and culture is just as unstoppable as the recirculation of physical matter. Having repeatedly ironized the nativist quest for pure and static origins, Ramanujan also warns that the quest for inviolable closure in death risks cultural sterility and claustrophobia. For individuals, poems, and cultures, Ramanujan envisions endings that can never be fully controlled or predicted, endings that are openings into new worlds, new metamorphoses.[51]

The imaginative relations between oneself and one's ending, oneself and one's beginning are, as we have seen in Ramanujan's poetry, crucially dependent on metaphor—on linguistic bridges that both traverse and mark the gaps between past, present, and future. As indicated by Ramanujan's metaphoric crossings between different tenses of his existence, the dislocation and relationality that metaphor metaphorizes as spatial are also temporal. The lyric subject constructs itself partly out of the resemblances between itself and the otherness of its bodily, psychic, and cultural pasts, partly out of the resemblances between itself and the otherness of its possible destinies—its imaginary afterlives in the bodies, works, and minds of the future. Crossings between now and then, here and there, one body and another are in turn isomorphic, as Ramanujan's poetic metaphors have shown, with passages between one's own culture and others. The family, an obsessive topic in Ramanujan's poetry, can be thought of as the primary institutional site for the diachronic transmission and synchronic codification of all these resemblances. A closer look at the interrelations between the family, metaphor, and postcoloniality in Ramanujan's poetry should help us to understand better the relation between vertical and horizontal likeness, between the many forms of displacement and transmission—hermeneutic, linguistic, genetic, bodily, geographic, and temporal.[52] While metaphor is metaphorized in terms of place, the metaphor of family is also, of course, key to our general understanding of metaphor. Indeed, family resemblance is a master trope in contemporary discussions of metaphor. "Family resemblances," Mark Turner speculates, "are perhaps the similarities that from infancy we notice most. And we use just this concept of similarity to help explain how things can bear a metaphorical relation or resemblance. In short, we explain *metaphor* to ourselves in terms of what we know about *family*."[53] In poems such as "Extended Family," as we shall see, Ramanujan illuminates this cross-pollination between our knowledge of the family and of metaphor.

Even critics who have clashed over Indian poetry in English, as did Homi Bhabha and R. Parthasarathy in the *Times Literary Supplement* (1978), agree that, in Parthasarathy's words, "The family is, for Ramanujan, one of the central metaphors with which he thinks," or in Bhabha's, "For Ramanujan, it is the metaphor of the family—bearer of ancient traditions, and source of love, change, regeneration—that aligns past and present and establishes his own history."[54] With its multiple reflections and opacities, its sameness and difference, the family is frequently the locus of Ramanujan's poetic acts of self-definition. Across a wide array of lyrics, the poet defines himself by sorting through his resemblances with his grandparents, parents, children, siblings, and wife. At one extreme, he sometimes tips the balance toward a sameness that threatens to obliterate identity. In "Self-Portrait," the reflections he sees in shop windows seem to be a stranger's portrait, "often signed in a corner / by my father" (23). With help from psychoanalysis, genetics, and Hinduism, Ramanujan weighs the leaden burden of the familial past.[55] Nor is the family's assimilative pressure only vertical; it is also horizontal. In dreams, the face of the poet's wife becomes "my own yet hers," until resemblance erases even gender difference, leaving him feeling "whole in the ambivalence / of being halfwoman half- / man . . . / androgynous as a god" ("Love Poem for a Wife" 2, 84). Commenting on the male "wish to be female," Ramanujan speculates that it is less repressed in Indian literature and religion than in Western: "Indian poetry and Indian saints' lives are full of female identifications, transvestite imagery, etc."[56]

At the other extreme, Ramanujan emphasizes the opaque differences separating himself from his familial alter ego. In the first "Love Poem for a Wife," nothing can ever make up for unshared childhood experiences, so the poet even ironically considers, as possible remedy to spousal estrangement, the ancient Egyptian practice of incestuous marriage. In the later "Love Poem for a Wife and Her Trees," he writes of his wife, "you're not me but Another, the faraway / stranger who's nearby" (182). Most of Ramanujan's family poems move dialectically between these poles of equivalence and difference, the metaphorical "is" and "is not." Family members are a source of both self-alienation and self-confirmation, "Clones subtly gone wrong," as Ramanujan puts it in the posthumously published "Lines":

> His, or is it her, parts
> are yours, but they do not add up
> to who you are, and you too
> are no longer you.
>   (267)

Already in the title and epigraph of his 1971 collection, *Relations,* Ramanujan signals the centrality of the family in his poetry, highlighting the Indian provenance of this preoccupation in the words of a classical Tamil poem: *"living / among relations / binds the feet"* (56). Drawing on the psychoanalytic findings of Alan Roland, Ramanujan surmises that Indians have an acute sense of a "familial self": they "carry their family-context wherever they go, feel continuous with their family."[57] The cover art of *Relations* reflects Ramanujan's characteristic blending of ancient Indian wisdom with Western psychoanalysis: the stark photograph of the author's face literalizes the parental imago, the poet's forehead containing an inset photograph of the poet's parents.[58] The cover invites us to compare the son's physiognomy with his parents', as well as the son's modern bare head with his father's turban and Śri Vaiṣṇava caste mark, his mother's sari. Comparing oneself with one's relations, Ramanujan's poetry suggests, may be the most basic of metaphorical activities. Further, Ramanujan explores how we think in family metaphors of our resemblances to other peoples. The trope of the "family of man" merely codifies one of the figures fundamental to our understanding of cultural alterity.

In the delightful poem "Extended Family," Ramanujan playfully likens the likenesses between family members and cultures, exploring the metaphorical basis of our understanding of both familial and intercultural community (169–70). "Extended" by a series of similes, as by family relations, the naked, bathing speaker humorously rediscovers himself in the discordant similarities between himself and his familial others:

> Yet like grandfather
> I bathe before the village crow
>
> the dry chlorine water
> my only Ganges
>
> the naked Chicago bulb
> a cousin of the Vedic sun

Here the word "cousin" is key. Metaphorizing as kinship the metaphorical relation of a Chicago bulb to the Vedic sun, it overtly relates intrafamilial relatedness to intercultural: put in the form of proportional metaphor, America is to India as the speaker is to his grandfather. In the ironic juxtapositions of chlorinated urban water and a sacred river, of a harsh interior light bulb and the natural yet divine sun, the speaker sees his life stereoscopically, as refracted through the prisms of metaphor and diaspora—a life that is a secularized, urbanized, americanized, comically diminished version of the family and culture from which he came. The poet's cross-cultural metaphors both bridge and reveal these distances in belief, environment, and geography. Some familial and cultural habits persist, despite changes in place and time, as exemplified by the son's bath time slapping of soap on his back and thinking in proverbs "like father," even as, "like mother," he hears "faint morning song." But in both cases, cultural otherness obtrudes to warp these intergenerational continuities. After likening himself to his father, the poet humorously bends inward the structure of the family simile:

> like me
> I wipe myself dry
>
> with an unwashed
> Sears turkish towel

His Brahman father, by implication, would never have violated codes of purity with an unclean towel. Cultural confusion and contamination—"Sears turkish"—signify the difficulty of sustaining his father's ritual practices in America. Similarly, the speaker may resemble his mother in listening to faint morning song, but "here it sounds / Japanese." The poem itself, moreover, alludes to the Japanese haiku in its compressed comparisons and spare short

lines and stanzas. From Chicago to India, Turkey to Japan, cross-cultural
connections, resemblances, and migrations make it increasingly difficult to
determine the precise location indicated by the word "here." Narrowly understood, "here" is Chicago, but memory, metaphor, and poetic form, as well
as trade and migration, explode geographical literalism. At the level of punc-
tuation, Ramanujan further loosens the poem's moorings by eschewing end-
stopped lines. The meaning of the lines "like me" and "like mother," for
example, syntactically migrates to the lines below and above, moving in different directions across the space of the poem and the world.

Metaphor, especially the trope of simile, is the rhetorical site not only of
geographical but bodily crossings in the poem. It spans physical differences
of generation and gender. Musically attentive like the woman who gave birth
to him, the naked speaker also finds in his body resemblances to the girl he
fathered:

> like my little daughter
> I play shy
>
> hand over crotch
> my body not yet full
>
> of thoughts novels
> and children

Humorously concealing his genitalia, the speaker reimagines himself in the
innocent, female body of his daughter, before it is filled with ideas, imaginings, and children, which will in turn perpetuate his identity after his death.
The penis, absented in his identification with his daughter, reappears as his
son's innocent "garden hose," the male conduit to a genetic future. The
speaker mockingly glances at the dependence of his future on his children's
not-yet-active sexual organs.

Having translated the poet back in time to his familial origins, simile
now propels him forward to his hypothetical progeny:

> like my grandson
> I look up
>
> unborn
> at myself
>
> like my great
> great-grandson

I am not yet
may never be

my future
dependent

on several
people

yet
to come

Dwindling ever since its beginning, the poem is finally honed to one- or two-syllable lines, as it sheds the known weight of the past for the airy unknown of the future. Again echoing the imagined song "Of what is past, or passing, or to come" at the end of "Sailing to Byzantium," Ramanujan acknowledges his dependence on future readers and poets, who, much as he reincarnates Yeats's words, will—he hopes—reincarnate his. Bound together by Ramanujan's allusion, both poems propound the resemblance between the crossing of distances in space—Ireland to Byzantium in one work, Chicago to India, Turkey, and Japan in the other—and the crossing of distances in time. Effecting one miraculous form of relocation, poetic metaphor also affords the other—in both cases, the emphasis on geographic displacement gives way to temporal. The word "like" functions as the connective tissue that grafts disjunctive places and temporalities—the figurative apotheosis of genetic, cultural, and migratory translation. Without metaphor, families might still inherit, cultures get passed down, and peoples migrate. But it is metaphor that reveals the family resemblances between these various forms of transmission and reproduction, as well as our need to conceive them in metaphors drawn from one another, creating multitudinous families of the mind.

Ramanujan's keen eye for the varieties of family resemblance—intergenerational, interpersonal, intercultural—is inextricable, as we have seen in poem after poem, from the postcolonial experience. Thus, his use of metaphor benefits from being understood within the context of the doubleness and displacement, the hybridity and interstitiality usually associated with postcoloniality. So too, his postcoloniality can profitably be explored through the prism of metaphor, the complex rhetorical site of resemblance and "double vision" in his poetry. While Ramanujan, like Walcott, glories in the connective power of poetic metaphor, he uses metaphor not only to suture but, even more than Walcott, to survey historical and cultural gaps, such as those embedded in the word "postcolonial" itself. The postcolonial experience helps to explain not only Ramanujan's metaphorical exuberance but also his ironic awareness of the edges and differences crossed by metaphor, as we have seen in his poignant fingering of the fissures that separate him from his origins and endings—from other times, other places, other traditions, even other members of his extended family. On the one hand, Ramanujan can write an indulgently metaphoric poem like "In the Zoo," in which he jocularly imagines that grey storks look "like Madras lawyers," white ones "like grandmother's maggoty curds," flying clumsily "like father" with his broken umbrellas (128). On the other hand, in the palinode "Zoo Gardens Revisited" (153–54), appropriately written in prose, Ramanujan fiercely scrutinizes such movements of metaphor:

> Once flamingoes reminded me of long-legged aunts in white cottons, and black-faced monkeys of grave lowbrow uncles with movable scalps and wrinkled long black hands. Now animals remind me only of animals. . . .

Ramanujan self-critically implicates the pathetic fallacy in the disregard that leads zoo visitors not to "gape at ostriches" but to "set their tail feathers on fire," even to feed endangered monkeys "bananas with small exquisite needles in them." The magic of metaphor, which can afford openings to other cultures, times, and even life forms, can also turn into black magic, used in the colonizing occlusion of the otherness of the other, perhaps even torture and destruction. At his best, Ramanujan fuses the contrary energies exhibited in his zoo poems—antimetaphoric questioning with metaphoric energy. His agility in fusing passionate attachment to metaphor with trenchant skepticism, rainbow-eyed postcoloniality with postcolonial irony, positions him to be read in coming decades as one of the leading poets of our transnational world. As the field of postcolonial studies attends to the significant interrelations between metaphor and postcoloniality, perhaps it will begin to grant Ramanujan and other Indian English poets like Adil Jussawalla, Arun Kolatkar, Eunice de Souza, Meena Alexander, Reetika Vazirani, and Agha Shahid Ali the close literary analysis that their work richly rewards.

CHAPTER FIVE

❦ Irony and Postcoloniality: Louise Bennett's Anancy Poetics

Irony has not always found a welcome home in postcolonial criticism. Condemning a novel by the Indian writer Amitav Ghosh, Javed Majeed argues, for example, that irony is "politically ineffectual" and "can have little place in the fashioning of post-colonial national identities."[1] This critique, frequently leveled against such postcolonial ironists as Salman Rushdie and V. S. Naipaul, is related to an older complaint about the social implications of irony. "Ironists have often been accused of elitism," according to Wayne Booth, who cites Kierkegaard's famous statement that irony "looks down, as it were, on plain and ordinary discourse immediately understood by everyone; it travels in an exclusive incognito."[2] Yet the links between irony and postcoloniality are profound and fertile, so much so that to ignore them because we assume irony to be more appropriate to Western bourgeois or postmodernist writing is to impoverish our sense of postcolonial literature's tonality and rhetoric, vision and politics. The intimate relationship between irony and postcoloniality is rooted in a mutual doubleness—a structural kinship like the one we traced in our earlier discussion of metaphor. Indeed, theorists of irony, like theorists of metaphor, often use tropes of double vision, meaning, and perception. But they represent the implicit tension within irony as less resolvable than in metaphor—the one is "additive," the other "subtractive."[3] Emphasizing the disharmony between parts, they characterize ironic cognition and rhetoric in terms of a "perceptual split" or *dédoublement,* "psychic scission" or "semantic disjunction."[4] As we saw in our discussion of metaphor, a comparable doubleness of vision, or layering of perspectives, characterizes the postcolonial condition, due to the forced convergence of colonial and "native" cultures. In an essay on postcolonialism and postmodernism, Linda Hutcheon briefly connects irony with the "twofold vision of the post-colonial. . . . This is the doubleness often represented in the metaphor of Prospero and Caliban. It is the doubleness of the colonial culture imposed upon the colonized. But it is also the doubleness of the colonized in relation to the colonizer, either as model or antithesis."[5] This suggestive line of analysis starts in binarism but need not remain there. Within the "contact zone" of postcoloniality or of irony, the crossings and conjunctures result in compound formations irreducible to either source. Hybridizing often contradictory cultural perspectives, postcolonial writers have in irony a potent rhetorical correlative for their bifocality and biculturalism.

Since theories of irony and of postcoloniality have been kept largely separate, it may be worth developing the homology between postcolonial and ironic doubleness, starting with concepts of the relation between irony's dual levels. In irony as in postcoloniality, the relation is described as being contradictory without being symmetrical or simply binary.[6] Irony, according to D. C. Muecke, "is a double-layered or two-storey phenomenon" with an "upper" and a "lower level." In complex or "double" irony, as opposed to merely "corrective" or "simple" irony, the difference between these layers or perspectives remains unresolved.[7] Interestingly enough, the hierarchical rhetoric of upper and lower constructs the ironic dyad as a relationship of power, with a "victim's" perspective at the lower end. Further, the dualities in irony don't cohere; they clash. Almost as if describing postcoloniality, Muecke finds in irony "the clash and shock as of two co-existing but irreconcilable, irrelatable 'realities.' Our minds which naturally seek to relate and synthesize are affronted."[8] In irony as in postcoloniality, the twin perspectives aren't merely juxtaposed; they are in a relation of antagonism, or at the very least of disharmony. Even when irony involves the negation of one perspective, Booth argues, that rejected meaning "is still somehow kept in mind, as part of our awareness of the irony." Thus the mind "clicks back and forth" between incongruous images.[9] Irony is said to involve an oscillation or "a kind of vibration between meanings."[10] In brief, a credible theory of irony, as of postcoloniality, must attend not only to the convergence of meanings but also to their persistence alongside each other, often in a relation of dynamic tension or even mutual exclusion.

In spite of critiques linking irony with Western bourgeois elitism or postmodernist dilatory play, the ancient notion of the *eiron* should help to remind us that, along with its potential for elitist conservation, irony can also be a powerful tool of subversion. Feminist, gay, and African-American critics have celebrated the potentiality of irony as transgressive "counterdiscourse," unsettling the dominant discourse from within.[11] Adapting this view, Linda Hutcheon sees irony as a trope neither of apolitical play nor of unqualified subversion but of "complicitous critique" in postcolonial literatures, a "trope that works from within a power field but still contests it."[12] Hutcheon's helpful model leaves open the question of identifying the "power field" within which postcolonial irony operates. Is it subversive of and complicitous toward imperial power alone, as Hutcheon implies? What of indigenous power? For Rushdie's *Midnight's Children,* is the power field that of the British empire and the West or is it postcolonial India and Pakistan? Rushdie's fate after the publication of *The Satanic Verses* indicates that his ironies were not felt to be exclusively anti-Western. In these and many other postcolonial texts saturated with irony, the power field engaged by a given work is often multiple and ambiguous. This is not to say that postcolonial irony is apolitical, but that its "edge"—to borrow Hutcheon's figure from her later book on irony—often cuts more than one way.[13] To view the irony of postcolonial literature as either apolitical or subversively anti-Western is to oversimplify it. Indeed, the multifaceted irony of writers like Rushdie and Soyinka, Naipaul and Walcott helps to explain why their work has been maddeningly barbed for readers of both the Third World and the First.

But postcolonial irony not only cuts; it also gathers. While offending, these writers have also helped local and foreign readers to imagine communities beyond what the state—whether Western or Third World—imagines for them. Irony's affiliative potential is another reason to reject concepts that schematize the trope as merely elitist, or subversive, or apolitical. In Wayne Booth's account of irony, "the building of amiable communities is often far more important than the exclusion of naive victims. Often the predominant emotion when reading stable ironies is that of joining, of finding and communing with kindred spirits." Thus, when Johnson calls Bolingbroke "a holy man," he "catches more of us in his net than he would have with 'Bolingbroke is an unholy man'": "unholy" is a harsher and narrower term, whereas "*holy* as irony can be accepted and enjoyed by everyone who is in any degree suspicious or critical of Bolingbroke."[14] Similar examples could be drawn from Walcott's ironic descriptions of self-serving politicians, Naipaul's of dictatorial regimes, or Okot's of nationalists fighting each other in the name of African unity. Such irony reflects a collective experience of postcolonial disenchantment with indigenous state politics, but its negative or subversive edge is inseparable from its affiliative force—the communal laughter that arises from seeing through the pretenses of native governments, as of their imperial predecessors.

In contrast to the view that irony "can have little place in the fashioning of post-colonial national identities," the Jamaican poet Louise Bennett exemplifies the central role a literary ironist can play in the formation of postcolonial community. A master of irony, Bennett is an outstanding example of the poet as public figure in the postcolonial situation. Though little known among poetry enthusiasts outside the West Indies, Jamaica's national poet is arguably one of the most significant English-language world poets in the middle decades of the twentieth century. Her stunning lack of foreign recognition—Jamaican critics have written nearly all the sustained criticism on her work, and she seldom makes it beyond regional anthologies—has been matched by the reverse reception on the part of the Jamaican public.[15] Bennett published poetry in Jamaica's national newspaper, the *Gleaner,* on a weekly basis through much of the 1940s. Later, she had her own regular radio show, "Miss Lou's Views" (1965–82), and a children's television program, "Ring Ding" (1970–82). Building a mass audience in Jamaica for performance genres, "Miss Lou" regularly delivered dramatic renditions of plays, folk songs, and pantomime, sometimes before tens of thousands. Jamaican schoolchildren have often recited competitively her dramatic monologues, sometimes with Bennett herself serving as judge. Although Bennett's cultural prominence has waned in recent decades with the ascendancy of Bob Marley and other heroes of reggae and dance hall, her iconic significance has persisted: in the year 2000, Bennett's recitations of her poetry occupied Air Jamaica's entire on-flight "folk" channel, and she was the "featured author" at Sangster's, the largest supplier of books in Jamaica. On the fiftieth anniversary of Bennett's professional debut, Jamaica's National Commercial Bank apostrophized her full-page image, "Jamaica wouldn't be the same without you."[16]

While we might expect such a public poet to be the composer of sonorous and solemn odes to the nation, to native political figures and institutions, Bennett's crafty poetry is nothing of the kind. Bennett builds an "amiable community" of Jamaicans not by aggrandizing but by wryly ironizing the emergent nation-state and its symbols, nationalists and antinationalists, the poor and the wealthy. Nor is she reluctant to deflate British administrators or visiting American politicians, American racism and British imperial arrogance. Like Yeats, Walcott, and Soyinka, Bennett directs her postcolonial irony both within and without, against the foibles of empire and of the indigenous nation. She embodies not only the emergent nation's cultural pride in itself but also its carnivalesque capacity for mockery and self-mockery.

Although irony may seem to be a Western formalist concept, one of the world's most vibrant figures for the ironist is the folk hero Anancy—the mythical spider who gives his name to animal tales and even to West Indian storytelling in general. Derived from a West African prototype, he is arguably the Afro-Caribbean counterpart to the Greek *eiron,* and comparable if distinct trickster figures exist in a wide range of postcolonial and American minority cultures.[17] The folklorist Daryl Dance writes of Anancy's social significance in the West Indian context: "Anancy is generally a figure of admiration whose cunning and scheming nature reflects the indirection and subtleties necessary for survival and occasionally victory for the Black man in a racist society."[18] By virtue of his ironic wiliness, Anancy is often able to triumph over stronger animals. Reimagined by such West Indian writers as Kamau Brathwaite, Dennis Scott, Andrew Salkey, and Wilson Harris, Anancy is of signal importance to Louise Bennett, almost as her mythical avatar.[19] As a folklorist, Bennett collected and published Anancy tales alongside her own in *Anancy Stories and Dialect Verse* (1950/1957), the title itself, like her subsequent *Anancy and Miss Lou* (1979), suggesting a correspondence between her poetry and the oral tales.[20] Carolyn Cooper insightfully links "the morally ambiguous craftiness of Anansi" with the "proverbial cunning of the Jamaican woman" and its manifestation in Bennett's poetry.[21] The comparison between the trickster hero and the poet is worth extending further to see if it sheds more light on both figures.

Because of Anancy's trickery and "unscrupulous cunning," some Jamaicans worried about his possibly degrading influence on the "national character."[22] Middle-class critics also accused Bennett of damaging Jamaica. They were particularly anxious about her celebratory use of Jamaican English, the lingua franca forged by slaves in the seventeenth and early eighteenth centuries through a blend of English dialects, other European languages, and such West African languages as Twi and Ewe.[23] Bennett's pride in the three-hundred-year-old language of everyday Jamaican speech was thought to be a baleful influence on people who should be trying to better themselves by using Standard English. Mervyn Morris cites a heated controversy as late as the 1970s over "Miss Lou's Views," Bennett's radio commentary: detractors claimed the program "tends to perpetuate ignorance in Jamaicans" and "is slowly destroying our young ambassadors of this great land."[24] Here, too, the connection with Anancy is suggestive, since in "dialect" stories the trickster often speaks a lisping, old-fashioned version of West Indian creole. Ventriloquizing Anancy, Bennett says, "'Im tawk wid a lisp tongue. 'Im tongue tie."[25] As the hero who out-dialects dialect in his tales, Anancy is arguably a regional emblem of dialect—of the wiliness and opacity of Caribbean English.

Anancy also personifies the close interconnections between irony and West Indian creole, once a toxic bond for some West Indian conservatives. In his clever ruses, Anancy ironically manipulates language, saying one thing while slyly meaning another, using periphrasis to prompt another animal to say a dangerous word, or deliberately distorting norms of pronunciation.[26] Exploiting the slipperiness and polyvalence of creole, he sometimes dupes other animals with double meanings and puns, but at other times falls into his own linguistic traps. Courageously choosing creole as the language of her poetry, Bennett suggests that it is a language more redolent of ironic and comic possibility, "rich in wit and humour," or as she put it in an interview, the "nature of Jamaican dialect is the nature of comedy"; not for her the dutifulness of a poetic vocabulary, tonality, and syntax that bow to the Queen's English.[27] When Kamau Brathwaite refers to Bennett's "teeth and lips tight and closed around the mailed fist of a smile," he encapsulates the laughter, aggression, and trickster-like disguise of her poetry.[28] According to Lloyd Brown, "The grinning mask of the oral tradition therefore represents a deeply ingrained irony that goes back to the original rebellion of the African slave through the Westerner's language."[29] This subversive appropriation of English may well recall Caliban—the most familiar paradigm for the West Indian writer. But whereas Caliban famously declares to Prospero, "You taught me language, and my profit on't / Is, I know how to curse," Anancy is perhaps a more adequate figure for the creolization, and not merely the appropriation, of the master's language, because of his hybrid, Euro-African speech. Further, the African-derived folk hero Anancy is free of Caliban's Western, high literary pedigree. Nor is he permanently trapped in a binary model, like the Caliban/Prospero dyad. If Caliban allegorizes the anti-imperial resistance of the West Indian writer, Anancy more accurately suggests the playful and polymorphous, all-ironizing folk wit of a creole poet like Bennett.

With her Anancy poetics, Bennett ran the perpetual risk of the ironist— the incomprehension and even anger of some members of her audience. On the eve of Jamaica's first elections under universal suffrage in 1944, Bennett wrote in the voice of an overconfident first-time voter, who boasts she will (incorrectly) mark the ballot by crossing out some names and leaving others.[30] Misreading the poem's final ironic flourish, several angry readers of the *Gleaner* wrote letters "accusing Miss Bennett of misleading the public on how to vote."[31] Bennett responded by composing a corrective poem that explains the "Rightful Way" to mark a ballot: "Yuh doan haffe cross out nutten . . . / Jus mark a X side o' de name."[32] But having first ridiculed her uneducated speaker, too impressed by the new-found power to vote, she redirects that irony toward the sort of "genkleman" and "destant, edicated / Smaddy [distant, educated Somebody]" who missed the ironies of her earlier poem. Even at the solemn first moment of universal suffrage, Bennett is unwilling to straightjacket the twists and turns, the multiply-directed ironies of her creole verse.

As creole ironist, Bennett resembles what the anthropologist Roger D. Abrahams has labeled the West Indian "man-of-words" or, more specifically, the "broad talker," who brings "the vernacular creole into stylized use, in the form of wit, repartee, and directed slander." Referring to West Indian joking practices like "giving rag, making mock, and giving fatigue," Abrahams attributes such aggressive joking and artful broad talk to Afro-Caribbean men. But as a major indigenous folklorist in her own right, Bennett both rectifies and exemplifies this ethnography: she proves broad talk to be a domain of female mastery, as demonstrated by the creole wordplay of her female personae.[33] Although "Jamaica Oman [Woman]" often strategically disguises her verbal and physical power, she "know she strong" and "Outa road an eena yard deh pon / A dominate her part."[34] Poetically adapting "labrish" or gossip and Anancy tales, Bennett shows these oral, yard-based, predominantly female discourses to be no less animated by irony and mockery, wit and verbal display than male broad talk. Abrahams's analysis of broad talk helps to illuminate the social purpose of Bennett's carnivalesque poetry. "By playing the fool or by describing the antics of the trickster Anansi," according to Abrahams, "the broad talker therefore enacts something of an anti-ritual for the community; he produces a needed sense of classless liminality and serves as a creative channel for antisocial community motives."[35] In her national role as poet—sometimes, indeed, her antinational national role—Bennett used irony to draw audiences from different classes into a humor-based liminal solidarity. "I think I speak to all Jamaica," she remarked, observing that "a large cross section of the community from the Governor-General to the man in the street can react to the lines and the situations I present. So I can't feel that I belong to any class or that I write for any class."[36] Like Anansi stories, carnival performances, and West Indian gossip, Bennett's doubly ironic poetry recalls a form of joking behavior that Abrahams calls "permissible rudeness."[37] Bennett would form a community of hearers and readers unafraid to laugh irreverently at the contradictions of either imperial or indigenous power and ceremony.

Despite—or perhaps because of—her extraordinary achievement in fusing such discourses as broad talk, gossip, and Anancy storytelling with formally accomplished verse, Bennett was barred from the ranks of West Indian "poets" during the period when she was writing her best poetry, from the 1940s through the early 1960s. She was never asked, she recalls, to a Jamaican Poetry League meeting, nor was she anthologized. Because of the creole orality of her work, she was scarcely acknowledged as someone who wrote, let alone as a poet.[38] Now widely recognized as a crucial precursor for a wide range of Caribbean poets, including more "literary" poets like Brathwaite and Dennis Scott and "dub" or performance poets like Michael Smith, Linton Kwesi Johnson, and Jean Breeze, Bennett explained her choice of language as enabling her to "express" herself "so much more strongly and vividly than in standard English."[39] She "persisted writing in dialect in spite of all the opposition," she told Dennis Scott, "because nobody else was doing so and there was such rich material in the dialect that I felt I wanted to put on paper some of the wonderful things that people say in dialect. You could never say 'look here' as vividly as 'kuyah.'"[40] Although Walcott referred approvingly to Bennett when he was working as a reviewer in Trinidad, her creole verse seemed subliterary to many poets drawing primarily on Anglo-American traditions.[41] After all, Bennett was ridiculing in her poetry the assimilationist adoption of an imperial language. At the same time, Bennett's Anancy-like irony, as well as her use of the ballad form, inhibited her natural allies—African-oriented, creole writers—from championing her wholeheartedly. She mocks West Indian Afrocentrism and black nationalism in poems like "Back to Africa": "Yuh haffi come from somewhe fus / Before yuh go back deh!" (104).[42] Bennett's combination of rudely unpredictable irony and folk-based creole endeared her to neither radical nor conservative West Indian poets and critics.

To track more closely Bennett's mercurial irony, I turn to four subjects about which she wrote with great vigor: language, race, emigration, and independence. In all these areas, she deploys an array of ironic strategies with multiple targets, energizing a language- and humor-based postcolonial solidarity. The shape-changing irony of her poetry defies preconceptions of the Third World writer as victimologist, anti-imperialist, or nationalist. The author of a large body of poetry that is robust and sometimes riotous in its language, humor, and pleasure, Bennett is an inspiring reminder that "laughter," as Bakhtin writes of the carnivalesque, has an "indissoluble and essential relation to freedom."[43]

Bennett thematizes language in self-reflexive poems that serve as a useful point of departure for a close reading of her work.[44] Although oral or performance poetry is sometimes assumed to be more suited to sociological or ethnographic overview than to "practical criticism," Bennett's best poems not only withstand but reward such engagement; as Mervyn Morris observes, they "use language with notable precision, cunning, force" in an art that is "both oral and scribal."[45] A stunning performer via the stage, radio, film, and television, Bennett has nevertheless insisted on being "recognized" as a "writer" above all, not someone who would "just stand up and say these things." After all, she adds, "I did start to write before I started to perform!"[46] By exploring her poetry as writerly inscription of broad talk, anancyism, and other oral modes, we slow it down and can thus analyze key features of Bennett's complex irony in relation to postcoloniality: perceptual doubleness, hierarchical inversion, and verbal mimicry; construction of an amiable community; resistance to the power fields; and provocative juxtapositions of Standard and Jamaican English.

Early in her career, Bennett wrote a creole defense of creole poetry, an *ars poetica* in a new key. "Bans a Killin" (1944) wittily counters attacks on Jamaican English as an inferior literary medium (4–5). The ironic target of this metapoem is a West Indian *alazon*, puffed up with pride about his knowledge of Standard English and its literature, blind to the implications of his ferocious desire to obliterate dialect. Noting that Mas Charlie has taken a "Whole heap a English oat [oaths] seh dat / Yuh gwine kill dialec," Bennett asks, with the feigned innocence of Anancy, "Yuh gwine kill all English dialec / Or jus Jamaica one?" Like many other members of the educated middle class, Mas Charlie hates dialect and loves the "English / Language," failing to recognize that dialect is the basis of all varieties of English, including the Queen's. The central irony of the poem is built around this self-contradiction in Mas Charlie's position:

> Dah language weh yuh proud a,
> Weh yuh honour an respec—
> Po Mas Charlie, yuh no know seh
> Dat it spring from dialec!

> Dat dem start fi try tun language
> From de fourteen century—
> Five hundred years gawn and dem got
> More dialec dan we!

Bennett enumerates Lancashire, Yorkshire, Cockney, Scots, and Irish dialect as evidence of this continuing plurality, despite centuries-old efforts at standardization. With the licensed rudeness of the broad talker, she reminds Mas

Charlie of the dialect used even by writers in the *Oxford Book of English Verse,* such as Chaucer, Burns, and Lady Grisel, let alone Shakespeare. In radio and stage performances, Bennett scoffs that the evolution of Standard English is described as "a derivation but Jamaica Dialec is corruption!"[47]

We can pinpoint Bennett's ironic strategies in "Bans a Killin" by looking at a single verb and a pun. Repeated through much of the poem, the verb "kill" at first represents the vehemence and violence of Mas Charlie's dialectophobia. But as the poem shows that the word's objects would logically have to include not only Jamaican but other dialects and even the "wit," "humor," "variety," and "Originality" of dialect verse (which now includes canonical English verse), "kill" becomes the ironic emblem of his imploding viewpoint. Far from narrowly targeting an ignorant group, his violent impulse turns out to be indiscriminate and finally self-directed:

> An mine how yuh dah read dem English
> Book deh pon yuh shelf,
> For ef yuh drop a "h" yuh mighta
> Haffi kill yuhself!

Bennett's punning rhyme on "yuh shelf" and "yuhself" brings the poem to its ironic climax. According to the *Dictionary of Jamaican English,* "Initial [h] is frequently lost in unemphatic contexts and used as a hypercorrection in emphatic contexts."[48] If Mas Charlie lets his guard down and drops an *h,* he might reveal himself as a Jamaican speaker, for all his hypercorrective efforts. In this climactic rhyme, the ironic disjunction between the poem's dialectophilic and dialectophobic perspectives is at its sharpest and wittiest. For this *alazon,* to drop an *h* would be to commit such a shameful mistake that he might have to redirect upon himself his ferocious desire to "kill" dialect. Anancy-like in her delight, the poet suggests the opposite meaning by her rhyme: that to drop the *h* would be for Mas Charlie finally to climb down from his high "shelf" and give life to his Jamaican "self," just as her punning subtraction of the letter *h* turns a space for his probably unread books into a word for identity. Verbally twinning these discordant perspectives, Bennett's irony is the rhetorical correlative for the "perceptual split" of postcoloniality.

Who are the targets of the poem's irony and who the co-conspirators? Humorously skewering a Jamaican mimic, Bennett deconstructs the linguistic distinctions and hierarchies that are the basis for Mas Charlie's feeling "inferior" about Jamaican dialect and dialect verse. Her irony resists the empire that initially codified these distinctions and hierarchies, as well as the Jamaican middle-class power field that perpetuates them. Yet the irony is also aesthetically "complicitous" with imperial power and its local props, in that the poem's terms of reference for undoing these distinctions remain the language and literature of the British isles, from Shakespeare to Burns. Even the characteristically hybrid form of Bennett's poem represents an ambivalent relation to empire, since its creole orthography and phonetics are emphatically Jamaican, but its ballad stanza and rhyme descend from British prototypes.

While targeting various "victims," does Bennett's irony also implicitly construct an amiable community? The first-order implied community is that of Jamaican creole speakers, joining the broad-talking poet in rudely laughing at the contradictions and pretensions of a mimic who forsakes his culture and language for the metropolitan center's. The power relations implicit in the poem's two-story irony invert the colonial hierarchy, placing the subaltern perspective at the upper level and the benighted imperial perspective at the lower. Outside readers like me temporarily join this local community, as members of an international audience competent to read Bennett's poem, perhaps with the help of dictionaries and commentaries and, thus, able to derive pleasure from the unmasking of Mas Charlie's affectations and misguided assumptions about linguistic hierarchy. The community-building efficacy of Bennett's irony becomes evident if we imagine a poem with the same viewpoint but without the irony. Earnestly attacking linguistic imperialists and indigenous mimics, solemnly lauding the virtues of Jamaican English, such a poem would likely have squandered the robust spirit of Jamaican creole and failed to catch so many readers in its web, to adapt Wayne Booth's metaphor to Anancy.

To dramatize the relation between Jamaican creole and Standard English in a variety of poems, Bennett brilliantly deploys strategies of linguistic juxtaposition. Other West Indian writers, as Katherine Wiggan observes, also "create comic situations on the level of language as the disparity between Creole and standard English is great and the social distance helps to enhance any potentially comic situation"; the same could be said, moreover, of traditions in British music hall and calypso.[49] Bakhtin theorizes such "double-voiced," "double-accented," and "double-languaged" writing as the "intentional hybrid": "two socio-linguistic consciousnesses . . . come together and consciously fight it out on the territory of the utterance." The goal of intentional hybridization, according to Bakhtin, is "the illumination of one language by means of another."[50] In "Dry-Foot Bwoy" (meaning thin-legged or inexperienced boy), perhaps the best among these poems about language, a group of creole-speaking women unmasks a boy who has adopted a pompous English diction and accent (1–2). The poem's Anancy-like speaker first pretends she thinks the imperially infatuated boy has caught a "bad foreign cole" and has "a bad sore-troat"; his English sounds like language emanating from a diseased body. Ultimately, she can only conclude from everything he says—"'Oh, jolley, jolley!'" "'Actually,' 'What,' 'Oh deah!'"—that it "is foreign twang / De bwoy wasa put awn!" Bennett deflates the seeming superiority of English English by inscribing it in a creole poem as "foreign twang." In this ironic inversion of imperial hierarchies, the "Standard" comes to seem deviant and the creole becomes the norm. The speaker's furious responses to the boy demonstrate the potential vigor of creole and the relative paucity of the mimic's empty rhetoric:

> No chat to me wid no hot pittata
> Eena yuh mout!
>
> . . . .
> No yuh name Cudjoe Scoop?
> Always visit Nana kitchen an
> Gi laugh fi gungoo soup!
> [Give laughter for pea soup!]

Juxtaposed with banal and hollow clichés like "Actually," "Oh deah," "How silley," the metaphorization of pseudo-British as hot potato–impeded speech instances the creative vitality of creole. Similarly, the boy's abstractions contrast with a creole diction that etymologically evinces the ancestral roots he would deny: a common Afro-Caribbean name, "Cudjoe" is from the Twi "day-name for a male born on Monday"; "Nana" is Twi for grandparent; and "gungoo" is from the Kongo word for pea.[51] Since "Cudjoe" can also mean "a heavy stick or cudgel," the word also hints at the force of the speaker's anger, as do the /k/ sounds and the emphatic masculine rhyme of *Scoop/soup,* especially in contrast to the boy's triple feminine rhyme: "'How silley! / I don't think that I really / Understand you, actually.'" Much as the speaker etymologically reroots the boy, so too her references to family and to food expose emotional and bodily dependencies on a culture he would forget. In ironic contrast to the boy's pretensions, the broad-talking poem displays creole flexibility, terseness, and phonemic vibrancy.

Bennett dramatizes the consolidation of a community of creole speakers, brought together by their ironic exposure of the mimic boy. Gossip- or labrish-based knowledge, produced and exchanged in the female realm of the Jamaican yard, equips the speaker and her friends for their spirited rite of unmasking. As the boy storms out of the room, they all mockingly "bawl out affa him" in his own empty imperial clichés: "Not going? What! Oh deah!"

Their ironic mimicry of his anglophilic mimicry joins them in laughter "from dat night till tedeh." Mimicry is a major issue in theories of both irony and of postcoloniality. Irony has been said always to involve an "echo," the as-if quotation of another person's words or thoughts, which the ironist pretends to sanction but repudiates.[52] Whereas earnest mimicry, like the dry-foot boy's, tries to reproduce faithfully colonial discourse, ironic post-colonial mimicry, such as that of Bennett's mocking women, self-consciously opens the gap between signifier and signified, making audible the dishar-mony between colonial original and postcolonial copy. Bennett anticipates similar scenes of collusive female irony in other postcolonial texts, such as the market girls' parodic appropriation of English-accented, anti-African patter in Soyinka's *Death and the King's Horseman*.[53]

Demonstrating her versatility in handling dramatic monologue, Bennett reverses the dramatic situation of "Dry-Foot Bwoy" in "No Lickle Twang": here the speaker is the *alazon,* sharing a negative view of Jamaican English with the dry-foot boy and Mas Charlie, but her vivid creole ironizes her fool-ish sense of inferiority about her indigenous language (2–4). She is deeply ashamed that her son has returned after six months in the United States "not a piece better," especially because he has failed to "improve" his speech: "Not even lickle [little] language, bwoy? / Not even lickle twang?" Like Mas Char-lie and the dry-foot boy, she has internalized the linguistic hierarchy that el-evates the Standard English of the metropolitan center (now the United States) above the "bad," creolized talk at the margins. Yet as soon as she de-scribes her shame—"Me proudness drop a grung [ground]"—she unwit-tingly instances the expressiveness of Jamaican English. Deploring her son's failure to return with an American coat, the speaker again blindly illustrates the wit and metaphorical resourcefulness of creole: a "pass de riddim coat" is so called, according to Mervyn Morris, because it is conceived as "a coat which ends below ('pass'/past) the buttocks ('de riddim'/the rhythm sec-tion)."[54] In contrast, her attempt to use a formal phrase from Standard English—when she refers to her "lamented son" lately returned from Amer-ica—ironically backfires, verbally killing off her son instead of merely ex-pressing her disapproval. Her blunders culminate when she tries to obviate her husband's imagined disappointment at returning home to find his son still speaks the same as ever:

> Ef yuh waan please him, meck him tink
> Yuh bring back someting new.
> Yuh always call him "Pa"—dis evenin
> When him come, seh "Poo."

Aspiring to the imaginary, superior discourse of empire, the speaker's failed mimicry abases the father instead of honoring him, since "poo" can be "a baby-language word for faeces."[55] By the trick of this last word, the Anancy-like poet brings to a climax the ironic disjunction between what the speaker intends and what she says. The speaker is so caught up in the allure of metropolitan language that she is in danger of losing her grip on the social embeddedness of oral communication: she would prefer for her son's speech to be incomprehensible, like her daughter's, who after only a week in America "talk so nice now dat we have / De jooce [deuce] fi understan."

The remoteness of "Standard English" from the Jamaican experience recurs as the source of considerable humor in Bennett's poetry. Bennett's code switching enacts this difference discursively, pasting together snatches of colonial song and poetry with creole gossip.[56] In these collage-like poems, the "perceptual split" or "semantic disjunction" at the core of irony again functions as the literary equivalent for postcolonial doubleness. In "Bed-Time Story," Bennett splices nursery rhymes into creole gossip or "labrish," abruptly shifting from one linguistic register to the other (6). The speaker of the poem tries to put her daughter to sleep by telling her Anglo-American nursery rhymes and at the same time tries to convey salacious gossip to a friend. The soporific rhymes and eye-popping gossip cross and clash, forming accidental semantic and syntagmatic connections that only highlight the gap between the discourses. Their friction verbally inscribes the forced political conjunctions that initially occasioned those juxtapositions.

While reciting "Mary Had a Little Lamb" and "Jack and Jill," the speaker also tries to tell her friend that Miss Mattie's son Joe has impregnated a girl named May and that Miss Mattie's daughter has given birth to a girl named Marta. Rhyme and meter weave the Anglo-American rhymes into the creole, only to make their distance even more apparent:

> Mary had a little lamb
> —Miss Mattie li bwoy Joe
> Go kick May slap pon har doorway—
> His feet was white as snow.
>
> An everywhere dat Mary went
> —Him Modder never know,
> An when she ear she ongle [only] seh—
> De lamb was sure to go.

The innocent world of Mary and her little lamb seems impossibly remote from the sexual encounter the speaker wants to relate. A signifier of this remoteness, snow is unknown in Jamaica, but numerous West Indian authors relate having to memorize English and American verses about this alien meteorological event. Imbedded in this context, the colonial nursery rhyme comes to stand for a fraudulent image of pastoral virtue and simplicity. The salaciousness of the Jamaican gossip ironizes this false purity, even as the Anglo-American nursery rhyme ironizes the gossip. The protestation of snow-white purity ironically confirms that Joe has penetrated not just May's "doorway." Similarly, "Jack and Jill," recontextualized within a story about birth out of wedlock, turns into a rhyme in which crown breaking is sexual intercourse, or "tumblin." Syntactically, lines of nursery rhyme promiscuously connect with adjacent lines in creole, so that Anglo-American rhyme and Jamaican gossip ironically warp or twist, amplify or undercut each other's meaning. Already an overtly "mixed" discourse, the creole in Bennett's poem further creolizes creole. Rhetorically echoing the fractured, jump-cut, collage-like experience of postcoloniality, the diglossic disjunctiveness of the poem intimates the difficulty of raising children in a world so linguistically and culturally split.

In "Sammy Intres," Bennett humorously runs together creole gossip not with children's verses but with "high art" poetry (7–8). Encouraged by a teacher to take an interest in her son's studies, Sammy's mother tries to memorize a poem that her son has been forced to learn: Longfellow's "Excelsior." Intercut with the mother's conversation, "Excelsior" metamorphoses into another ironic signifier of the remoteness of such colonial verses from the Jamaican experience. Here again the "snow an ice" of the poem remind us of the strangeness of this imposed discourse in the West Indian context, like the "banner wid de strange device" borne by Longfellow's hero. The speaker refers to "singing wid—de accent / Of dat unknown tongue," not realizing that she is commenting on her own efforts at colonial ventriloquism. The primary target of the irony in both this poem and "Bed-Time Story" is the Jamaican speaker who recites rhymes either that she cannot grasp or that accidentally comment upon her gossip in ways that escape her. Thus, in a certain sense, each benighted speaker could be seen as the "victim" of a colonial discourse that betrays her ignorance. But to read the ironic resistance this way would be to miss the implied targets of the irony—namely, the colonial power that imposed these English verses and the local elite that continued to perpetuate their enshrinement as a discourse higher and better than indigenous bed-time Anancy tales or poems. Bennett's broad-talking irony is doubly resistant, beholden to neither power field.

In Bennett's self-reflexive poems about poetry, language, and postcolo-

nial society, creole is the primary ironizing discourse, surrounding and sub-
suming the discourse of the colonizer. To incorporate the didactic, poetic,
and cliché discourse of the colonizer and native mimic within a sea of creole
is to reverse the colonial hierarchies of standard and deviation. Bennett's poems thus linguistically enact in their code switching and diglossia a kind of
reverse colonization. Bennett's creole interacts synergistically with the "aggregative" function of irony: her irony constitutes an "in-group" that "gets
it" over against those who do not—*alazons,* mimics, and implicitly the colonizers themselves.[57] So too, her Jamaican creole projects an in-group of indigenous speakers, as well as honorary insiders who are willing to achieve
competence in the language. Irony is often said to be "culture-specific," to
the extent that it is almost like a "dialect" among the people who share it.[58]
The irony and creole in Bennett's poetry thus function as twin dialects, reinforcing each other's power to constitute collusive communities of laughter.

Although many Jamaicans deny paying attention to skin color, race continues
to shape the destiny of individuals and groups in Jamaica, as in much of the
West Indies.[59] According to Aunty Roachy, Bennett's frequent radio persona,
"de real fac a de matter when it come to class an colour eena Jamaica is dat
plenty people still a judge dem one anodder class by de colour a dem skin!"[60]
Bennett wrote a series of sharply ironic poems about race after the end of the
Second World War, when the Allied fight against ethnic hatred elsewhere, the
treatment of interracial "war babies," the increase in emigration, and the upsurge in Jamaican nationalism made the contradictions in Anglo-American
and Jamaican thinking about race increasingly evident. As a serious and consequential matter, race might not seem to admit readily of ironic treatment,
but irony, like race, works through oppositions, reversals, and symmetries.
Bennett can thus hammer an ironic wedge into the racial binary, splitting it
open in poem after poem. The ironic force of her poetry about race is directed
primarily at the racial distinctions, false symmetries, and hierarchies originally put in place by colonial regimes in Jamaica, dating back to the Spanish
conquest. But, to her mind, black nationalism perpetuates such racialized
thinking, even as it inverts its values. Her poems about race help to elucidate
further the powerful connections between irony as a double-voiced rhetorical structure and the postcolonial inheritance—specifically, the experience
of racial division, hierarchy, mixture, and passing.

One of Bennett's most humorous, if painful, poems on race, "Pass fi
White" (1949), is brilliantly built around a pun on the word "pass" (101–2).

Theorists indicate that puns share with irony in a "simultaneity" and "super-imposition of meanings." Puns can be conceived in terms of a "homonymic collision," in which "the messages converge and clash in an irresolvable dis-location of meaning."[61] Such a description of colliding, clashing, dislocated meanings is especially evocative in the postcolonial context. The primary target of the poem's ironic punning on "pass" is Miss Jane's daughter, who has been sent to the United States for an education. She proudly writes to her parents "Fi seh she fail her exam, but / She passin dere fi white!" In the course of the poem, the word "pass" clicks back and forth between its so-cioacademic and its racial meanings:

> She couldn pass tru college
> So she try fi pass fi white.
>
> She passin wid her work-mate-dem,
> She passin wid her boss,
> An a nice white bwoy she love dah gwan
> Wid her like seh she pass!
>
> . . . .
> Some people tink she pass B.A.,
> Some tink she pass D.R.—
> Wait till dem fine out seh she ongle [only]
> Pass de colour bar.

In its semantic doubleness, the word "pass" enacts the duplicity of the daughter's racial passing; it seems to be one thing but then suddenly and un-predictably turns into another. That is, the strange passage of "pass" from one meaning to another is the verbal correlative for the undecidability of her racial identity. Miscegenation has resulted in the daughter's racial double-ness, which Bennett in turn recasts in the simultaneity and superimposition of her postcolonial irony. While the humor of the poem is constructed around the differences between passing in the theaters of race, the academy, sexual relations, and social class, the circulation of the word from one realm to another highlights the false parities between one set of hierarchies and boundaries and another. To fail or pass an exam, to win or lose as a sexual ob-ject, to get ahead or fall behind in the economy—the pun on "pass" reveals how the daughter conceives all of these as being symmetrical with and com-parable to failing or succeeding at being white. In the poem's parody of the colonialist mentality, all these hierarchies are linked, confused, and erro-neously seen as equivalent, as suggested by Bennett's telling rhyme:

Jane get bex [vexed], seh she sen de gal
Fi learn bout edication,
It look like seh de gal gawn weh
Gawn work pon her complexion.

While the ironic edge of the poem is clearly directed against Jane's daughter, the girl may be no more than what theorists of irony call a "pseudo-victim," since Bennett attacks not so much her as the colonizer's racist hierarchies, which make possible the girl's confusion and distortion of values. Indeed, the father's perspective on her racial passing suggests that there may even be method in her seeming foolishness:

De gal puppa dah laugh an seh
It serve Merica right—
Five year back dem Jim-Crow him, now
Dem pass him pickney [child] white.

Him dah boas all bout de distric
How him daughter is fus-class,
How she smarter dan American
An over deh dah pass!

Surely the father here, too, is the butt of the poem's irony, since he can't see that his desire for revenge ends up reinforcing the racial hierarchy that victimized him in the first place. Yet perhaps he and his daughter are also taking an Anancy-like delight in fooling a system that treats whiteness as socially superior and that confuses racial, academic, and social hierarchies. Possibly because of the more graded, if still racist, hierarchy of color in Jamaica, the father perceives the falsity of the severe racial binary in the United States. The daughter seems to be both the dupe of racism and the duper of American racists, both stooge and stealthy manipulator. The dual irony of the poem is directed both at home and abroad, both at the daughter's internalized racism and at the American racism that rewards it. The community of readers formed by this irony sees through both the girl's misguided emphasis on racial over other forms of "improvement" and the racist system that rhymes "edication" with "her complexion."

If "Pass fi White" mocks the desire of Afro-Caribbeans to assimilate to whiteness and repudiate blackness, "Back to Africa" is no less ironic in its treatment of the reverse desire: to "return" to Africa and repress other aspects of West Indian identity (104–5). Written in 1947, Bennett's poem suggests that the "Back to Africa" movement, strong at this time in Jamaica, may also

fall into simplistic racial polarities, merely inverting the essentialism of colonialist racism. In its final stanza, the poem leans heavily on the word "homelan," ironizing both the concept of an originary, ancestral home in Africa and
its Eurocentric prototype in the concept of an imperial "homelan": to go either to Europe or to Africa is to "Go a foreign," since a Jamaican's "homelan"
is "right deh." From the start of the poem, Bennett humorously deconstructs
the Garveyite notion of the return to African origins by literalizing "coming
from" and "going back":

> Back to Africa, Miss Mattie?
> Yuh no know what yuh dah seh?
> Yuh haffi come from somewhe fus
> Before yuh go back deh!

An Afrocentric *alazon,* Miss Mattie is betrayed by the very words she uses to
describe her racial quest for origins: not having come from Africa, she can't
very well go back. If Miss Mattie were to follow consistently the logic of ancestral return, she would have to acknowledge, the poem indicates, not only
her African but also her English, Jewish, French, and indeed Jamaican-born
forebears. If she goes to Africa on the basis of her face's "great resemblance"
with Africans', then, by the same token, blue-eyed, white Americans should
return to England. Ably exploiting the symmetrical structure of the ballad
quatrain, Bennett wields the hyperlogical ironies of an eighteenth-century
wit.

Suddenly shifting strategies, Bennett amusingly piles up a series of ono-
matopoeic words to suggest phonemically the massive confusion that would
be caused if all people tried to return to their place of ancestral origin:[62]

> What a debil of a bump-an-bore,
> Rig-jig an palam-pam
> Ef de whole worl start fi go back
> Whe dem great grampa come from!
> [What a devil the pushing and jostling,
> The lively crowded dance and noisy confusion . . .]

The echoic form of these words for confusion and dance also suggests
bouncing back, return to origins. But since each echo transforms the preceding phoneme, these words also hint that no return is without change and revision. Bennett ironizes the black nationalist idea of an essential racial
identity, traceable to a single place, by pitting it against the ineluctable reality of racial mixture and displacement throughout the world, particularly in

Jamaica. Her own lively intermingling of the French "parlez-vous" with creole words like "Bun Grung" [a place name meaning Burnt Ground], of ele-
vated English words like "countenance" and "resemblance" with homely
Jamaican "yuh" and "deh," suggests at the level of diction the very creolization and postcoloniality that she thematizes.

Whether using interracial blending for ironic leverage against quests for
pure origins or denials of mixed origins, Bennett treats racial mixture with a
humor that contrasts with the agonized meditations of other West Indian poets, most famously Walcott's "A Far Cry from Africa" and "The Schooner
Flight." Witness her poem "Colour-Bar," about the "torment" of the "mu-
latta" or "red-kin nayga":

> Me sorry fe po' red-kin, for
> Dem don' know wey dem stan'
> One granpa w'ite, an t'oder grampa
> Big, black, African.
>
> Wat a debil of a mix-up!
> Wat a dickans of a plight!
> Dem sey dat dem noh nayga,
> Nayga sey dat dem noh w'ite.[63]

Bennett is no less aware than other Afro-Caribbean poets of the "plight" of
the "mulatto," but she satirizes the racial divisions and social demarcations
that create this predicament. Here, the speaker inverts the typical social
stratification by taking pity on those normally considered higher on the
racial totem pole in Jamaica. She is relieved to have been "bawn nayga,"
solidly on one side of the "colour-bar": unlike red-skin blacks, she suffers
neither demeaning desires to affiliate with whiteness ("bex dat dem noh
w'ite" [vexed that they're not white]), nor fears of being rejected by whites,
nor discomfort with her blackness:

> Wen red-kin hitch too much pon w'ite
> W'ite peple tun dem back,
> An dem fraid fe talk to black people
> Less people tink dem black.

In another 1949 poem, "White Pickney," Bennett again addresses the
fate of the racially mixed: "Dem half a dis an half a dat, / Dem neider dose nor
dese—" (98). But her homely vernacular, and in particular the mechanical
symmetries implied by her consonances and alliterations ("dis" and "dat,"
"dose nor dese"), evacuates any tragic seriousness. This poem's improbable

plot hilariously fuses the denial of and the quest for origins. The speaker has read in the newspapers that after the war, "Five tousan black baby dah lef / Britain fi Merica." Here is the obverse of the Afrocentric theme of return to origins—namely, being returned to "black" origins by the force of British racism. The irony of the poem centers on a false symmetry between the fate of these offspring of black American fathers and white British mothers and the Jamaican offspring of white fathers and black mothers. The speaker reasons that if the "war babies" are classified as racially the same as their father and returned to their paternal home, then, by the same logic, Miss Mary's mixed race daughter should be classified "white" and sent to England, presumed homeland of her father:

> Ef dem-deh baby mumma call
> Dem "black" den is awright,
> Since him puppa is white man,
> Fi call fi-yuh pickney "white."

The poem mocks the speaker's dim understanding of the racial binary, which, far from evenly dividing mixed race children as black and white according to their paternity, labels them all black. Sure of her erroneous inferences, she jubilantly offers to help Miss Mary pack up her "baby tings": "newspaper tell me broad / Seh dat yuh baby white." But the poem suggests that to label the baby "black" is just as false as labeling it "white." The Afro-Jamaican speaker is again the pseudo-victim of the poem's irony. Her innocent reasoning reveals the harsh illogic at the heart of the imperially drawn racial order. It demonstrates that this order depends on symmetrical oppositions—black and white, home and abroad—and on asymmetrical hierarchies that warp and weight these differences.

While Bennett is skeptical toward black nationalist and white imperialist assumptions about origins, toward Afrocentric and pass-for-white suppression of racial heterogeneity, her irony does not always dissolve collective political identifications. As the emphatically creolized language of her poetry suggests, Bennett also wants to affirm Afro-Jamaican identity. Many of her poems enact a delicate balance between skepticism and pride toward the African inheritance in Jamaica. The poem "Nayga Yard" (1948) favorably expounds on African heritage and accomplishment in Jamaica (102–4). Here again Bennett satirizes the essentialist racial thinking behind the Jamaican diaspora, "Dese days when white man 'comin home' / An nayga 'gwine back.'" But using the West Indian concept of "yard" to cast the Jamaican nation as a collective home, the speaker asks, "Is who-for yard Jamaica is?" Citing the preponderance of African achievement in Jamaica, she surveys athletics, the judicial system, and the schools and finds in each case the "greates" is "a nayga man":

> Call fi Jamaica fastes sprinters,
> Gal or bwoy, an den
> De foremos artis, doctor, scholar—
> Nayga reign again!

But "Nayga Yard" is not so simple as a black nationalist anthem. After all, the celebratory refrain proclaiming the greatness of "nayga" relies on a word that, though deliberately transvalued, still retains its "derogatory" associations, "commonly implying extra blackness, backwardness, laziness, stupidity, etc."[64] Each time the poem proclaims the greatness of "nayga," it both furthers and retards racial affirmation. Moreover, at the end of this enumeration of black accomplishments, the catalog goes humorously awry:

> Go eena prison, poor house, jail,
> Asylum—wha yuh see?
> Nayga dah reign predominant!
> De place belongs to we!

This sort of "predominance" is hardly what the speaker set out to tally. While ratifying black self-esteem in Jamaica, Bennett draws back from unqualified dogma, suspicious toward excessive racial pride of any kind. Her characteristically dual irony is directed both against the refusal to recognize the black record of accomplishment in Jamaica and against blind racial presumption that fails to recognize the blemishes in this record. Bennett's poetry exemplifies what Bakhtin calls the freedom of "folk laughter" from dogmatism, piety, and official truth: "It is universal in scope," "directed at all and everyone," including "those who laugh."[65] "Caliban as Poet" is an inadequate model for the anti-ideological ideology, the antipolitical politics of Bennett's polymorphous irony.[66] Bennett gives powerful expression, through the antiritual of her Anancy poetics, to the hybridity, the irreverence, and the unorthodoxy of Jamaican creole language and culture—and it is to these that she is most loyal.

Relying on verbal, dramatic, and citational irony, Bennett also uses situational irony as skillfully as any modern poet. Not that situational and verbal irony can be kept neatly distinct, since poets as disparate as Bennett and

Thomas Hardy use the tensions of verbal irony to perform in language the seeming contradictions of history. In her stunning poem "Colonization in Reverse," Bennett ironically superimposes the midcentury Jamaican migration to England on the three-hundred-year English settlement of Jamaica. Even the word "colonization" in her title verbally enacts the irony of the historical "situation," yoking together the empire's forcible and exploitative occupation with the economic migration of Jamaicans seeking to rise out of their colonial poverty.

The first wave of mass Jamaican migration to Britain began on 21 June 1948, when the *Empire Windrush* arrived near London with 492 Jamaicans. Encouraged by the postwar labor shortage in England and the scarcity of work at home, 300,000 Jamaicans followed before the doors closed in 1962, many of them skilled and semi-skilled workers, braving the journey to the "motherland" in search of better economic opportunity. England's official national policy allowed for the free entry of all "British" subjects. But the British government betrayed intense anxiety over the arrival of "coloured colonials," assumed to be racially and socially inferior to whites: officials referred to the *Windrush*'s landing as an "incursion" that should not be followed by further "influxes."[67] "That nearly five hundred people could simply board a ship and come," writes the historian Kathleen Paul, "presented officials with a premonition of a limitless, uncontrollable invasion."[68] Although colonial education in the British West Indies had encouraged the colonized to conceive of themselves as British and of Great Britain as their "home," they encountered upon migration a sharply different attitude, which defined black or West Indian Britishness as a separate sphere of national identity from that of white British subjects. Formally British, Jamaican immigrants found themselves classified as "alien" intruders.

In Bennett's "Colonization in Reverse," England's apprehension implicitly shadows the speaker's ebullient tone (106–7). The poem humorously turns on its head the British alarm over the Jamaican "invasion":

> What a joyful news, Miss Mattie;
> Ah feel like me heart gwine burs—
> Jamaica people colonizin
> Englan in reverse.
>
> By de hundred, by de tousan,
> From country an from town,
> By de ship-load, by de plane-load,
> Jamaica is Englan boun.

> Dem a pour out a Jamaica;
> Everybody future plan
> Is fi get a big-time job
> An settle in de motherlan.
>
> What a islan! What a people!
> Man an woman, ole an young
> Jussa pack dem bag an baggage
> An tun history upside dung!

In another ironic twist, the speaker's euphoria inverts a long history of Jamaican bitterness over the violence of empire: that she greets the news of colonization with glee is a striking historical paradox. The migratory bursting of geographic boundaries finds its bodily equivalent in the speaker's feeling that her heart will burst for joy. At the level of the poetic line, the strong caesurae and syntactic parallelism in the second and fourth stanzas reinforce the sense of mirror-like inversion, as if the poem were an hourglass. These rhetorical, rhythmic, and stanzaic symmetries form the scaffolding for the poem's ironies of historical reversal.

At the level of the word, the poem ironically repossesses the rhetoric of colonization, starting with the word "colonize" itself. To call this influx of Jamaicans into Britain a "colonization" is to ironize the exaggerated British sense of the migration as a threat to English identity. Bennett's verbal irony decolonizes the word "colonize," appropriating it for the use of the colonized in their triumphant countercolonization of the "motherland." Similarly, to "settle" is no longer the prerogative of the colonizers; the colonized now furnish England with new inhabitants as the English once did Jamaica. To demonstrate verbally how Jamaicans "tun history upside dung" after three centuries of British rule, Bennett turns the language of colonization upside down. Jamaicans are "shippin off" their "countryman" to "immigrate an populate / De seat a de Empire." The word "populate" here ironically echoes its colonial usage, going back to the sixteenth century: "To furnish or supply (a country, etc.) with inhabitants; to people."[69] Perhaps less obviously, the speaker's exclamations wittily recall the language of colonial "discovery": "What a islan! What a people!" Seeming to be about joy at the Jamaican "discovery" of England, the referent of the line pivots from metropole back to colony when, in a further reversal, the next line describes Jamaicans preparing to migrate. These mirrorings, inversions, and verbal echoes humorously focus the differences between the imperial occupation and the peaceful postcolonial migration.

Mocking the British colonial enterprise and fears of the Jamaican "invasion," Bennett also turns her irony on her fellow Jamaicans, now that they have become postcolonial settlers.[70] Characteristically suspicious of lofty pretensions swaddled in abstract nouns, Bennett pokes fun at Jamaican profiteers who "open up cheap-fare- / To-Englan agency," ostensibly to "show dem loyalty." In "shippin off / Dem countryman like fire," these travel agents are no more pure in their motives than were their supposedly high-minded British counterparts. In an ironic "tunabout" of Jamaican history, the exploited now exploit their former exploiters, as vivified by Bennett's colorful metaphor: "Jamaica live fi box bread / Out a English people mout." Continuing to play on the word "settle," Bennett ironically uses the word in two more senses: "Some will settle down to work / An some will settle fi de dole." The migration of the word from one meaning to another—"to establish a colony," "to take up residence," and finally "to be content with"—is emblematic of the shifts in the direction of the poem's irony. The Jamaican settlement of England couldn't be as exploitative as the English settlement of Jamaica, yet neither is it altruistic.

A character named Jane exemplifies the reverse exploitation of the colonizers: she is paid

> Two pounds a week fi seek a job
> Dat suit her dignity.
>
> Me seh Jane will never fine work
> At de rate how she dah look
> For all day she stay pon Aunt Fan couch
> An read love-story book.

From Jamaica's imperial masters, Jane appropriates not only money but also highfalutin welfare rhetoric about one's "dignity." People like Jane, the poem suggests, are doing unto others what was done unto them. But in a further twist, the once-jubilant tone of the poem goes a little sour: economic parasitism may be debilitating and unattractive, whoever commits it. Having highlighted differences between Jamaican migration and British imperialism, Bennett inverts the emphasis of her ironic counterpoint, wondering if colonization in reverse may resemble colonization plain and simple, though on a vastly different scale. In a final, Anancy-like turnabout, Bennett recurs in the poem's last quatrain to the anxieties of the imperial center. Her tongue twirling in her cheek, she offers her mock sympathy for English fears of being swamped by black Britons:

What a devilment a Englan!
Dem face war an brave de worse;
But ah wonderin how dem gwine stan
Colonizin in reverse.[71]

The rhetoric of reversal, at its strongest in the doubly ironic structure of
"Colonization in Reverse," is central to Bennett's poetics more generally. Her
irony oscillates in the gap between a series of mirrorlike oppositions—between colonizer and colonized, center and metropole, white and black, dialect and standard. As we have seen, Bennett marshalls a variety of poetic
devices to encode formally these oppositions and inversions, from the symmetrical structure of the ballad stanza and lexical antitheses to syntactic repetitions and verbal echoes. Indeed, her poetry more often looks like a hall of
mirrors than like John Donne's "little rooms." In her array of ironic inversions, Bennett locates a language and poetic form to express that sameness-
with-a-difference at the heart of postcolonial experience.

The rhetorical reversals of Bennett's emigration and independence
poetry crystallize a question that has long been important in discussions
of postcoloniality—namely, the inverse relationship between colonizer
and colonized, particularly during nationalist struggles for independence.
Frantz Fanon theorized this relationship in terms of reciprocal violence: "The
violence of the colonial regime and the counter-violence of the native balance
each other and respond to each other in an extraordinary reciprocal homogeneity."[72] Because the Jamaican struggle for independence was itself relatively nonviolent, Bennett is less often concerned with the violence of this
"reciprocal homogeneity," revealing its many other manifestations. But in one
poem, "My Dream," violent nationalist reaction comes to the fore (112–13).
Written in the decade before independence, "My Dream" is a dream allegory
of resistance to the British empire. A humble washerwoman, personifying Jamaica, watches indignantly as Cousin Rose, or imperial England, greedily devours abundant provisions and "never gi me none!" Cousin Rose then starts
to "tease," "taunt," and hit the washerwoman. The speaker's feelings reflect
the upsurge of Jamaican nationalism in 1949 and after:

An when de lick-dem bun me, an
Ah feel me jaw dah swell,
Me temper bwile, me vengeance grow,
Me heart bawl out "Rebel!"

Acting out nationalist impulses, the washerwoman wants to reciprocate
Cousin Rose's violence, so she "start maltreat de clothes." Up to this point,

the poet's sympathy has been entirely on the side of the oppressed Jamaicans, but once the washerwoman tears up the clothes, merely provoking Cousin Rose to laughter, the speaker begins to look like the butt of the poem's irony. As Fanon would write, the violence of empire goes "far beyond in horror and magnitude any answer the natives can make": the washerwoman's violence is symmetrical without being equivalent.[73]

But in contrast to Fanon, Bennett wonders if this reciprocal violence in the Jamaican context, instead of being cleansing and purifying, is self-defeating. After her revolt, the speaker vividly pictures her island nation as victimized by both colonizer and herself, floating buglike in a toxic sea. Her sudden recognition of the mutual suffering in Jamaica and war-ravaged England finally lifts her out her despair:

> Ah feel just like a bug een a
> Big pool a D.D.T.,
> Den ah hear a vice seh, "Keep heart:
> Yuh no wusser off dan she."
>
> Dog a sweat but long hair hide i,
> Mout a laugh, but heart a leap!
> Everyting wha shine no gole piece.
> An me jump out a me sleep.

The strikingly divergent readings of the poem's end by Bennett's principal editors help to illustrate the poem's ambivalence toward both imperialist suppression and reciprocal nationalist violence. For Rex Nettleford, the final proverbs are about the washerwoman's and, hence, Jamaica's concealed "undercurrent of dissatisfaction."[74] Mervyn Morris reads them as referring instead to Britain's hidden weakness after World War II, which makes Cousin Rose not so different from the struggling washerwoman.[75] Bennett's dual irony supports both readings. Thematizing protective concealment, the proverbs themselves exemplify Anancy-like disguise, as if the poet were aiming at deliberate occlusion, to remain inassimilable to nationalist or imperialist dogma.[76] Bennett's allegorical figuration further imbeds the meaning of the poem in layers of hermeneutic disguise.

Allegory, disguise, opacity—these are key features not just of Bennett's poem but of creole itself, according to Edouard Glissant, who refers to the necessity of furtive communication among slaves to explain why creole "has at its origin" a "conspiracy to conceal meaning."[77] If so, then Bennett's sly strategies of saying and unsaying, of ironic and unpredictable turnabout, are true to a "counterpoetics" that extends well beyond her personal aesthetic.

In Glissant's view, "the Creole language was constituted around this strategy of trickery," resulting in specific qualities that are effectively harnessed throughout Bennett's poetry: "Improvisations, drumbeats, acceleration, dense repetitions, slurred syllables, meaning the opposite of what is said, allegory and hidden meanings."[78] In a radio monologue, Bennett relates how "we African ancestors," having been forced to speak English, "pop [outwitted] we English forefahders-dem. Yes! Pop dem an disguise up de English Language fi projec fi-dem African Language in such a way dat we English forefahders-dem still couldn understan what we African ancestors-dem wasa talk bout when dem wasa talk to dem one annodder!"[79] Rejecting both Cousin Rose's imperial thuggery and the washerwoman's reciprocal violence, Bennett ultimately sides with the laughter-filled counterpoetics embedded within the creole language itself. What this allegiance will mean for her poetry at the moment of political decolonization is one of the most fascinating episodes in Bennett's career.

Does postcolonial poetry find its ideological fulfillment in the moment of independence? Perhaps, if we look to a poem like Walter DeSouza's "This Is My Land," published in the *Gleaner* on the eve of Jamaica's independence:

> This is my nation—pure and proud
> New born—a land unspoiled by war and strife
> Arising now to take its rightful place
> An inspiration to her people's life[80]

No hint of irony complicates the poem's clichéd and idealizing celebration of Jamaica's formal decolonization on 6 August 1962. Except for its rhyme and pentameter, the poem is almost indistinguishable from many prose statements in the *Gleaner*, such as the rhapsodic lead article, "Midnight Tonight—a Date with Destiny":

> *Tonight the people of Jamaica will speak of God in their own different ways, will sing the national anthem and watch the Flag of its new nation rise proudly into the skies while bonfires on the peaks of the island's mountain ranges will blaze forth triumphantly to the stars as fireworks spangle the whole heavens in an outburst of joyous celebration. And in the cities and towns and villages and hamlets of the island, made bright with special illumination, there will be singing and rejoicing, localised reflections of the national centre of rejoicing at the National Stadium where the Princess Margaret will represent the Queen at the handing over of sovereign powers to the people of Jamaica.*

> The coming moment is one to be pondered by every Jamaican with humil-
> ity and with pride. It is the hour of our coming of age. It is the hour in which
> we will begin our greatest political adventure.[81]

Poetically endowing its prose with syntactic layering and delay, with confla-
grations in heaven and earth, the editorial engulfs all Jamaicans in an unambivalent joy and pride at the moment of independence. Every inch of social
space in Jamaica reflects the "national centre." The symbols of nationhood—
the anthem, flag, and stadium—gather all Jamaicans into a single identity;
indeed, later in the same issue of the *Sunday Gleaner,* these and other national symbols were given a full-page pictorial spread.[82] There is nothing
accidental in the emergence of the new Jamaica: at midnight, "the efforts of
many men will have climaxed with achievement" and "culminated in the attainment of Independence." This is not a day for equivocation or criticism.
As another writer puts it: "Today is no bad day to count our virtues. Tomor-
row is time enough to acknowledge our defects. But until the flag breaks at
the masthead a few seconds after midnight, we can justifiably indulge our
proper pride and take note of the positive qualities we possess and from
which we hope to create an original nation."[83] Joining the univocal chorus of
celebration are the official congratulations not only from the queen but also
from Khrushchev, Chiang Kai-Shek, and many other world leaders, official
letters reprinted on the front pages of the newspaper.

At this moment of political decolonization, literature can itself function
as a symbol of newfound and rightful independence alongside the flag, the
anthem, and the stadium, as indicated by the publication (and review in the
Sunday Gleaner) of the *Independence Anthology of Jamaican Literature.*[84] But
Bennett's poetry, though also often published in the same newspaper, seems
irreducible to this symbolic economy. How does her poetry about Jamaican
independence compare with the independence poetry and prose printed
in the *Gleaner,* governed by the historiographic rhetoric of culminating
achievement and destiny, by ideological principles of nationalist pride and
idealization, and by the symbolic subordination of difference in totemic
emblems of unity? Though herself a powerful cultural force for Jamaican decolonization, Bennett responds to Jamaica's grand moment of political independence with ironic guile and Anancy-like complexity, turning inside out
the dominant rhetoric, ideology, and symbolism of the moment. Her fine sequence of poems on independence reveals Bennett to be no less ironic in her
treatment of Jamaica's official self-representation than she is of the British
empire's.[85]

"Jamaica Elevate" recalls but deranges the rhetoric of the decolonizing struggle and destiny (113–15). Compare this speaker's historiography with the *Gleaner*'s:

> So much tings happen so fas an quick
> Me head still feel giddy!
> Biff, Referandum! Buff, Election!
> Baps, Independence drop pon we!

Far from being a glorious achievement and attainment of Jamaican heroes, independence is almost accidental, dropping like fruit from a mango tree. Not that the speaker is immune to national pride. She seems impressed by the international chorus of "congratulation / From de folks of high careers" and glad that Jamaica's politicians "Dah rub shoulder an dip mout / Eena heavy world affairs." But her conflation of metaphors for such contact humorously literalizes and thus deflates them. In reporting how Jamaica responds to other nations, she uses verbs that betray her newly bloated sense of national prerogative: "we meck" world bodies "know" we will join them, "we meck Merica know" we support them, and "tell Russia," "tell Englan" we dislike or disdain them. But in her overidentification with the newly independent nation, this *alazon* exaggerates both her own power and the Jamaican state's in independence. "Any nation dat we side wid," she claims, "Woulda never need to fret," though all she can enlist for the national defense is "half a brick," a "broken bottle," and a "coocoomaca stick." Her credibility undone by this contradiction, the speaker further contradicts herself by swinging suddenly from belligerence to pacifism. Years earlier, after the 1944 Constitution gave new power to Jamaican political leaders, Bennett was already satirizing such delusions of grandeur, as in this scathing quatrain:

> I is de rulin powah, gal!
> I is Authority!
> I meck dis country jump wid joy,
> Or rock wid misary![86]

Parodying the collective identification with symbols of independent nationhood, as in the *Gleaner*, the speaker of "Jamaica Elevate" boasts the key indices of Jamaica's newfound autonomy, including the stadium constructed in time to be the ceremonial site for transferring sovereignty from Britain to the new state. Obsessively repeated, the word "owna" suggests not only her identification—"our own"—but her possessive sense that she now "owns a" series of powerful new totems:

> We got we owna Stadium,
> We owna Bank fi save,
> We owna National Anthem
> An we owna flag a wave.
>
> We owna Governor-General,
> A true-bawn Native Son. . . .

For the speaker, the new governor general is the most impressive of all these symbols of nationhood, chiefly because of his blackness. At first she mistakes his newspaper picture for that of a family member, Bada John-John:

> De fus day im picture print, de
> Paper drop outa me han;
> Me heart go boop, me bawl out
> "Someting bad happen to John!"

Humorously playing on the racist homogenization of black faces, Bennett mocks the speaker's foolish misidentification, as well as her assumption that a black face in the news is bad news. Only at this point is the speaker revealed to be illiterate, unable to read the caption. But Bennett's irony is once again double-edged, directed not only at the speaker but at the racist colonialism that has made a black face in the newspaper so rare that it looks like a family member's in trouble—a colonialism that has made a black political leader's face nearly inconceivable for an Afro-Jamaican.

As this and other examples suggest, Bennett's independence poetry does not accord easily with received histories of postcolonial literature and decolonization. In the 1950s and 1960s, according to a chronicler, "Many writers in English from the African and Caribbean colonies took up the call to include literature as a moving spirit in the nationalist struggle. Anti-colonial resistance became for them a rallying cause, an enabling context, and a focal subject."[87] Surely Bennett's poetry is broadly "nationalist" insofar as it indigenizes literary language, personifies vibrant local voices, and ironizes colonial domination. Yet the independent nation is hardly the telos of the poetry. In "Independence Dignity," Bennett celebrates independence and at the same time pries open the ironies of the national celebrations (116–17). Implicitly critiquing the official celebrations, she stages a poetic celebration that is richly ambivalent, concerned to preserve a space for the independence of the poet's and other individuals' nonconformist irony and doubt, even at a moment of massively orchestrated collective feeling. As in "Jamaica Elevate," the poem takes the form of oral news-telling to someone who is missing the actual events, thus overtly competing with the official print news. The as-if "reporter" relates to Cousin Min how "Independence Celebration / Capture Jamaica." For Bennett, the moment of decolonization is ironically one of capture: the nation is recolonized by the fomented fervor for independence.[88] Not that such ironic insight should be mistaken for *pro*-colonialism. Bennett parodies the colonially inherited poem "The Burial of Sir John Moore," a Napoleonic war elegy by Charles Wolfe:

> Not a drum was heard, not a funeral note,
>   As his corse to the rampart we hurried;
> Not a soldier discharged his farewell shot
>   O'er the grave where our hero we buried.[89]

Bennett humorously transfigures a death lament into a nativity ode. She tropes the empire as death and Jamaica as birth:

> Yuh waan see how Jamaica people
> Rise to de occasion
> An deestant up demself fi greet
> De birt a dem new nation!

> Not a stone was fling, not a samfie sting,
> Not a soul gwan bad an lowrated;
> Not a fight bruck out, not a bad-wud shout
> As Independence was celebrated.

Reincarnating the threnodic rhetoric of anaphora, negation, and caesura, Bennett ironizes the colonial poem, the excessively reverential and conformist spectacle of the independence celebration, as well as her people's frequent stone flinging, fighting, and cursing.

Yet the poem is not immune to the collective joys of independence day:

> Concert outa street an lane an park
> Wid big-time acs performin,
> An we dance outa street
> From night till soon a mornin.

The polysyndeton "street an lane an park" suggests the sweeping scope of the shared revelry. So too does the prepositional reach of "From night till soon a mornin," a rhetorical pattern reinflected as spatial expanse in "From Packy Piece to Macka Town." The poem verbally reenacts this spreading joy. But Bennett worries lest this collectivism be so all-encompassing as to defeat the very principle of independence being celebrated. Newspaper advertise-

ments linked banking, real estate, alcohol, and many other products and
services to Jamaican independence, a commodification that Bennett humorously questions:

> Independence pen an pencil,
> Cup an saucer, glass an tray;
> Down to Independence baby bawn
> Pon Independence Day.

How does Bennett's independence poem distinguish itself from these independence products? By opening up a space for ironic reflection on just
such incongruities as the unindependent celebration of independence. The
epistrophic repetition of "ting" (thing) in the line "Everyting was Independence ting" suggests the paradoxical risk of hemming in independence. The
preposition "up," repeated with finite verbs throughout the poem, suggests
verticality, the collective attempt of the Jamaican people to rise above their
usual selves in accordance with the pride and decorum of the occasion: they
"deestant [decent] up demself" and the lights "pretty up" and "sweeten up"
the crowd; unruly Jane "stan up straight," and lazy Joe "Serious up him face,"
both of them to sing the national anthem. But this temporary upward movement builds to suggest the inevitable slump into normalcy that will follow.
Bennett constructs the last two lines of the poem out of four substantives,
suggesting that everything and everyone in Jamaica freezes in a temporary
pose:

> Jamaica Independence
> Celebration dignity.

In brief, while Bennett's poem shares in Jamaica's joy over independence, it
resists the totalizing and programmatic orchestration of univocal affect.
Bennett knew that this joy was complicated for many Jamaicans by other
feelings, such as regret over the collapse of the short-lived West Indies Federation (1958–61), elegized in her poem "Dear Departed Federation."[90] In
contrast to the nationalist subordination of all human difference in the seamless identity of the new state, Bennett reimagines the individual acts of self-
overcoming required for this evanescent conformity. "Teet an tongue was all
united," she writes, "Heart an soul was hans an glove," but these humorously
conflated idioms for undifferentiated cohesion indicate the suspect nature of
attempts to merge with the homogeneous, mass, fabricated identity of the
postcolonial nation. As Lloyd Brown remarks, Bennett gives expression in
her poetry to the "Jamaican's national consciousness" not by offering "an

overview of a collective consciousness" but by expressing "the contradictions, self-conflicts and uncertainties" within and among individuals.[91]

"Independence finds a ready Jamaica," proclaimed a headline in the independence issue of the *Sunday Gleaner.*[92] The article returns to this claim over and over, as if by repetition to convince the author and the readers of its veracity. "After 300 years of tutelage in the British way of life and in the development of a parliamentary democracy," begins the piece, "Jamaica is ready for independence." Independence means a state of political maturity and self-sufficiency. "Socially, too," the article goes on, "Jamaica is ready for independence," because of its mature racial and religious tolerance. "Economically, Jamaica is also ready for independence," because of its industry and raw materials. "With all these assets, spiritual as well as material, sophisticated Jamaica is ready for independence." But in the most compact poem in the series, "Independance," Bennett allows herself to wonder about the nation's readiness (117–19):

> Independance wid a vengeance!
> Independance raisin Cain!
> Jamaica start grow beard, ah hope
> We chin can stan de strain!

Instead of adopting a pose of unflinching self-assurance, Bennett gives voice to doubts about the preparedness and fate of the postcolonial nation. Literalizing the clichéd association of national with personal maturity, Bennett humorously depicts independence as a newly sprouted beard that a man's chin may or may not be able to support. She makes visible the masculinist assumptions behind the gendered rhetoric of national development and self-sufficiency.

The prime minister of Jamaica, Sir Alexander Bustamante, referred in his independence message to the "heavy responsibilities ahead of us. Independence means the opportunity for us to frame our own destiny and the need to rely on ourselves in so doing. It does not mean a licence to do as we like. It means work and law and order."[93] "What Independance mean" is also a question that Bennett joins in her poem:

> Mattie seh it mean we facety.
> Stan up pon we dignity,
> An we don't allow nobody
> Fi teck liberty wid we.
>
> Independence is we nature
> Born an bred in all we do,

> An she glad fi see dat Government
> Tun independant to.

The word "facety," meaning impudent and cheeky, continues the face trope from earlier in the poem (the bearded chin). If the prime minister hoped that independence would mean not only self-reliance but orderliness, Mattie projects her own more assertive, brash, even overbearing self-conception onto the new nation. For her, independence is independence from disrespect and imposition. Like the speakers in Bennett's other independence poems, Mattie undergoes an inflation in her self-conception, seeing her fantasies of personal power and heedlessness fulfilled in the political realm. Much as the speaker of "Jamaica Elevate" makes bullying use of verbs like "tell" and "meck know," so too Mattie wants to "tell" the personified "map" how to represent her nation, and implicitly herself:

> She hope dem caution worl-map
> Fi stop draw Jamaica small,
> For de lickle speck cyaan show
> We independantness at all!

> Moresomever we must tell map dat
> We don't like we position—
> Please kindly teck we out a sea
> An draw we in de ocean.

The poem mocks Mattie's naivete about maps, but it also suggests that behind each of her foolish assumptions is, paradoxically, a shrewd insight. While Mattie is mistaken to believe that graphic size on a map absolutely corresponds to a nation's relative "independantness," colonial mapmakers did bloat the size of Europe's nations by comparison with their colonial outposts. England hardly appeared as a "little speck" in British maps of the world. Similarly, Mattie foolishly believes that such depictions can be changed at will, yet colonial powers have often wilfully manipulated maps of their nations for political purposes. Her mistaken assumption that maps are humanoid betrays the insight that maps are constructs, subject to the geopolitical self-perceptions of their makers. Here as elsewhere in Bennett's independence poetry, the irony that cuts against the colonized cuts no less against the colonizers. But for Bennett, to reverse the colonizer's grand self-perception is not enough; little will have changed if Caliban is as blindly self-aggrandizing as Prospero. She would not only "reverse the maps of domination," in Susan Willis's phrase, but also reveal the assumptions behind all such mapping, whether by colonizer or colonized.[94]

Bennett recalls a different developmental model of the nation toward the poem's end, humorously recalling the frequent association of independence with birth: "Jamaica people need a / Independance formula!" If Jamaica is gaining its independence because of its mature readiness, then why is it, like other emergent nations, often metaphorized as a newborn baby, in need of a special infant "formula"? Bennett mockingly suggests the inadequacy of either the maturation or the birth metaphor for the newly independent nation:

> No easy-come-by freeness tings,
> Nuff labour, some privation,
> Not much of dis an less of dat
> An plenty studiration.

The speaker's recipe for successful independence strangely mixes ingredients appropriate to the newly matured male (self-restraint, hard work, economy) and the newly born child (the finger-wagging behest, "Not much of dis an less of dat," and subsequent study in school). At the end of the poem, Bennett returns to the literalized figure of competent nation as mature male:

> Independance wid a vengeance!
> Wonder how we gwine to cope?
> Jamaica start smoke pipe, ah hope
> We got nuff jackass rope!
> [We've got enough local tobacco!]

In her independence poetry, Bennett intimates that nationhood has taken so long to arrive that it is almost anticlimactic, yet at the same time its arrival is almost violent in its suddenness ("wid a vengeance!"). Despite all the journalistic posturing about "readiness," Bennett allows for feelings of uncertainty, even helplessness, in the once colonized population.

If the independence ceremonies attempt to form a sense of national community around officially structured events, galas, and symbols, Bennett evokes in her poetry the reverse kind of community-formation, revolving around ironic insight into the follies of the nation's self-representation and self-aggrandizement. Even at the moment of independence, she, like the West Indian broad talker, rudely questions the self-importance, pomp, and gaudy grandeur of the national celebrations. As a national poet, Bennett joins officials in seeking to inspire a sense of liminality across lines of class and gradations of color, but in place of their cultural rites of universal reverence and submission, she offers poetic "antirituals" that are closer to what Abrahams calls the broad talker's "wit, repartee, and directed slander"—tactics that serve as "a creative channel for antisocial community motives." Bennett's antinationalist irreverence dovetails with her anti-imperialist wit in helping to evoke and form a carnivalesque community of the once colonized. Her poetry builds, as Bakhtin rhapsodically writes of carnival, "a second world and second life outside officialdom," on the basis of a laughter that "knows no inhibitions, no limitations," that "boldly unveil[s] the truth": "Laughter purifies from dogmatism, from the intolerant and the petrified; it liberates from fanaticism and pedantry, from fear and intimidation, from didacticism, naïveté and illusion, from the single meaning, the single level, from sentimentality."[95]

Admittedly, Bennett's complex irony makes her as hard to pin down as the trickster Anancy. As we have seen, the double structure of her irony is a central way in which she aesthetically embodies postcoloniality, insofar as both are "to double business bound." In this regard, she exemplifies the power of an ironic poetics that is shared by other Caribbean writers, such as Walcott and Naipaul, and indeed a host of other postcolonial writers across the Third World. India, for example, has given rise to many of the most powerful contemporary ironists, including poets like Ramanujan and Eunice de Souza and novelists like Rushdie and Arundhati Roy. Unwilling to settle for a poetry of nationalist dogma or imperial rhetoric, Bennett frustrates the effort to track her ever-shifting ironies from one poem to another or, indeed, from one stanza or line to the next. Even the model of double irony hardly does justice to the variety of her ironic strategies. The full measure of her accomplishment can only be found in the specific texture and structure, the verbal fabric and rhetorical play of individual poems in relation to their informing historical contexts.

"Dialect" poets like Bennett are often condescended to in poetry criticism, assumed to be primarily of "local" interest. Only recently have African-American "vernacular" poets like Sterling Brown and Langston Hughes received the kind of close literary analysis their work deserves. American and British critics have been still less welcoming of postcolonial poets who represent the variety of modern English. But to regard Standard English as the common language from which a world poet should not deviate is to reimpose an outdated imperial norm, disguised as a formula for universal accessibility. This normativist critical view is entangled in the old European concept denounced by the poet David Dabydeen (Guyana/United Kingdom): that black people are "linguistically illiterate" and "ignorant of the rules of grammar. Their language is mere broken, stupid utterance." Along with other Afro-Caribbean poets like Walcott, Brathwaite, Mervyn Morris, Dennis Scott,

Lorna Goodison, Grace Nichols, Michael Smith, and Dabydeen himself, Bennett exemplifies what Dabydeen calls the "energy, vitality, and expressiveness of creole."[96] The first Caribbean poet to make consistently brilliant and ebullient use of creole, Bennett is long overdue for recognition beyond the West Indies—as master ironist, as master poet, as a major anglophone poet of our time. Indeed, her poetry, at once subversive and aggregative in its creole irony, is one more index of the range, the heterogeneity, and the promise of post-colonial poetry.

CHAPTER SIX

🌱 The Poet as "Native Anthropologist": Ethnography and Antiethnography in Okot p'Bitek's *Songs*

The vexed relation between postcolonial literatures and anthropology has sometimes been condensed in one of two conflicting propositions: that postcolonial literatures are ethnographic or that they are nonethnographic. According to the first formulation, advanced primarily by Western critics, postcolonial literatures are saturated with ethnographic information, conveying for a foreign readership the customs and beliefs of native cultures. Reviewing Achebe's *Things Fall Apart* and other African novels, Charles Larson finds "anthropological passages," "anthropological overview," and "ethnological background" woven into their narrative fabric: "The anthropological is indeed important. Without it there would be no story."[1] More recently, Christopher Miller has argued that "francophone African literature has always practiced some form of anthropological rhetoric," using "devices such as footnotes, parentheses, and character-to-character explanations in order to provide the reader with the necessary cultural information." While conceding the troubled, "imperialist" history of anthropology in Africa, Miller believes that "a fair Western reading of African literatures demands engagement with, and even dependence on, anthropology."[2] According to the contrary view, advanced primarily by postcolonial writers themselves, Western critics have, in Kwame Anthony Appiah's words, "been all too eager to attend to the ethnographic dimension of African literature."[3] In specifying their social milieu, postcolonial texts are no more ethnological, argues Appiah, than are Scott's *Ivanhoe* or Flaubert's *Madame Bovary*. The popularity at home of postcolonial writers like Soyinka and Achebe indicates that they intend not a foreign but a local audience.[4] Haunted by anthropology's complicity in the colonial enterprise, many postcolonial writers reject any recolonization of postcolonial literatures under the rubric of Western anthropology.

Each of these arguments illuminates an aspect of the

interrelation between postcolonial literatures and anthropology, but neither may be adequate in itself to the complexities of their dynamic engagement. Strangely, postcolonial theory, for all its vigorous and far-ranging explorations, has thus far failed to grapple with the large implications of this relationship. Perhaps one place to start reconceptualizing the tangled skein that binds and divides the two discourses is the postcolonial literary texts produced by professional anthropologists. Having been trained as ethnographers, typically in the diaspora, these writers return home in their imaginative works, but to a "home" defamiliarized by anthropological modes of understanding. Their work crosses the boundaries that constitute "native" literatures on the one hand and "anthropological" discourse on the other. Most important for our purposes, these writers make visible the intense dialogue with ethnography latent in much postcolonial writing in European languages.

When "native anthropologists" write "postcolonial literature," do they incorporate ethnographic assumptions into their literary work, thereby revealing the compatibility of anthropology and postcolonial literatures? Or are such writers disqualified from the postcolonial and the "native" by virtue of their diasporic investment in anthropology? Despite their anthropological training, do these poets and novelists resist Western ethnographic codes in their imaginative writing, thus confirming the antagonism between the two discourses? What can we learn about the promise and the limitations of anthropology from the responses of the poet-ethnographer?

Recently, the Indian novelist Amitav Ghosh, trained at Oxford in anthropology, has deepened the complexity of the relationship between the two discourses. His story "The Imam and the Indian," in particular, has influenced the Western anthropological theorizing of James Clifford and David Scott, raising anew the question of how we should position anthropology in relation to the "native" text—above, before, within, or after it? As anterior or posterior discourse? As metadiscourse or intrinsic discourse?[5] Two decades before Ghosh worked on his thesis in anthropology at Oxford, an East African poet wrote a thesis at Oxford on Acoli and Lango traditional songs, after studying with some of the most famous anthropologists in the English-speaking world.[6] Okot p'Bitek is also the author of the most celebrated East African poem in English. Often deemed "nativist," his poetry seems to inhabit the opposite end of the postcolonial literary spectrum from Ghosh's intercultural, decentered work. The broad contrast between these two writer-anthropologists indicates the difficulty of trying to arrive at pat conclusions about the nature of "ethnographic literature" or "literary

ethnography." Because Okot published significant field research and theoretical texts in anthropology, and because his literary work intensely engages
ethnographic assumptions and practices, his masterpiece, *Song of Lawino*
(1966), in addition to the briefer companion poem *Song of Ocol* (1967), may
be a most revealing case study in the twisted relationship between anthropology and postcolonial literatures.

A poem astonishingly popular in Africa and abroad, Okot p'Bitek's *Song of
Lawino* has long been hailed as one of the most authentically native works
of the postcolonial world. In their polemical *Toward the Decolonization
of African Literature,* Chinweizu, Onwuchekwa Jemie, and Ihechukwu
Madubuike celebrate the "traditionalist" Okot's *Song of Lawino* as "possibly
the best rounded single work of African poetry in English today," "using
authentic African imagery and Acholi dramatic rhetorical devices." They
denounce, by contrast, "Euromodernists" like Soyinka and the early
Christopher Okigbo for having "assiduously aped the practices of 20th-
century European modernist poetry."[7] The words "authentic African" converge repeatedly in discussions of Okot, as when Ngugi wa Thiong'o praises
the poet's expression of "an authentic African self."[8] The contrast with the
Euromodernists is also recurrent. Introducing an important essay on the
poem, Bernth Lindfors sets Okot apart from "cultural mulattoes": "When he
sang, no European echoes could be heard in the background. His *Song of
Lawino* was the first long poem in English to achieve a totally African identity." He adds, "It is a thoroughly indigenous poem in form, content, style,
message and aesthetic philosophy."[9] Also redeeming the communal, rooted
Okot from the company of narcissistic, displaced Euromodernists, Nkem
Okoh proclaims *Song of Lawino* "a thoroughly homebred and autochtho-
nously African literary work."[10] "There is a grave danger" for English-language African writers, warns G. A. Heron, "that with the tool of language
they will borrow other foreign things," but Okot succeeds in using English
"without borrowing foreign elements that distort his message."[11] Deeply
rooted, indigenous in form and content, uncompromised by alien influences, *Song of Lawino* would seem to be the epitome of African cultural authenticity.

Okot's own pronouncements about the dangers of "apemanship" have
helped to shape the reception of his poetry as a preeminent indigenous artifact. Numbering himself among Africa's "cultural revolutionists" and "gal-
lant nationalists," Okot celebrated their dedication "to the total demolition

of foreign cultural domination and the restoration and promotion of Africa's proud culture to its rightful place."[12] But not all of Okot's prose can be assimilated to the nativist paradigm. In the same essay collection, he recalls a 1967 festival at Uganda's National Cultural Centre in Kampala, which featured African pop groups like the Mods and Jets, the Echoes and Slingers, and the Vibrations, their members wearing "tight jeans and large studded belts," miniskirts and blond wigs. As director of the center, Okot was accused of promoting a cultural "slave mentality": "Where is your nationalism, man?" asked an enraged revolutionary student.[13] But while Okot obviously favors the "popular arts of the countryside" and disdains the "aping" of Western song, he also concedes the growing influence of Western music, film, and other forms on Uganda's village youth.[14] The songs of town and village youth, according to Okot, are "equally valid and significant": thus, the Uganda Cultural Centre "must not be reactionary like some old men who reject all foreign art forms, nor must it reflect the bigoted ideas of some miseducated men who despise all things African."[15]

Okot has too often been taken for the type of the reactionary who rejects all foreign art forms. His first written work was a Mozart-inspired opera. Asked about the influence of African oral tradition on *Song of Lawino* and *Song of Ocol*, Okot responded with some exaggeration, "I don't think they are very much influenced by the African oral tradition; they cannot be sung, for instance." He repeatedly cited instead Longfellow's *Song of Hiawatha* and the biblical *Song of Solomon*.[16] While he also recalled the influence of his mother, who had often composed new songs and was known, among other names, as Lawino, he humorously recounts his frustration in reading to her the first draft of *Song of Lawino*:

> I took it to her with great pride and said, "I've got a song for you." And she completely surprised me by asking me to sing it! Of course, I couldn't, and my balloon just collapsed. She went on and asked, "Is it a love song?" I couldn't answer that. "Is it a war song? Is it. . . . What kind of song is it?" So I said, "You shut up. Let me read it to you." She shut up and I read it aloud. She was very pleased but kept on saying, "I wish there was some tune to it." You see, it was not really like an Acholi song.[17]

Certainly Okot's *Song of Lawino* and *Song of Ocol* are influenced by and even incorporate various Acoli genres. In a piece of intrinsic genre criticism, Lawino enumerates "Provocative songs, / Insulting and abusive songs / Songs of praise / Sad songs of broken loves," and she might also have mentioned satirical beer-party songs, dance songs, war songs, and funeral dirges (42).[18] Yet

Okot's heteroglossic poems are not Acoli oral songs, any more than Langston Hughes's "The Weary Blues" is an "authentic" blues or Salman Rushdie's *Midnight's Children* is an oral Indian narrative. Generically hybrid, Okot's poems compound the oral, brief, communal, occasional, proverb-laden songs of the Acoli with the written, single-authored, long dramatic monologues of the West.

Although critics have tended to laugh off Okot's statements that *The Song of Hiawatha* was a primary inspiration for his "songs," the seemingly improbable connections between an African nativist and Longfellow might help us to reopen the question of Okot's cultural sources and his relation to the discourse of anthropology.[19] For Longfellow starts his poem much as if he were an ethnographer, who will "repeat" native American "songs," "legends and traditions" as he "heard them / From the lips" of a native American singer:

> Ye who love a nation's legends,
> Love the ballads of a people,
> That like voices from afar off
> Call to us to pause and listen,
> Speak in tones so plain and childlike,
> Scarcely can the ear distinguish
> Whether they are sung or spoken;—
> Listen to this Indian Legend,
> To this Song of Hiawatha![20]

The idea of the long poem as a simple, nearly oral conspectus of a native people's lore—traditional ways that are endangered—undergirds Okot's *Song of Lawino*. But whereas Longfellow crosses a cultural gulf to transcribe the indigenous "voices from afar off," Okot presumably listens to the lore and legends of his "own" people. Okot reverses Longfellow's imperial perspective on "childlike" oral culture by singing and writing from "within" it. He performs for the Acoli the roles of both listening ear and scribal hand, voice and text. The postcolonial poet nevertheless absorbs *Hiawatha's* generic premise that the long poem is the proper form for relating, explaining, and dramatizing songs and traditions of a non-Western culture.

Exposed at an early age to this proto-anthropology as part of a colonially imposed Western canon, Okot was later immersed in the prescriptions and assumptions of modern British anthropology. Yet the relation between Okot's anthropological and literary work remains largely unexplored. It shouldn't escape our notice that Okot was awarded the degree of B.Litt. in anthropology only a few years before he published *Song of Lawino*. How did an Acoli writer wind up reading anthropology at Oxford in the early 1960s? Britain's African empire may have been breaking up at this time, but imperial patterns of cultural and educational dissemination persisted in the relations between metropole and decolonizing outpost. Thus, having found his way to Britain as a member of the Ugandan national soccer team that played barefoot at the summer Olympics of 1956, Okot first studied education at the University of Bristol and then received a law degree at Aberystwyth in 1960. From 1960 to 1963 he read at Oxford's Institute of Social Anthropology, headed by the social anthropologist E. E. Evans-Pritchard, author of the pathbreaking trilogy on Nuer religion and social practices (1940, 1951, 1956). Godfrey Lienhardt, whose renowned *Divinity and Experience: The Religion of the Dinka* was published in 1961, supervised Okot's research, which included fieldwork in Uganda in 1962. Plunged into British anthropology during some of its headiest days, Okot wrote a thesis entitled "Oral Literature and Its Social Background among the Acoli and Lang'o" (1964), which provided the basis for his books *Religion of the Central Luo* (1971) and *The Horn of My Love* (1974), a collection of Acoli oral poetry with extensive commentary. In 1970 he published his most searching book on anthropology, *African Religions in Western Scholarship*.[21]

Although Chinweizu, Ngugi, and others portray Okot's poetry as a pure, rooted, authentically indigenous touchstone of African literature, *Song of Lawino* and *Song of Ocol* are poems of split vision, part of yet parted from the culture they describe. "Many an African leader is split," Okot remarks, "between his African background, of which he is secretly proud but publicly ashamed, and the so-called 'modern way of life,' of which he is publicly proud but secretly unsure."[22] Okot's inner division may be much the same, although the values are reversed. Insofar as Okot's poems record and explain the village culture of Acoliland, anthropology inflects their apprehension of a native culture threatened by change. Okot admits that Acoli war songs and dance songs "are now socially irrelevant": "If all that can be done is to record them on tape, to be preserved like specimens in the laboratory, then that at least we must do."[23] Are Okot's literary songs in effect laboratory vials, preserving specimens from a vanishing East African village heritage? In what specific ways is Okot's literary work shaped by his training in Western anthropological techniques for selecting and conserving cultural samples? To what extent is *Song of Lawino* in harmony with the disciplinary assumptions of anthropology?

The poem's anthropological affiliations run deep. Social anthropology, writes Okot in *African Religions in Western Scholarship,* has been based on "the study of the so called 'tribal' peoples," and thus, as he quotes Joseph H. Greenberg, "The basic technique [is] field study, by observation and partici- pation and verbal interviews of relatively small groups typically organized on a tribal basis."[24] Okot offers in *Song of Lawino* an "intensive, in-depth study of a small community 'from the inside,'" in accordance with this an- thropological norm after Malinowski, as described by Sally Falk Moore.[25] In *Song of Lawino,* the unit of description and exploration is a single "tribal" vil- lage. The communities studied by the anthropologist, Moore states, needed to be "small enough to be treated as closed systems."[26] Villages, as James Clifford observes of anthropology, "have long served as habitable, mappable centers for the community and, by extension, the culture. . . . The village was a manageable unit. It offered a way to centralize a research practice, and at the same time it served as synecdoche, as point of focus, or part, through which one could represent the cultural whole."[27] By limiting the "field" of *Song of Lawino* to an Acoli village, Okot can represent intensively and com- prehensively the social and religious practices of Lawino and her clan. A concrete and bounded cultural space, her village serves as vivid synecdoche for the cultural whole of Acoliland, and sometimes even for sub-Saharan Africa. This circumscription of the field is as useful to the imaginative writer as it is to the anthropologist, helping to make the living social world both comprehensible and representable.

Lawino's vehement defense of her native culture and rejection of West- ern ways also resemble the culturally conservative stance of much social anthropology. Although her perspective has been assumed to be "autochtho- nous," it could also be seen as strongly allied with the anthropologist's ten- dency, until recently, to valorize and study what Moore calls seemingly "ancient and fixed 'traditions' and 'customs.'"[28] Lawino's proverb for this tra- ditionalist position, repeated often, is "Let no one / Uproot the Pumpkin" (56). Lawino addresses her Westernized husband:

> Listen, Ocol, my old friend,
> The ways of your ancestors
> Are good,
> Their customs are solid
> And not hollow
> They are not thin, not easily breakable
> They cannot be blown away
> By the winds
> Because their roots reach deep into the soil.

I do not understand
The ways of foreigners
But I do not despise their customs.
Why should you despise yours?

Listen, my husband,
You are the son of a Chief.
The pumpkin in the old homestead
Must not be uprooted!
    (41)

Almost as an anthropologist to the estranged Ocol, Lawino would reintroduce her husband to Acoli customs, as Okot would his readers, both Acoli and foreign. Lawino's "live and let live" or "to each his own" philosophy conforms to a bedrock assumption of anthropology. Defending her right to practice her people's ways, Lawino naturalizes cultural difference by referring to the vivid biological diversity around her. Even this anthropomorphic comparison of differences between animal species to differences between peoples is not alien in the history of ethnography:

No leopard
Would change into a hyena,
And the crested crane
Would hate to be changed
Into the bold-headed,
Dung-eating vulture,
The long-necked and graceful giraffe
Cannot become a monkey.
    (56)

But the assumptions shared in Okot's poetry and in anthropology—tolerating difference, preserving traditional culture, and focusing on the village—are insufficient to prove that Okot's imaginative eye was disciplined and directed by his anthropological training. After all, imaginative works by Achebe, Soyinka, and other nonanthropologists share some of these general features. Indeed, before he left for Britain, Okot had already drafted, in 1956, a small portion in Acoli of what would later grow to be his English *Song of Lawino* (1966) and his Acoli *Wer pa Lawino* (1969). Even so, *Song of Lawino* as a whole reflects the strong influence of anthropology in more specific ways. The latter sections of the poem, mostly added or amplified in the wake of Okot's ethnographic research, not surprisingly resemble anthropological discourse more than the earlier sections. Whereas Lawino had focused, in

sections 1–5, on her feelings of betrayal by her wanna-be-white husband, who is intoxicated with a new Westernized wife humorously named
Clementine, her emphasis shifts in these latter sections to an ethnographic
outline of Acoli culture. In a long passage new in the 1966 English version
and partly excerpted below, she describes in detail her mother's house:

> Look,
> Straight before you
> Is the central pole.
> That shiny stool
> At the foot of the pole
> Is my father's revered stool.
>
> Further on
> The rows of pots
> Placed one on top of the other
> Are the stores
> And cupboards.
> Millet flour, dried carcasses
> Of various animals,
> Beans, peas,
> Fish, dried cucumber . . .
>
> Look up at the roof,
> You see the hangings?
> The string nets
> Are called *cel*.
> The beautiful long-necked jar
> On your left
> Is full of honey.
> That earthen dish
> Contains simsim paste;
> And that grass pocket
> Just above the fireplace
> Contains dried white ants.
>   (59)

Even the shift in voice in these sections indicates a greater degree of objectification, the poet relying less on urgent and directed second-person address,
more on depersonalized second- and third-person description.[29] Here Lawino invokes an abstract "brother" and almost seems to be talking beyond him
to a non-Acoli audience. Whereas agitated apostrophe to her husband and

clansmen verbally encoded Lawino's full participation in her village community, the diminishment and attenuation of this rhetorical device implicitly
open a space between Acoli village culture and the poet, even as the poem
paradoxically becomes most "indigenous" in content. Swollen with pain and
pride in the early sections, Lawino's voice is tinged in these later sections
with a detachment that, coupled with ethnographic inventory, resembles the
tone of anthropology's "participant observer."

Among the most important footprints left by anthropology in *Song of
Lawino* are the categories of knowledge that structure Lawino's representation of Acoli ways. In the later versions of *Song of Lawino*, Okot gathers together Lawino's views on cooking and eating from seven previously scattered
short sections and concentrates them all in the sixth section, adding passages like the one quoted above, which almost reads like culinary anthropology. Here as elsewhere in *Song of Lawino*, the mode of apprehension and
narration is governed by a recognizably anthropological topos. Lawino's poetic ethnography of Acoli customs for preparing and consuming food also
informs us that her people use "grinding stones" to pound "millet / Mixed
with cassava / And sorghum" (59). Lawino details the different kinds of
wood and whether they serve for cooking or for making axes or canes. She
explains that the Acoli stove is "dug into the earth" and that half-gourds and
earthen dishes are used for food and drink (61). At mealtime among the
Acoli, except for the father seated on his stool, everyone sits on papyrus mats
on the earth. But first,

> We wash our hands clean
> And attack the loaf
> From all sides.
> You mould a spoon
> And dip it in the gravy
> And eat it up.
>   (62)

Each of the ensuing sections addresses one or more anthropological
concepts. Some critics have complained that the later sections of *Song of
Lawino* fail to sustain the narrative of conflict among Lawino, her husband,
and her rival wife. In view of Okot's revisions and additions after his ethnographic schooling, the shift in narrative mode can be explained. As the struc-
turing logic of these sections, anthropological tableaux supplant dramatic
tension and plot. One of Evans-Pritchard's principal strategies in his famous
ethnography of the Nuer, as Sally Falk Moore surmises, was "to take a West-

ern concept, such as the concept of time, and to address the variety of ways in which Nuer thought of it."[30] This technique is only slightly veiled in "There Is No Fixed Time for Breast Feeding," where Lawino expounds the "customs of our people" in relation to time, referring to the agricultural patterns of the daily routine and the seasonal round of wet and dry (68). Similarly, in the next section she parses the different classes of names among the Acoli, responding to the apparent meaninglessness of Christian names: Bull names are passed to the children of the chief, *Jok* or divinity names are given to "deeply respected" twins, titles like her father's are acquired through battle, and there are also sorrow names, praise names, and mourning names (82–83). In the sections on religious beliefs and medicine, Lawino describes some of the healing and apotropaic practices of diviner-priests like her father and Acoli herbalists. To ward off maladies, the Acoli pray to the ancestors for intervention and wear charms like elephant tails, rat toes, cowry shells, and colobus-monkey hair. She even recounts the different roots, greens, and juices that she applies to stomachaches, sore throats, wounds, difficult childbirth, impotence, and the evil eye. If a child falls ill with fever, a jealous woman or relative is most likely to blame for having "hidden / The child's excreta in a tree fork," or buried the boy's hair in a riverbed, or trapped the girl's shadow or head (97).

Thus, in the latter sections of *Song of Lawino,* the poet's practice has much in common with the anthropologist's: carefully describing specific village customs, gathering them together under one conceptual rubric, and relating them to the broader nexus of a people's beliefs. So ethnographically rich and wide ranging is Okot's survey of the Acoli in *Song of Lawino* that it makes his professional monograph *Religion of the Central Luo* seem narrow by comparison. At least for Okot, poetry ironically seems a more efficient medium for ethnography than professional ethnography itself. As one indication of the vast anthropological ground Okot covers in *Song of Lawino* and *Song of Ocol,* most of the crucial concepts that he lists in a table of *Religion of the Central Luo,* along with their corresponding indigenous words, are recognizable from the poetry: "Dominant Deities, Chiefdom Deities, Ancestral Ghosts, Ghostly Vengeance, Curse, Blessing, Totems/Emblems, Pestilences, Certain Diseases, Rain, Lightning, Ritual Observances (Respect), Fault/Sin, Sacrifice, Witch, Evil Eye, Fetish, Medicine/Poison, Diviner, Priest, Prophet."[31]

Lawino's commentary on death also condenses considerable ethnographic knowledge. Although Lawino vaunts the efficacy of herbs, charms, and sacrifices, when it comes to last things, she is a fatalist, as she explains in a long passage new in the English version of the poem:[32]

when the day has dawned
For the journey to Pagak [the place of no return]
No one can stop you,
White man's medicines
Acoli medicines,
Crucifixes, rosaries,
Toes of edible rats,
The horn of the rhinoceros
None of them can block the path
That goes to Pagak!

When Death comes
To fetch you
She comes unannounced,
She comes suddenly
Like the vomit of dogs. . . .

. . . .

You may be the fastest runner,
A long distance runner,
But when Death comes
To fetch you
You do not resist,
You must not resist.
You cannot resist!
       (102)

Here as elsewhere, Lawino deprivileges Western "crucifixes, rosaries" by juxtaposing them with similarly apotropaic devices used by the Acoli, such as rat toes and rhinoceros horns. Her figuration of death as the sudden vomiting of dogs is characteristically vivid and tactile. The fatalism of the Central Luo, once all devices and rites have failed, was also the final subject of Okot's *Religion of the Central Luo,* providing a useful point of comparison:

> When danger threatened, the Central Luo did all they could to avert it, and to rid the homestead of it. The beliefs and practices I have described and certain knowledge of medicines were used to diagnose, explain, interpret the individual causes of misfortune and ill-health, and they also provided means and ways of coping with the individual situations of anxiety and stress. But when all these failed, when the game of ritually acting out their deeply felt needs and desires and hopes had produced no satisfactory results, at this level, the Central Luo became sceptical and irreligious, and preferred to face the facts of life cooly and realistically. When your son died you wept, but amid tears, you declared, "*Wi-lobo*"; "This is the way of the world"![33]

Do we learn more about Luo fatalism from Okot's anthropological or his poetic account? At an analytic remove, his professional narrative relies on objectifying abstractions like "the Central Luo," "fatalism," "situations," "ritually acting out," "satisfactory results," "sceptical and irreligious," until he adds the last flourish of a poetic apostrophe with a specific example, the poet's voice finally overtaking the ethnographer's. Ironically, the poem may afford a more immediate apprehension of Acoli fatalism, because of its more intrinsic perspective (Lawino's dismissal of the indigenous medicines she has been promoting) and lively metaphors (the victim as doomed runner, death's suddenness as dog vomit). These rough distinctions between ethnographic and literary discourse should not serve to harden boundaries that are unstable and permeable; on the contrary, they indicate once again that Okot the poet may paradoxically "out-ethnograph" Okot the ethnographer.

In addition to the broad influence of anthropological strategies, does the discipline leave more specific discursive traces in *Song of Lawino*? Perhaps. Sometimes Lawino objectifies her cultural environment as "our People" and "the Acoli." She constructs her culture as an ethnological unit, related to yet distinct from others both nearby and far away. She compares, for example, the Acoli stove dug in the ground with the three mounds of clay used by the Lango—a type of stove she has learned to use from the "wife of my mother's brother" (61). Admittedly, the extent of ethnographic influence is difficult to measure here, since this self-understanding can also be viewed as intrinsic. Another example of the undecidability of the ethnographic or the oral in Lawino's rhetoric is her description of her culture's habitual rites of time:

> When the sun has grown up
> And the poisoned tips
> Of its arrows painfully bite
> The backs of the men hoeing
> And of the women weeding or harvesting[,]
> This is when
> You take drinking water
> To the workers.
>   (64–66)

> When the baby cries
> Let him suck milk
> From the breast.
>   (68)

> Among our People
> When a girl has
> Accepted a man's proposal
> She gives a token,
> And then she visits him
> In his bachelor's hut
> To try his manhood.
>   (90)

These passages can be seen as the didactic instructions that an oral culture uses to transmit its customs—prescriptions for acts to be repeated whenever certain conditions are present. Without reiterating when and how certain actions should be performed, an oral culture cannot sustain itself. But in such passages Lawino may also sound as if she were explaining herself to a foreign audience. Her specific rhetorical strategy—the use of subordinate adverb clauses in the habitual present—is also key in anthropological writing, freezing actions in time as perpetual events. In works like Godfrey Lienhardt's *Divinity and Experience* and Evans-Pritchard's *Nuer Religion*, many pivotal sentences take the form, "When boys reach manhood they take the colour-names of oxen . . ." and "When a spirit gets a cow, . . . the cow ought to be disposed of."[34]

Granted the uncertain provenance of some of the poem's rhetorical forms, we can summarize by saying that Okot's *Song of Lawino* abounds not only in "Acoli ways" but also in anthropological ways, from general assumptions to detailed observations. If *Song of Lawino* is often cited as a preeminent example of authentic African culture, then its participation in anthropological techniques, attitudes, and categories of knowledge suggests that "nativist" literatures may be deeply and pervasively intertwined with Western ethnographic discourse. Paradoxically, the poem's "nativism," like the "nativism" of negritude and other recuperative postcolonial movements, betrays the force of Western influence.[35]

But to gauge the full measure of the complex relationship between *Song of Lawino* and anthropology, we need to probe the ways in which the poem, though steeped in ethnographic practices and ideas, may also be actively antiethnographic. "To the gallows / With all the Professors / Of Anthropology," demands Ocol in one of his bombastic tirades against the preservers and defenders of African culture (129). As a professor of anthropology himself, Okot was undoubtedly more sympathetic to the discipline than Ocol. But Okot's own relationship with the discipline of anthropology was vexed, perhaps offering clues to understanding the ambivalences in his poetry. This sentence concludes the preface to Okot's *African Religions in Western Schol-arship:* "Lastly, I would like to thank my Oxford teachers, especially Profes-sor Evans-Pritchard, Dr. Godfrey Lienhardt and Dr. John B[e]attie for their personal friendship, and for the challenge they threw at me."[36] Gracious as this acknowledgment is, it comes after Okot has indicated how troubled his relationship was with his teachers, whose disciplinary rhetoric and assump-tions he found offensive:

> I first met a number of Western scholars at Oxford University in 1960. During the very first lecture in the Institute of Social Anthropology, the teacher kept referring to Africans or non-Western peoples as barbarians, sav-ages, primitives, tribes, etc. I protested; but to no avail. All the professors and lecturers in the Institute, and those who came from outside to read papers, spoke the same insulting language.
>
> In the Institute Library, I detested to see such titles of books and articles in the learned journals as *Primitive Culture, Primitive Religion, The Savage Mind, Primitive Government, The Position of Women in Savage Societies, Institutions of Primitive Societies, Primitive Song, Sex and Repression in Savage Societies, Prim-itive Mentality,* and so on.

Later in the same work, Okot ridicules the anthropological defenses by Lucy Mair and Evans-Pritchard of words like "primitive" as "value-free."[37] Okot's quarrel with his teachers went deep. Their "insulting language" and assump-tions, he recalls, "caused me so much suffering" and "often led to bitter ex-change in lecture rooms and during seminars."[38] As indicated by Lawino's strategic use of the word "primitive," this "bitter exchange" spills over into *Song of Lawino.* "He says Black People are primitive," laments Lawino of her self-despising husband, and she goes on to discredit this view by her intelli-gence, her perspicuity, and her brilliant use of metaphor (36). For all its ethnographic inflections in form and content, *Song of Lawino* mounts a pow-erful rebuttal of several key tenets of social anthropology.

Okot anticipates by decades the postcolonial critique of anthropology and the intensified self-scrutiny within the discipline. In his scholarly writ-ing, Okot attacks Western anthropology because of its colonial complicity, its religious investments, and its assumptions about the anthropological ob-server. Regarding the first of these he writes: "Social anthropology has not only been the handmaiden of colonialism in that it analysed and provided important information about the social institutions of colonised peoples to ensure efficient and effective control and exploitation, it has also furnished and elaborated the myth of the 'primitive' which justified the colonial enter-prise" (1–2). In a bracing historicist critique, Okot traces the nineteenth-century foundation of the discipline to the requirements of French, German, British, and other European colonial administrators. In a more widely read book of anthropology published two years later, *Anthropology and the Colonial Encounter,* Talal Asad alludes to "wild remarks about anthropology being merely the handmaiden of colonialism," yet he concedes that anthropologists have contributed "towards maintaining the structure of power represented by the colonial system," as reflected in their "mode" of "objectifying alien societies."[39]

Elaborating this line of argument from the decolonizing era, Edward Said has more recently claimed that anthropology, like other specialized disciplines about the cultural "Other," continues to be "an often direct agent of political dominance."[40] Said doubts that anthropology can shed its colonial inheritance: "Perhaps anthropology as we have known it can only continue on one side of the imperial divide, there to remain as a partner in domination and hegemony."[41] Thus Okot answers the question, "Is there a place for social anthropology in an African university?" with a definitive "no," even though he was himself a member of such a department (6). In an epilogue to Okot p'Bitek's *African Religions in Western Scholarship,* Ali Mazrui, former dean of the faculty of social sciences at the University of Makerere, quarrels with Okot's harsh view: the sympathies of anthropologists, according to Mazrui, were partly responsible for the "cultural toleration" of British colonial rule (131). But even Mazrui has to admit that anthropology's "respect" for African ways "was essentially parental" (132). Okot's historicist and anticolonial critique of anthropology should alert us that his ethnographically informed poetry nevertheless seeks to disentangle itself from disciplinary norms conducive to perpetuating colonial domination.

As for the religious bias of anthropology, Okot doesn't hesitate to label his teachers "Christian apologists": Evans-Pritchard and Lienhardt "use African deities to prove that the Christian God does exist, and is known also among African peoples" (41). Conceding that African intellectuals had also hellenized and christianized African deities, he hammers Western anthropologists like Lienhardt, Evans-Pritchard, and Placide Tempels for having forced the independent, multiple, and distinct African deities into the mold of the Christian God: "There is no evidence to show that [the Nilotes] regard the named *jogi* as refractions, or manifestations, or hypostases of a so-called High God" (71). In contrast to the metaphysic that anthropologists have imposed, Okot argues that traditional Africans have "no thought of another world" and could even be described as "atheistic" (99–100). Lawino is, as we shall see, Okot's most forceful corrective to this wrongheaded anthropology, exemplifying the this-worldliness of many African religions.

Okot traces the source of such misconceptions about African culture to a key disciplinary assumption of Western anthropologists—namely,

> that a student should carry out research among a people other than his own. This, they say, provides a certain distance between him and those people, so that, although he tries to get as close as possible to their way of life, there is what they call "detachment," which is supposed to ensure objectivity. . . .
>
> In my view the student of African religions needs to soak himself thoroughly in the day-to-day life of the people whose thought-systems and beliefs he wishes to study. He must have a deep knowledge of their language. When attending ceremonies, he must not stand apart as a spectator, but join in fully, singing the songs, chanting the chants and dancing the dances. Let our students experience the real thing, for only then will the full meaning and significance of the songs and chants and invocations come through. It is obvious that if he is going in for studies in "depth," then in studying his own people he starts off with a great advantage, in that he knows the language and much of the customs and the attitudes of his people; and they may know him as well. This helps a great deal, because often there exists a barrier between the people and a foreign researcher, who mumbles half-understood sentences; for this barrier disappears when a researcher returns to his home among his own people.

As late as 1989, Edward Said could complain that "the problematic of the observer" was still "remarkably underanalyzed" even in revisionist anthropology, which typically evaded the questions, "Who speaks? For what and to whom?"[42] Whereas Okot calls for the anthropologist's full participation in the community under study, James Clifford, who has helped to foreground the "problematic of the observer," describes the approach of the Malinowskian generation in terms of "the controlled empathy of participant-observation": "An understanding rapport and measured affection were favored. Expressions of overt enthusiasm and love were circumscribed." The normative fieldworker was Western and white, "a homebody abroad."[43] As Kirin Narayan writes, "Those who are anthropologists in the usual sense of the word are thought to study Others whose alien cultural worlds they must painstakingly come to know."[44] In the period of decolonization, Okot and other "native anthropologists" put new pressure on the binary distinctions that had been constitutive of the discipline—native and researcher, home and abroad, insider and outsider. In *Song of Lawino* and *Song of Ocol*, Okot practices a kind of counteranthropology, blurring the cultural boundaries between observer and observed, eroding the tonal detachment prescribed by his elders at Oxford.

Even so, the dichotomies that structure anthropology also infect the oppositional discourse used to attack it. Curiously enough, Okot's rhetoric, as well as that of other postcolonial critics, is often consistent with these binary assumptions while it inverts their values, celebrating the authentic voice of the native insider as opposed to the outsider perspective of the Western researcher. But the anthropologist who returns from Oxford to conduct field-work, or what has been termed "homework," is distinct from either a "pure" indigenous insider or an outside observer.[45] "How 'native' is a native anthropologist?" asks Kirin Narayan, deconstructing the received disciplinary dichotomy: those who are "'native,' 'indigenous,' or 'insider' anthropologists are believed to write about their own cultures from a position of intimate affinity." But amid the multiple currents moving information, capital, language, and education across North/South and East/West borders, the "native" anthropologist should be seen as having complex and multiple identifications and origins.[46] Although Okot writes nostalgically that "this barrier disappears when a researcher returns to his home among his own people," he knows that the reunion is seldom so simple. This anthropologically trained poet is self-critical enough to recognize himself in the Western-ized, self-alienated Ocol, whose name echoes Okot's, as does his affiliation with Makerere University (87): "Ocol is more like me and my age-mates who have been through the school system. The great debate in the poem is one which takes place inside us."[47]

Still, Okot's sympathies clearly lie with the more "native" Lawino, who is the indigenous anthropologist's best solution to his disciplinary and cultural predicament. If, as Okot believes, anthropology has been led astray by its preference for "detachment," if the better practice is immersion in the culture being studied, and if the person speaking for and about that culture should belong to it, then the answering form may be the imaginative literary work in which an African village woman speaks in her own voice about her society and customs. On the one hand, she represents a native authenticity that the Westernized Acoli anthropologist can no longer lay claim to. On the other, she rebuts the Western anthropologist's effort to impose an alien voice and vision on Acoli culture. Gender difference is in part a figure for cultural difference: like many nationalist and negritude writers who reimagine the African homeland as mother, Okot genders as female the authentic Acoli voice, as opposed to his and Ocol's masculine detachment, thereby marking the author's distance from the ideal of African cultural integrity.[48]

As deployed in *Song of Lawino,* dramatic monologue as a genre has an antiethnographic function. Okot's critique of Placide Tempels's famous *Bantu Philosophy* spotlights the problem of voice in anthropology. Okot

quotes Tempels's patronizing assertion that the Bantu lack "an adequate vocabulary" for their own ethnophilosophy: "It is we who will be able to tell
them, in precise terms, what their innermost concept of being is."[49] An of-
fended Okot responds:

> A crucial question arises as to the attitude and role of the student of African
> thought. It is, to say the least, an unhelpful conceit to start off by holding that
> a people do not know what they believe, or cannot express it; and that it is the
> student—who, after all, is the ignorant person—who will tell the people
> what they believe. It seems to me that the role of the student of traditional re-
> ligion and philosophy is, as it were, to photograph, in as much detail as pos-
> sible, the way of life of the people; and then to make comments, pointing out
> the connexions and relevances of the different parts, and their ultimate rela-
> tion to the whole of life. In this way the beliefs of a people, whether in one god
> or in a number of gods, in witchcraft and magic, will emerge.[50]

Song of Lawino is a more radical solution to this problem of voice than is
Okot's own anthropological work: it endows a village woman with her own
vibrant and compelling voice, seemingly abolishing the role of intermediary.
Insofar as *Song of Lawino* wrests voice from the anthropological observer and
bestows it on a native insider, his "autoethnography" powerfully resists the
ethnographic norm of *speaking for* another culture.[51] Against the anthropological standard of "controlled empathy," it seems to provide access to direct
speech. Gone is the ethnographic metadiscourse of "tribalism" and "the
primitive mind," along with any metaphysical filter for African religion. But
dramatic monologue affords this victory over the Western ethnographer's
voice precisely because it allows the poet to disguise his own more complex,
more anthropologically informed relation to Acoli culture. Critics often say
Lawino is the poet's mouthpiece, but her difference from Okot is almost as
important as her similarity in waging the poem's antiethnographic battle.

Dramatic monologue characteristically emphasizes the subjectivity of
the speaker. Because it dramatizes utterance, it calls attention to the emergence of the subject through vocalization. In the first few lines of *Song of
Lawino,* the speaker vigorously asserts herself as voice:

> Husband, now you despise me
> Now you treat me with spite
> And say I have inherited the stupidity of my aunt;
> Son of the Chief,
> Now you compare me
> With the rubbish in the rubbish pit,
> You say you no longer want me

Because I am like the things left behind
In the deserted homestead.
You insult me
You laugh at me
You say I do not know the letter A
Because I have not been to school
And I have not been baptized

You compare me with a little dog,
A puppy.

My friend, age-mate of my brother,
Take care,
Take care of your tongue,
Be careful what your lips say.
          (34)

Apostrophe, a primary rhetorical tool of both dramatic monologue and Acoli
songs, establishes Lawino's voice by putting her into a performative relation
to an absent addressee.[52] The abundant use of anaphora ("Now," "You,"
"Take care") and other figures of repetition further heightens the impression
of living speech, the pained and agitated spouse unleashing a torrential response to her absent husband. By calling attention to her illiteracy ("You say
I do not know the letter A") and to Ocol's tongue and lips, Lawino highlights
the act of utterance from the poem's start. She incorporates Ocol's abusive
words within her own, thus increasing our sense of overhearing an agitated
response to her interlocutor's taunts. Lawino's specific familial points of reference—aunt, son, brother—situate her within a concrete social space that
lends credibility to her speech-acts. By all these means, Okot creates a character whom we listen to as vocalizing subject, not as ethnographic specimen.
If the "native informant" is typically reduced to a supporting role in the anthropologist's work of scholarly inscription, here the native informant takes
center stage, her robust speaking voice almost seeming to eclipse any scribal
or interpretive function.

    Even so, we cannot forget for long that Lawino's voice is a fiction, cre-
ated by the poet's written language. At the same time that Okot creates the illusion of unmediated talk, he also calls ironic attention to the inscription of
this antitextual "voice" in his text. To Lawino, books look so strange that
they seem like old smelly trees with their bark peeling, some with frightful
pictures on them, "Dead faces of witch-looking men and women" (114). Of
course, we have access to Lawino's antibibliographic viewpoint only from

just such a book, plastered with the picture of the author on its back. Lawino attacks book learning at length as both Westernizing and feminizing. Of young Acoli men, she says,

> Their manhood was finished
> In the class-rooms,
> Their testicles
> Were smashed
> With large books!
>   (117)

From this perspective, the young Acoli author of *Song of Lawino* must have immolated himself before literary and ethnographic books to give life to Lawino's voice. Insofar as the poem as dramatic monologue is antiethnographic, fashioning an authentic and illiterate Acoli spokeswoman, it can only renounce ethnographic scholarship and other forms of Western discourse through its own written language. The poem as book, as written object, is at least as much kin to the ethnographic textuality it repudiates as it is to the unmediated vocalization to which it aspires. Similarly, we cannot help but notice the irony that Lawino rails against English in English. Through dramatic monologue, Okot may seem to remove the linguistic "barrier" he disapproves between the anthropologist and the people, creating the illusion of an Acoli woman who speaks in her own language for her own culture. But it is in English that we read her complaint about Ocol: "He abuses me in English, / And he is so arrogant" (35). For Lawino, the English language is a sign of colonial subordination: "The dogs of white men / Are well trained / And they understand English!" (115). Is *Song of Lawino*—rendered in English by a Western-trained poet-ethnographer—symptomatic of the very condition Lawino decries? By mediating between speech and writing, illiteracy and literacy, Acoli and English, is Okot's dramatic monologue complicitous in Western anthropology? As Gayatri Spivak provocatively asks, "Can the subaltern speak?"[53]

In short, to see Okot's use of dramatic monologue as unambiguously antiethnographic would be a distortion. Indeed, dramatic monologue is arguably the most ethnographic of poetic genres. Much has been said of the deeply historical nature of dramatic monologue as a genre: it situates the speaking subject within a particular moment and a particular set of social relations. "Historical contextualization," Herbert Tucker astutely points out, is "the generic privilege of dramatic monologue" and indispensable in the "construction of character." What is overheard in Western dramatic mono-

logue is history.[54] In postcolonial dramatic monologue, by extension, what
is overheard is culture. Cultural contextualization is the generic privilege of
postcolonial monologue, since the genre is particularly suited to conveying
the cultural imbeddedness of character. The rise of dramatic monologue in
nineteenth-century Europe has been attributed to increasing relativism,
since the genre enables the performance of a variety of perspectives and values. Similarly, its recent resurgence in and beyond the West can be ascribed
in part to a multipolar, multicultural age. Indeed, the ethnographic potentiality of the genre was evident long before the rise of postcolonial literatures.
Intended to widen the Western reader's sympathies, exotic monologues such
as Joseph Warton's "The Dying Indian," Felicia Hemans's "The Indian
Woman's Death Song," Robert Browning's "Through the Metidja to Abd-el-
Kadr," and Maria Jewsbury's "Song of the Hindoo Women" are exercises in
the ethnographic imagination.[55] Far from exoticizing her own culture, Lawino speaks for it as norm, but even she, as we have seen, sometimes sounds
as if she were explaining Acoli values to outsiders:

> Ask me what beauty is
> To the Acoli
> And I will tell you;
> I will show it to you
> If you give me a chance!
>   (51)

Lawino speaks for her culture, however, as one among many, and dramatic
monologue formally embodies her awareness of being culturally located.
The genre enables the poet to vaunt a specific outlook and to acknowledge
its cultural relativity.

Although Okot resists ethnographic norms in ceding expressive authority to an Acoli woman, dramatic monologue not only offers a wellspring of
personal utterance but also, paradoxically, objectifies the speaking subject,
locating her in a culture, a society, a history. Loy Martin writes of the "divided
subject" in dramatic monologue: the "person-as-process" who enacts sub-
jective being through speech and the "person-as-object" who is absorbed
into a totality larger than herself.[56] As speaker, Lawino is less objectified
than Ocol, whose dramatic monologue exemplifies the use of the genre to articulate and analyze a "case" of psychopolitical disturbance: he is, like the
colonial subject in Fanon's *Black Skin, White Masks*, excessively identified
with white culture and thus aggressively turned against himself as a black
man.[57] But even without the ironic leverage wielded in *Song of Ocol*, *Song of*

Lawino is the utterance of a woman whom we experience both as vital, sub-
jective being and as discursive nexus of habits, beliefs, and values of the
Acoli. Indeed, this division helps to pinpoint one aspect of the poem's simul-
taneous embrace of ethnography and rebuff to it.

Another key area of ethnographic ambivalence in *Song of Lawino* is religion. The religious anthropology that Okot attacked in prose is a significant
intertextual presence through much of his poem. Okot's Oxford teachers, as
we have seen, represented Africa's multiple deities as emanations of a single
God. But Lawino forcefully rebuts this Westernization by her distinctions:

> And when it is *Jok* Omara
> That has caused madness,
> Or Odude or Ayweya
> That has brought troubles,
> When *Jok* Rubanga
> Has broken someone's back
> Or *Jok* Odude
> Has tied up a woman's womb,
> And the husband
> Cries over his lost bridewealth,
> Saying,
> What is marriage without childbirth?
>   (94)

For Lawino, there is no single, overarching Being who connects these *jogi*. In
enumerating the types and functions of *Jok*, Okot could be seen as practicing
a kind of poetic ethnography, but it is an ethnography that sharply corrects
the views of his teachers. "How did *Jok* come to be called God?" asks Okot;
his answer traces the misunderstanding from Evans-Pritchard and Max
Müller back to early Christian missionaries baffled by the necessity of finding African equivalents for their supreme deity.[58] Further, these beings are
not metaphysical but local, causing specific ailments and difficulties. Metaphysical speculations about who created the earth strike Lawino as nonsensical (89). Her religion is entirely this-worldly:

> All misfortunes have a root,
> The snake bite, the spear of the enemy,
> Lightning and the blunt buffalo horn,
> These are the bitter fruits
> Grown on the tree of Fate.
> They do not fall anyhow,

> They do not fall at random,
> They do not come our way by accident,
> We do not just run into them.
> When your uncle curses you
> You piss in your bed!
> And you go on pissing in your bed
> Until you have taken him
> A white cock!
>   (98)

That Lawino's religion is a matter of cause and effect in the everyday world is rhetorically emphasized by such graphic images as "pissing in your bed"; it tells her what occasions specific misfortunes and how to redress them.

In matters of religion, Okot often wields translation, mistranslation, and nontranslation as antiethnographic devices in *Song of Lawino*. Admittedly, in translating his own Acoli poetry for initial publication in English, Okot may be seen as participating in the ethnographic quest to decode non-Western "tribal" languages. Moreover, in sprinkling his English text with transliterated Acoli words that are key to understanding Acoli religion and culture, Okot recalls the modest diglossia of classic anthropological studies. One of Evans-Pritchard's primary strategies was "to take a word from the Nuer vocabulary that had no direct translation into English, and to elucidate its various referents."[59] Less accommodating to the Western reader than his teachers, Okot mockingly mistranslates some key religious terms. Counteracting the distorting effects of imposed anthropological and missionary words, he bizarrely names, for example, the Christian God the *Hunchback* throughout *Song of Lawino*. Baffled by missionary metaphysics, Lawino asks,

> Where did the Hunchback
> Dig the clay for moulding things,
> The clay for moulding Skyland
> The clay for moulding Earth
> The clay for moulding Moon
> The clay for moulding the Stars?
> Where is the spot
> Where it was dug,
> On the mouth of which River?
>
> And when the Hunchback
> Was digging the clay
> Where did he stand?
>   (87)

Elsewhere Okot recounts the riveting story of how the Christian God came to be called *Rubanga* in Acoli (or Luo):

> In 1911, Italian Catholic priests put before a group of Acoli elders the question "Who created you?"; and because the Luo language does not have an independent concept of *create* or *creation,* the question was rendered to mean, "Who moulded you?" But this was still meaningless, because human beings are born of their mothers. The elders told the visitors that they did not know. But, we are told that this reply was unsatisfactory, and the missionaries insisted that a satisfactory answer must be given. One of the elders remembered that, although a person may be born normally, when he is afflicted with tuberculosis of the spine, then he loses his normal figure, he gets "moulded." So he said, "*Rubanga* is the one who moulds people." This is the name of the hostile spirit which the Acoli believe causes the hunch or hump on the back. And, instead of exorcising these hostile spirits and sending them among pigs, the representatives of Jesus Christ began to preach that Rubanga was the Holy Father who created the Acoli.[60]

In *Song of Lawino* the deliberately strange translation of God as Hunchback wittily recalls a mangled history of cultural imposition and misunderstanding. Behind Okot's "retranslation of missionaries' mistranslations of the vocabulary of Christian belief," Heron observes, "lies the history of the blunders of the missionaries in their first dealings with the Acoli at the beginning of this century."[61] The word "hunchback" captures the weirdness of the concept of God within Acoli culture, both for the people who first encountered it and for an individual like Lawino who still cannot easily make sense of it within her cultural framework. For Okot to have written "God" for *Rubanga* might have been to reiterate an act of cultural imperialism and to have papered over the gap between antithetical cultural perspectives.

Okot defamiliarizes other key terms of Christianity by rendering them in humorously skewed translations. Lawino recounts her alienating experience of both Protestant and Catholic indoctrination, starting with the Catholic missionaries:

> When I was in the Evening Speakers' Class
> We recited the Faith of the Messengers
> And Our Father who is in Skyland,
> We sang Greetings to Maria
> We learnt:

> > *Glory shine on the body of the Father*
> > *And on the body of the Son*
> > *And on the body of the Clean Ghost*

We recited the Prayer for saying Yes
And the Prayer for Love,
The Prayer for Trust,
The Greetings of the beautiful men
With birds' wings,
And the Dekalogu,
The Ten Instructions of the Hunchback.
　　　(84)

The English-language reader has to decipher each term, momentarily expe-
riencing a fraction of the hermeneutic bafflement of the Acoli: the "Faith of
the Messengers," we infer, is the Gospel, "Skyland" is heaven, the "Clean
Ghost" is the Holy Ghost, the beautiful men with birds' wings must be the
angels, and the Ten Instructions, the Ten Commandments. Returned to English through the detour of Acoli, these revised English terms are bidirectional, recalling both the stock English original and its literal rendering in
another language. Their linguistic strangeness for the English reader echoes
some of their cultural peculiarity for the Acoli. Okot's partial retranslations
into English represent a kind of discursive anticolonialism. They embed and
mock a linguistic history of missionary efforts to identify local equivalents
for religious concepts, often literal translations of Western abstractions. Like
their missionary forebears, anthropologists are, according to Okot, "intellectual smugglers": mistranslating African concepts like the Acoli *Jok* or the
Akan *Borebore* as God, "strong" as "omnipotent," or "wise" as "omniscient,"
they introduce "Greek metaphysical conceptions into African religious
thought."[62] At least Lienhardt and Evans-Pritchard acknowledge that they
can only see African religions through the prism of their own beliefs; "it is
wise to bear in mind," Okot says of many Western anthropologists, "that
they are active members of their own churches and other institutions, and
their first allegiance is to their God, whom they believe to be supreme."[63]

Perhaps the most powerful antiethnographic device in *Song of Lawino* is
Okot's inversion of the ethnographic gaze. At a time when the norm of anthropology was the study of "primitive" societies in the non-Western world,
Okot "anthropologizes" the West. "Although social anthropology has been
described as the study of man and his works," he writes, "in Western scholarship it has been, until very recently, the study of the so called 'tribal'
peoples, and has shown very little interest in western industrialised societies."[64] Where Western anthropologists assimilate Luo religion to their
preconceptions, Lawino aggressively redescribes their religion from her perspective. She recounts her first experience of communion, led by a large
robed Protestant:

He held a little shiny saucer:
It had small pieces of something.
The name of the man
Was Eliya
And he was calling people
To come and eat
Human flesh!
He put little bits
In their hands
And they ate it up!

Then he took a cup,
He said
There was human blood
In the cup
And he gave it
To the people
To drink!

I ran out of the Church,
I was very sick!
O! Protestants eat people!
They are all wizards,
They exhume corpses
For dinner!
          (75)

Slyly inverting the Western stereotype of African cannibalism, Okot irreverently literalizes a Christian ritual, stripping away its metaphysical meaning.
The humor of the scene lies in defamiliarization, in the dissonance between
the habitual Western rite and the impression it first makes on an Acoli village
woman. As Lindfors writes, "Lawino focuses attention on some of the arbi-
trary and seemingly irrational aspects of western behaviour which would
very likely baffle any non-westerner encountering them for the first time.
She forces us to recognize the illogicality of our ways. Her incomprehension
is both a warning and a protest against cultural arrogance."[65]

Similarly, Lawino's puzzlement over the Christian calendar denatural-
izes a Western custom:

My husband says
Before this man was born
White men counted years backwards.
Starting with the biggest number

Then it became
One thousand
Then one hundred
Then ten,
And when it became one
Then Jesus was born.

I cannot understand all this
I do not understand it at all!
(73)

Lawino's complaint comes at the end of a long rebuke to her husband for trying to impose an industrialized society's concept of time on an African village, where time is a function of agricultural life and seasonal return. She
tells time by sunrise and sunset, harvest and hunger. This section's reflection
on time may well be, as we saw earlier, indebted to an ethnographic category
of knowledge. But instead of merely submitting to a Western anthropological norm, Lawino casts a defamiliarizing, ethnographic glance in the reverse
direction. "Time has become / My husband's master / It is my husband's husband," she laments (68); Ocol monitors every moment according to a fixed
sequence of minutes, hours, days, and years:

If my husband insists
What exact time
He should have morning tea
And breakfast,
When exactly to have coffee
And the exact time
For taking the family photograph—
Lunch-time, tea time,
And supper time—
I must first look at the sun,
The cock must crow
To remind me.
(64)

Listen
My husband,
In the wisdom of the Acoli
Time is not stupidly split up
Into seconds and minutes,
It does not flow

> Like beer in a pot
> That is sucked
> Until it is finished.
>   (69)

Lawino astutely juxtaposes Acoli and Western practices for observing and regulating time. In her stereoscopic vision, she resembles yet reverses the anthropologist, whose underlying source of insight is the sometimes unannounced splicing together of divergent cultural perspectives. Perhaps Lawino isn't quite disinterested here, but neither is the anthropologist, whose "ethnocentrism," according to the postcolonial novelist and anthropologist V. Y. Mudimbe, is neither "an unfortunate mishap, nor a stupid accident, but one of the major signs of the possibility of anthropology."[66]

If we were ignorant of Western codes of cooking and eating, we might learn a lot from Lawino's mock-ethnographic account. From Ocol's "apemanship," we glean that Westerners eat with spoon and fork though Lawino does not (56), sit at meals not on the earth like her but "on trees / Like monkeys" (61), cook standing up (58), preserve meat in ice (58), keep foods in tins (58), use dangerous coal and electric stoves (57–58), and cook with flat-bottomed pots and pans "Because the stoves are flat / Like the face of the drum" (59). Lawino is repulsed by the texture of Western foods: a fried egg "Is slimy like mucus," cooked chicken makes "You think you are chewing paper," and the standard mushy fare seems like "Foods for the toothless, / For infants and invalids" (58). In a strategy explored earlier in my discussion of Ramanujan, Okot's metaphors vividly enact at the level of the word and the image the uncanniness of postcolonial perception.

Perhaps Lawino's most aggressive counterethnographic ethnography is a propos of Western love, beauty, and dance. Lawino proudly declares Acoli ways of adorning the female body, against which Western makeup seems frightful. Of Ocol's new, Westernized wife, Lawino observes:

> Her lips are red-hot
> Like glowing charcoal,
> She resembles the wild cat
> That has dipped its mouth in blood,
> Her mouth is like raw yaws
> It looks like an open ulcer,
> Like the mouth of a field!
> Tina dusts powder on her face
> And it looks so pale;

She resembles the wizard
Getting ready for the midnight dance.
        (37)

Lawino delights in the abundant and astonishing use of simile. By figuratively
reconceiving lipstick and face powder, she associates habits meant to soften
and beautify the face with violence, death, and destruction. Her similes mimic
the to-and-fro flight of the mind from an unfamiliar sight to daily experiences
and back again, attempting through trope to make sense of the seemingly
nonsensical habits of the West. In the poem's third section, "I Do Not Know
the Dances of White People," Okot extends this cluster of figurative associations, fiercely defamiliarizing Western practices of love and dance:

You kiss her on the cheek
As white people do,
You kiss her open-sore lips
As white people do,
You suck slimy saliva
From each other's mouths
As white people do.

And the lips of the men become bloody
With blood dripping from the red-hot lips;
Their teeth look
As if they have been boxed in the mouth.

Women throw their arms
Around the necks of their partners
And put their cheeks
On the cheeks of their men.
Men hold the waists of the women
Tightly, tightly . . .
        (44)

Lawino's horror and astonishment have ethnographic content, but not of the
sort that a pre-1960s textbook would have emphasized: Westerners kiss on
the lips, unlike peoples in some other parts of the world; they dance holding
each other, a strangling violation of dance codes for the Acoli. Further, they
dance inside:

It is hot inside the house
It is hot like inside a cave
Like inside a hyena's den!
        (45)

Throughout this section, such repetitions effectively reproduce Lawino's sense of claustrophobia and confinement within Western rites.

If these passages amount to a kind of reverse ethnography, Lawino comes closer to an outright parody of the discipline in graphically describing the latrine in a Western-style dance hall, her figurative abundance rivaling the most resourceful scatological literature in English:

> The entire floor
> Is covered with human dung
> All the tribes of human dung!
> Dry dungs and dysentery
> Old dungs and fresh dungs
>
> Young ones that are still steaming,
> Short thick dungs
> Sitting like hills,
> Snake-like dungs
> Coiled up like pythons.
> Little ones just squatting there,
> Big ones lying on their sides
> Like tree trunks.
>
> Some dungs are red like ochre
> Others are yellow
> Like the ripe mango,
> Like inside a ripe pawpaw.
> Others are black like soil,
> Like the soil we use
> For smearing the floor.
> Some dungs are of mixed colours!
>   (46)

Even before Lawino has categorized the varieties of excrement, the phrase "tribes of human dung" is our first clue that anthropology is being mocked. In *African Religions in Western Scholarship*, Okot scornfully surveys anthropological definitions of "tribe," including Evans-Pritchard's, and concludes that the term, though a cornerstone of the discipline, is analytically meaningless and an "insult" that "ought to be dropped."[67] With his descriptive rainbow of excremental tribes, Okot excoriates anthropological practices for demarcating one group of human peoples over against another according to key characteristics. To anthropologize non-Western societies as "tribes," he suggests, is to risk treating them as objectified "others," things to be eliminated from the world's body.

In *Song of Ocol* Okot still more forcefully connects anthropological classification with imperialist destruction. The self-alienated Ocol aggressively surveys East African peoples, employing catalogs that bizarrely cross anthropological textbook with Walt Whitman:

> You Maasai warrior
> Honing your spear
> And polishing it with ghee,
> You naked Jie
> Studying the sick cow,
> You Turkana scout
> Perched on the termite mound
> Ijakait from Toposa,
> You Dodos General
> Presiding over the war council;
>
> You Suk youth
> I hear you singing
> Praises to your black ox,
> Your hands raised
> In imitation of its horns;
>
> You men on Nandi hills
> Tending cattle in the rocky pastures
> Always suspecting an impending raid,
> You Pokot hordes
> Driving home the stolen cattle;
>
> Kipsigis men
> I see colourful shields
> Surrounding a thick bush
> In which I see
> A lion's tufted tail . . .
>
> You proud Kalenjin
> Chiefless, free,
> Each man the chief
> Of his hut.
>   (135)

Ocol's ethnographic overview of "tribes" might seem value neutral. But in each case, he parodically reduces a people to a single characteristic: an African people comes to seem little more than a favorite weapon, headdress, animal, or method of political organization.

Most tellingly, his ethnographic reductionism soon turns into rancorous calls for the extermination of the customs and peoples he has classified:

Listen,
We will not simply
Put the Maasai in trousers
To end twenty five thousand years
Of human nakedness,
Dynamiting the ochre quarries
Is only the starting gun,

We will arrest
All the elders
The tutors of the young
During circumcisions,
The gathering of youths
In the wilderness for initiations
Will be banned,
The council of elders
Will be abolished;
The war dance . . .
The blowing of war horns
Will be punished
With twelve strokes
Of the cane
For each blast;

All the men with *moi* names
And those with "killer" marks
On their backs
And on their arms
Will be hanged for murder.
        (136–37)

The violence of Ocol's verbs intensifies as he calls for traditional African peoples to be "jailed" and "shaved," their customs to be "destroyed" and "stamped out," until he is so carried away he promises to "blow up / Mount Kilimanjaro," to "uproot" the trees and "fill the Valleys" (146). What happened to Ocol's seemingly careful and particularist surveys of different tribes? By interweaving them with hyperbolically imperialist calls for the blanket destruction of traditional African cultures, Okot unforgivingly highlights the most negative potential of anthropology—a discipline of ethnographic cleansing.

This extreme indictment might seem to rule out any accommodation of anthropology within *Song of Lawino* or *Song of Ocol,* but these texts are, as we have seen, often ethnographic in their antiethnography. Lawino, after all, indulges in her own rough form of ethnographic classification in defending Acoli hairstyles as naturally suited to Acoli hair:

> Listen,
> Ostrich plumes differ
> From chicken feathers,
> A monkey's tail
> Is different from that of the giraffe,
> The crocodile's skin
> Is not like the guinea fowl's,
> And the hippo is naked, and hairless.
>
> The hair of the Acoli
> Is different from that of the Arabs;
> The Indians' hair
> Resembles the tail of the horse;
> It is like sisal strings
> And needs to be cut
> With scissors.
> It is black,
> And is different from that of white women.
>   (51)

Lawino's defense of her kind of "vigorous and healthy hair / Curly, springy and thick / That glistens in the sunshine" relies in part on the logic of distinction and classification, even though it might seem uncomplicated self-affirmation (54). To each people, its own style of existence and self-representation.

So long as we perceive *Song of Lawino* as a "homebred" manifesto, we obscure the dialectical impact of the objectifying gaze of the ethnographer on the poem's self-affirmations. A defense, Lawino's representation of her own culture cannot be conceived as pure or unmediated. When Lawino describes Acoli ways, she presents them to us always in relation to Western culture. Her "native" culture is anthropologized by its placement side by side with the West's. I return once more to an example of Lawino's proud assertions of her culture:

> I do not know
> How to keep the white man's time.
> My mother taught me
> The way of the Acoli

>   And nobody should
>   Shout at me
>   Because I know
>   The customs of our people!
>   When the baby cries
>   Let him suck milk
>   From the breast.
>   There is no fixed time
>   For breast feeding.
>   (68)

Lawino may not know exactly how to keep time in Western fashion, but she knows enough to realize that Western time differs from her own customary practices. Her vision of her own culture is mediated through the knowledge of the white man's "fixed time." She cannot conceive of her culture except through the detour of another. She continually presents her culture to us in terms of what it is not—whether in food or religion, dance or dress. Witness such section titles as "I Do Not Know the Dances of White People," "There Is No Fixed Time for Breast Feeding," and "I Am Ignorant of the Good Word in the Clean Book." In *Song of Lawino* traditional Acoli culture is not simply "there" but "under erasure," threatened by Western influences, constantly having to justify itself in relation to them. Thus, even in its nativist defenses, *Song of Lawino* is a poem of split vision, facing at once inward and outward, resisting and incorporating ethnographic norms.

Close attention to Okot's conflicted dialogue with anthropology in *Song of Lawino* and *Song of Ocol* demonstrates that the poem is profoundly intercultural, despite the well-meaning claims on behalf of its "African authenticity," "autochthony," and "nativism." In an intelligent reading of *Song of Lawino*, K. L. Goodwin claims that cultural "syncretism" is beyond Lawino's "conceptualization, and is perhaps alien to Okot p'Bitek's own beliefs."[68] Like other Western and postcolonial critics, Goodwin believes that the power of the poem lies in its fidelity to Acoli culture. In another fine introduction to *Song of Lawino*, Gerald Moore similarly sees "total participation by the poet in the still flourishing culture of his people."[69] While the poet's participation in traditional Acoli culture is indeed vigorous, it is not total but, as we have seen, highly mediated. Okot's poem is ineluctably hybrid in genre, cultural perspective, and language. If even this touchstone of the "authentically African" is deeply syncretic, then the distinction between the "culturally native" poem and the "culturally mulatto" poem in English is unlikely to continue to be useful.

Perhaps the most immediate evidence of the poetry's hybridity is its language, to which I recur by way of conclusion. A bilingual poet, Okot is brilliant in his linguistic interleaving of English and only partially translated Acoli idioms, as we saw in his antiethnographic non-/mis-/semi-translations of Acoli religious terms. Like other postcolonial writers and like Western anthropologists, Okot sprinkles his text with apparently untranslatable native words. Sometimes explaining them in a brief note, he more often leaves them to be puzzled from context.[70] But Okot also makes use of a more risky strategy for hybridizing English—namely, he renders Acoli words and phrases with insistent literalism. Discussing Nigerian writers, Michael C. Onwuemene terms this strategy "transliteration" or, perhaps more helpfully, "translexification" and sees this implanting in English of idioms and tropes from African ethnic languages as comparable to what is called in translation theory semantic translation, which emphasizes the source text, as opposed to communicative translation, where the target culture is primary: "Semantic translation . . . is a Janus-faced interstitial operation between the word level and the idiom or trope level of language use; the words are translated, but the idiom is only transferred."[71] Okot wields this strategy with remarkable effectiveness, as we can see by looking at one last passage from *Song of Lawino*:

> My husband's tongue
> Is bitter like the roots of the *lyonno* lily,
> It is hot like the penis of the bee,
> Like the sting of the *kalang*!
> Ocol's tongue is fierce like the arrow of the scorpion,
> Deadly like the spear of the buffalo-hornet.
> It is ferocious
> Like the poison of a barren woman
> And corrosive like the juice of the gourd.
>   (35)

In English it is nonidiomatic to talk of bees with penises, scorpions with arrows, or hornets with spears. But these literal translations vividly recover the metaphorical content of Acoli expressions and at the same time bring striking metaphors into English. Taban lo Liyong, Okot's Acoli rival and near-contemporary, attacked his "Acholi-English" for losing the meaning of native proverbs and idioms by rendering them into English "*word for word, rather than sense for sense, or proverb for proverb.*"[72] In a largely sympathetic account of *Song of Lawino*, Heron also bemoans the "curious obscurities" and "lost meaning" in Okot's "unnaturally literal translation."[73] Examples include the repeated proverb about not destroying traditions—"The pumpkin in the old homestead / Must not be uprooted" (41); idioms such as "to eat" instead of simply "to win" a praise name or title (82–83); and words such as "moons" for "months" (69–70). But instead of losing meaning, these renderings afford a literary gain that no mere one-to-one substitution could afford. Okot serves the languages of both colonizer and colonized, reinvigorating the language of English poetry by infusing it with Acoli metaphors, while vivifying the metaphoricity of Acoli—a metaphoricity obscured by everyday use. The double "poetry" of *Song of Lawino* thus enacts and exemplifies the intercultural energies of postcolonial poetry. Through its Acoli-English, the bilingual poet africanizes the master's language by persistent reference to the partially absented native tongue. In the creolized language of Okot's poetry, English no longer exists without its African shadow.

As with language, so with the disciplinary assumptions of anthropology, we've seen that Okot simultaneously embraces a Western colonial inheritance and vigorously repudiates it. Indeed, the power of *Song of Lawino* can be traced in part to its robust dialogue with anthropology, helping to reveal the limitations of the controversy over whether postcolonial literatures are ethnographic. Without Okot's ethnographic attentiveness to specific Acoli customs, his grouping of them in ethnographic clusters, his relating of them to general assumptions, his continual counterpointing of them with Western ways, *Song of Lawino* would be a less compelling work than it is. Nor would it be as vital and intense without its dramatization of the indigenous voice, its pointed repudiation of Christian ethnography, its humorously skewed translations, its inversion of the ethnographic gaze, and its mock-ethnographic catalogs. The poem's often brilliant response to anthropology sharpens our awareness of the discipline's capacity to distort, reduce, contain, and oversimplify the non-Western world; yet it also heightens our appreciation for anthropology's ability, like that of the postcolonial poetry it enriches, to convey the lived density and cultural distinctness of Third World societies. *Song of Lawino* and *Song of Ocol* are not ethnographies of the Acoli but neither are they merely antiethnographies, just as they are neither Acoli oral songs nor Western literary artifacts. They are "both/and," not in a merely formulaic and predictable balancing of opposites, but in actively engaging these intertexts, whether to repudiate, revise, or remake them.

Song of Lawino and *Song of Ocol* are perhaps atypical in addressing anthropology as a disciplinary discourse in such a sustained manner. But this "special case" may help us to consider how a host of other prominent postcolonial writers, such as Léopold Sédar Senghor, Chinua Achebe, V. Y.

Mudimbe, Kamau Brathwaite, and Amitav Ghosh, also draw directly on anthropology's findings and practices, while chafing at some of its disciplinary
norms. In the ambivalent relation between postcolonial writers and anthropology, the story of Wole Soyinka's experience at Cambridge is illustrative: in
1973–74 he delivered a series of lectures entirely in the department of anthropology, having been declined by an English department apparently unable to "believe in any such mythical beast as 'African Literature.'"[74] Soyinka
was more readily welcomed by English anthropologists than by literary
scholars. But even his most "ethnographic" poetry published before this dis-
agreeable episode both incorporates and contests disciplinary assumptions
of anthropology. Like a religious anthropologist, he centers his long poem
Idanre (1967) on such key orishás (or Yoruba deities) as Ogun and Shango;
but far from presenting these figures as members of an "ancient and fixed"
pantheon from an immutable past, Soyinka emphasizes their hybridization
with modern technologies, such as electric wires. Similarly, in a gripping
poem ironically entitled "Pleasure," Ramanujan offers an ethnological portrait of a Jaina monk, who masochistically immolates himself by standing on
an anthill, having

> smeared his own private
>
> untouchable Jaina
> body with honey
> thick and slow as pitch. . . .[75]

No doubt Ramanujan's sketch of the monk is indebted to anthropological
codes of representation. But his emphasis on the psychology of pain as pleasure also complicates the poem's objectification of the monk as ethnological
specimen, just as the wider range of Ramanujan's poetry both answers and
deconstructs the question, "Is There a Hindu Way of Thinking?" Sharing the
recuperative ethnographic zeal of many earlier postcolonial writers, Yeats
and Bennett are among those at the forefront of efforts to collect, promote,
and revalorize the folklore of their peoples. Even so, Yeats digests Irish myth
within an idiosyncratically personal vision, and Bennett feminizes performance genres described as male by professional anthropologists. All told, the
tribes of the literary and the ethnographic are no more isolated from one another than are today's national literatures. The ethnographic and counterethnographic crosscurrents that flood Okot's *Songs*—and perhaps other
postcolonial poems of Africa, India, and the Caribbean—deepen and complicate their intellectual and literary substance, helping to make them rich
and enduring contributions to world literature in English.

CODA

🖊 On Hybridity

The poets discussed in this book share a language, a genre, an education, an empire and its collapse. Yet the differences among them are vast, starting with their location on different continents, their birth into distinctive local cultures, and their experience of divergent colonial histories. Yeats is more closely affiliated by geography and history to the metropolitan center than are the four poets of the so-called Third World. Although I have tried to complicate such distinctions as "oral" and "literary," "native" and "Western," the poets most indebted to the Western postromantic lyric—W. B. Yeats, Derek Walcott, and A. K. Ramanujan—write dense, inward, scribal poetry that looks and sounds very different from the more dramatic, communal, satiric poetry of Louise Bennett and Okot p'Bitek. The two West Indian poets featured in this book could hardly seem more different from each other. Most of Walcott's poetry is in slightly inflected Standard English; Bennett's is pervasively in Jamaican English. Bennett's characters are representative Jamaican types; Walcott's creolize heroes from classical literature. Next to the quiet, carefully modulated ironies of Ramanujan's lyrics, Okot's poetry can seem hortatory, even harsh. Next to the urgent and dramatic spokenness of Okot's poetry, Ramanujan's or Yeats's contemplative verse can seem hermetically self-contained.

Such distinctions could be elaborated endlessly. By examining these authors in sequence, I've wanted to honor each writer's literary and cultural specificity, while engaging a series of distinct, if interlinked, questions about the relation between poetry and postcoloniality. Yet, I've tried to show that all of these writers, in spite of their many differences, enact the cross-cultural energies and complexities of postcoloniality in their poetry's hybrid forms, figures, and vocabularies. Sometimes they overtly thematize the postcolonial condition of cultural and linguistic inbetweenness—Walcott famously writes, for example, of being "divided to the vein," "schizophrenic," "mulatto," even "mongrel." But their most significant accomplishment lies less in announcing their hybrid experience than in forging aesthetic forms that embody it, some of which I've delineated in the chapters of this book: literary archetypes that interweave disparate genealogies, metaphors that splice discordant cultural perspectives, ironies that rhetorically twin warring meanings, and genres that conjoin the disciplinary and literary forms of the colonizer with the inherited oral traditions of the colonized.

The critical paradigm of hybridity has been central to my analysis of postcolonial poetry. Yet the metaphor of hybridity, as any reader of recent postcolonial criticism and theory knows, is fraught with risks. Having tried to rebuild a case for hybridity in piecemeal fashion, I return to the principal charges against it once more, addressing them in general terms, while also summarizing how my primary readings bear on this vexed issue. A number of theorists have developed ever-more subtle criticisms of the hybridity model and of such overlapping concepts as creolization and diaspora, but, as we have seen, a few salient points recur.[1] First, the hybridity model is said to create the false impression of symmetry between unequal terms, cultures, or nations, distorting and diluting the persistent power struggle between colonizer and colonized. It seems to me that postcolonial criticism can keep this potential problem in check by continually referring back to the colonial and postcolonial matrices of violence, inequality, and oppression, even as it reveals the cultural interchange across the colonial divide. Surely, the hybridity model cannot stand alone; it needs to be politically and historically contextualized in each instance. The significance of Yeats's hybridization of place names, poetic forms, poetic inheritances, vocabularies, and mythologies, for example, would be unreadable outside the sociopolitical context of his Anglo-Irish mediation between an imperial culture and a civilization it dominated and ruthlessly suppressed for seven hundred years. Against this backdrop, the hybridity paradigm can help us to analyze the intricate, janus-faced artifacts that Yeats wove out of his deeply conflicted relation to England and Ireland.

As this example indicates, attention to hybridity and awareness of sociopolitical context, instead of being mutually exclusive, can be mutually supplementing, even corrective. Moreover, the knotted and tensile fabric of postcolonial poetry itself evinces chronic historical and political inequities. The power of Walcott's intercultural, intertextual trope of the wound inheres in its agile crossing of the boundaries between the unequal cultures of white and black, European and Afro-Caribbean, so that the asymmetries of colonialism are part and parcel of his poetry's vibrant hybridity. His repeated references to Greek culture as a culture of slavery should make it hard to miss the irony and bravura of his appropriation of a Greek hero, Philoctetes, as an emblem of West Indian suffering under European colonialism.

Another oft-repeated charge is that the concept of hybridity replicates the binaries it is meant to supersede, perpetuating such dichotomies as colonizer and colonized, or First World and Third, even as it attempts to articulate a post-Manichean space of interculturation. If, according to the first criticism, hybridity theory too readily dissolves and thus depoliticizes the divisions between colonizer and colonized, the second, nearly opposite criticism is that the hybridity model reiterates and thus hardens these divisions, however much it may seem to eclipse them. But the supposed defect of closet binarism can also be seen as one of the advantages of the hybridity model: it acknowledges the Manichean structure of the colonial divide, while also allowing for the sometimes frenzied traffic across it. Theories that purport to move completely "beyond the binary" or "beyond hybridity" risk obscuring the severity of the racial, cultural, and religious divisions put in place by colonialism's structures of domination. The hybridity paradigm should continually oscillate back and forth between this dichotomous structure and the intersticial forms it has produced. It should acknowledge the binaries that frame postcolonial experience and the irreducibly intercultural and composite effects of transregional contact and collision. I see Ramanujan's metaphors as poetic sites of split vision, aesthetically exemplifying in their mediative work the transnational, transtemporal, and translingual vision of the postcolonial. His metaphors surely move beyond the binary in that they create a third space of cultural convergence, but they are also within the binary in that they alert us to the crossing itself, to what is gained and lost, to the gaps brilliantly and boldly traversed between histories, geographies, and languages in the best postcolonial poetry.

The potentially dichotomizing effects of hybridity theory can also be restrained if we remind ourselves that each of the cultural spaces conjoined in any discussion of hybridization—British, African, East Indian, West Indian—is itself hybrid even before the more intensely creolizing experience of colonialism. Indeed, a third critique of the hybridity trope is that all cultures are hybrid and none can claim homogeneity; as such, the biological trope depends on a false norm of purity. I embrace a view of the world's cultures as "always already" hybridized. Hyphenated terms such as "Anglo-Norman" and "Anglo-Saxon" remind us of the foundational hybridity of British culture, and we know that Indian civilization was multiple, layered, and heterogeneous long before the arrival of the British East India Company. But I don't believe this perspective should rule out a more nuanced understanding of degrees and modalities of hybridity. In the wake of the European colonization of India, Africa, and the Caribbean, the syncretism of cultures is graphic and tumultuous, because of the enormous differences in outlook, religion, language, geography, and power that are crossed in the postimperial contact zone. Even as empire forces Western and Third World cultures together, occasioning the creation of new mediative cultural forms, these forms visibly embed within themselves a relation of on-going friction, tension, even rupture.

We should be able to postulate that all cultures are hybrid, while also allowing that some are more vividly and inorganically hybrid than others. Perhaps we ought to think of the varieties of hybridity as a continuum, from instances where the terms conjoined already have much in common with each other (e.g., two relatively equal European or Asian cultures, or a metropolitan and a settler culture), to instances where the differences are sharp, dramatic, and irreducible. In the double vision, psychic schism, and verbal dissonance of Bennett's creole irony, the historical collisions of colonizer and colonized are, as we've seen, put to cultural work. English is itself, as Bennett reminds us, a creole compounded of multiple languages and dialects, but Bennett's overt creole—the primary fuel of her irony—is in our era more obviously hybridized than its metropolitan counterparts. Okot p'Bitek's poetry confirms that even the most "native" cultural artifact is, at least in the postcolonial context, ineluctably multicultural, in this instance shot through with ethnographic modes of thought and perception, as well as traditional oral practices and idioms. Even Okot's vehemently antiethnographic defense of traditional Acoli culture understands itself in relation to the European disciplinary and literary contexts against which it would define its difference.

The theoretical debate will continue over the liabilities and benefits of the necessarily imperfect paradigm of hybridity, but the best proof of the concept's critical value is likely to be the quality of the readings, cultural insights, and commentaries that it affords. Used in conjunction with the literary discourse of poetics and the historical, theoretical, and interdisciplinary strategies of postcolonial studies, this critical tool can help to deepen our apprehension of the animated intercultural congress and exchange in the structures—archetype, metaphor, irony, dramatic monologue—that are the contact zones of postcolonial poetry.

Moreover, if we embrace the hybridity of postcolonial poetry, we hybridize our understanding not only of Third World poetry in English but also of anglophone poetry more generally. The hybrid muse, as I suggested at the outset, can help to internationalize a field of study that has remained relatively insular in the West. What happens if we hybridize our canons of modern and contemporary poetry in English, giving due space in our courses, personal libraries, and anthologies to Third World poets? If we place them cheek by jowl alongside confessional poets and poets of the Movement, neoformalists and experimentalists? If we see Anglo-American poets born around 1920—Robert Lowell, Gwendolyn Brooks, and Philip Larkin—as contemporaries of a witty Jamaican poet named Louise Bennett? If we place First World poets born around 1930—Adrienne Rich, Thom Gunn, Geoffrey Hill, and Sylvia Plath—cover by cover, class by class, poem by poem together with their distinguished contemporaries in the Third World, including A. K. Ramanujan, Derek Walcott, and Okot p'Bitek? If we rethink the polyglot cosmopolitanism of Eliot, Pound, Stein, H.D., and other migrant modernists from the perspective of the later intercultural bricolage of postcolonial poetry? If we compare First World appropriations of the Persian ghazal, the Malayan pantoum, and other non-Western forms with the postcolonial indigenization of European literary paradigms?

These are among the questions that those of us who read, teach, and relish poetry in English will need to address in the coming years. They are questions that have stimulated me in my own development as a scholar and teacher, continuing my work on Irish, British, and American poetry alongside research and teaching in postcolonial literatures. As we learn more about the wide range of anglophone poets from around the world, our narratives of continuity and breakthrough in modern and contemporary poetry, or of internecine strife, may well begin to seem increasingly provincial unless they take into account the world-wide scope of poetry in English. Its horizons globalized, poetry criticism will be in a better position to trace the accelerated circulation of tropes, vocabularies, and forms in the modern and contemporary world, from Eliot and Auden to Elizabeth Bishop and Louise Bennett, A. K. Ramanujan and Li-Young Lee.

By the same token, how do our courses and collections of postcolonial literatures change when we hybridize them generically by giving due weight to poetry? If in reading the plays of Wole Soyinka and the fiction of Chinua Achebe, Michael Ondaatje, and Vikram Seth, we also read their poetry? If in studying African literature in English, we set Okot p'Bitek, Christopher Okigbo, and Kofi Awoonor beside Achebe, Buchi Emecheta, and Ben Okri? If in surveying South Asian literature in English, we include A. K. Ramanujan, Eunice de Souza, and Agha Shahid Ali alongside Anita Desai, Salman Rushdie, and Arundhati Roy? If in discussing West Indian literature, we explore not only Derek Walcott but also Louise Bennett, Kamau Brathwaite, Lorna

Goodison, and Grace Nichols? Perhaps postcolonial poetry can help to sharpen our eye for the modalities of literary hybridization in other genres of postcolonial writing, making us more responsive to the specific aesthetic strategies and idioms through which writers creatively articulate their postcoloniality. Once we see how Third World poetry in English concentrates and distills the ambiguities, tensions, and discrepant temporalities of postcoloniality, we may be more willing to move the genre from the margins of the field to its center. The hybrid muse has been prolific, has traversed an astonishing geographic range, and has produced diverse and heterogeneous forms. It is time that we listened to what this muse has to say about aesthetic possibility and intercultural experience in our era of transnational imagination.

NOTES

Chapter One: Introduction

1. Okot p'Bitek, *"Song of Lawino" and "Song of Ocol"* (Oxford: Heinemann, 1984), 35.

2. T. S. Eliot, "The Social Function of Poetry," in *On Poetry and Poets* (New York: Farrar, Straus & Giroux, 1957), 8. On Herder's concept of the *Sprachgeist* (literally, the spirit of the language), see Kwame Anthony Appiah, *In My Father's House: Africa in the Philosophy of Culture* (Oxford: Oxford University Press, 1992), 50, 56.

3. John Palattella, "Atlas of the Difficult World: The Problem of Global Poetry," *Lingua Franca* 9, no. 4 (1999): 52–58; Thomas Babington Macaulay, "Minute on Indian Education," in *Macaulay: Prose and Poetry*, ed. G. M. Young (Cambridge, Mass.: Harvard University Press, 1952), 722. The anthologies discussed were Clifton Fadiman, Katharine Washburn, and John Major, eds., *World Poetry: An Anthology of Verse from Antiquity to Our Time*, 1st ed. (New York: Norton, 1998); Jerome Rothenberg and Pierre Joris, eds., *Poems for the Millennium: The University of California Book of Modern and Postmodern Poetry*, 2 vols. (Berkeley: University of California Press, 1998), vol. 2; J. D. McClatchy, ed., *The Vintage Book of Contemporary World Poetry* (New York: Vintage, 1996). Of these anthologies, only McClatchy's makes a serious attempt at representing the global scope of poetry in English. Rothenberg and Joris make passing introductory references to the "'postcolonial' world," but only make room—amid well over two hundred poets—for a few English-language postcolonials in their map of avant-garde poetry after World War II (8). *World Poetry* provides a similar allotment and tellingly shifts its postcolonial poets out of the section "Modern Poetry in English," which is defined as exclusively Western.

4. A. Poulin, Jr., "Contemporary American Poetry: The Radical Tradition," in *Contemporary American Poetry*, ed. A. Poulin, Jr., 6th ed. (Boston: Houghton Mifflin, 1996), 647.

5. Paul Hoover, introduction to *Postmodern American Poetry: A Norton Anthology*, ed. Paul Hoover (New York: Norton, 1994), xxvii, xxxiv.

6. Grace Nichols, "Epilogue," in *I Is a Long-Memoried Woman* (London: Karnak House, 1983), 80.

7. This quoted phrase, discussed in the ensuing chapter on Yeats, is from Benedict Anderson's influential *Imagined Communities: Reflections on the Origin and Spread of Nationalism* (London: New Left, 1983). Some of these concerns are shared by "ethnic" poets in the United States and Britain, whose ascendancy may help to open up the boundaries of contemporary poetry, even though the geographic, historical, and cultural bearings of "minority" and "postcolonial" poetry are distinct. See, e.g., Alfred Arteaga, *Chicano Poetics: Heterotexts and Hybridities* (Cambridge: Cambridge University Press, 1997); and, on "black British" poets, Peter Childs, *The Twentieth Century in Poetry* (London: Routledge, 1999), 192–204.

8. See the early essays by Bruce King, "The Emergence of Post-independence Modern Nigerian and Indian Poetry," *World Literature Written in English* 26 (1986): 331–40; and H. H. Anniah Gowda, "'Refin'd with the Accents that are Ours': Some Reflections on Modern English Poetry in India, Africa and the West Indies," in *The Colonial and the Neo-Colonial: Encounters in Commonwealth Literature*, ed. H. H. Anniah Gowda (Mysore: University of Mysore, 1983), 21–32. Half of the writers discussed in a book about "Commonwealth" poetry are from the Third World, the other half from the white dominions: see James Wieland, *The Ensphering Mind: History, Myth, and Fictions in the Poetry of Allen Curnow, Nissim Ezekiel,*

A. D. Hope, A. M. Klein, Christopher Okigbo, and Derek Walcott (Washington, D.C.: Three Continents Press, 1988).

9. Ian Adam and Helen Tiffin, eds., *Past the Last Post: Theorizing Post-colonialism and Post-modernism* (Calgary: University of Calgary Press, 1990); and Jonathan White, ed., *Recasting the World: Writing after Colonialism* (Baltimore: Johns Hopkins University Press, 1993).

10. Ania Loomba, *Colonialism/Postcolonialism* (New York: Routledge, 1998).

11. Leela Gandhi summarizes: "The novel becomes a sort of proxy for the nation" (*Postcolonial Theory: A Critical Introduction* [New York: Columbia University Press, 1998], 151). Like Gandhi and other critics, I reserve the word "postcolonialism" for the theory, "postcoloniality" for "the condition it addresses" (Gandhi, 4). See also Bart Moore-Gilbert's discussion of the differences and convergences between the subfields "postcolonial theory" and "postcolonial criticism" in *Postcolonial Theory: Contexts, Practices, Politics* (London: Verso, 1997), 169–70; 11–33, 169–84.

12. For critiques of the terms "postcolonial" and "Third World," see, e.g., Ella Shohat, "Notes on the Postcolonial," *Social Text* 31/32 (1992): 99–113; Anne McClintock, "The Angel of Progress: Pitfalls of the Term 'Post-colonialism,'" *Social Text* 31/32 (1992): 84–98; and Aijaz Ahmad, "Jameson's Rhetoric of Otherness and the 'National Allegory,'" *Social Text* 15 (1986): 65–88. Arguing against "postcolonial," Shohat nevertheless differs from Ahmad in endorsing the heuristic value of the term "Third World" (111), a term used by diverse writers in postcolonial studies, including Edward Said, Gayatri Spivak, Chandra Talpade Mohanty, Timothy Brennan, and Homi Bhabha. Despite the obviously hierarchical implications of "Third World," I employ the term strategically to indicate parts of the world that are economically dependent and impoverished, preferring it to the evolutionary implications of "developing world" and the neocolonialist force and socioeconomic obscurity of "Commonwealth." In using the term "postcolonial," I limit its historical scope to the period of decolonization and afterward. To use the term too narrowly—meaning strictly after the moment of political independence—would be to separate this period artificially from the era of decolonization immediately preceding it, even though we now know the continuities were greater than the changes. Moreover, the achievement of independence from the British empire often involved various stages of relative autonomy. To use the term too broadly—meaning any time after the initial onset of colonialism—would be to dilute it beyond meaningful use. Engaging these and other definitions, I offer more extended consideration of the term "postcolonial" in the ensuing chapter.

13. There are a number of helpful overviews of English-language poetry in regional and national contexts, but I limit myself, for economy's sake, to four texts per region. For the anglophone West Indies, see Lloyd W. Brown, *West Indian Poetry* (Boston: Twayne-G. K. Hall, 1978); Paula Burnett, introduction to *The Penguin Book of West Indian Verse in English*, ed. Paula Burnett (New York: Penguin, 1986), xxiii–lxiv; J. Edward Chamberlin, *Come Back to Me My Language: Poetry and the West Indies* (Urbana: University of Illinois Press, 1993); and Laurence A. Breiner, *An Introduction to West Indian Poetry* (Cambridge: Cambridge University Press, 1998). For anglophone Africa, see R. N. Egudu, *Modern African Poetry and the African Predicament* (New York: Barnes & Noble Books, 1978); K. L. Goodwin, *Understanding African Poetry* (London: Heinemann, 1982); Robert Fraser, *West African Poetry* (Cambridge: Cambridge University Press, 1986); and Tanure Ojaide, *Poetic Imagination in Black Africa: Essays on African Poetry* (Durham, N.C.: Carolina Academic Press, 1996). For anglo-

phone India, see *Contemporary Indian English Verse,* ed. Chirantan Kulshrestha (Atlantic Highlands, N.J.: Humanities Press, 1981); Bruce King, *Modern Indian Poetry in English* (Delhi: Oxford University Press, 1987); Vinay Dharwadker, "Some Contexts of Modern Indian Poetry," *Chicago Review* 38 (1992): 218–31; and John Oliver Perry, "Contemporary Indian Poetry in English," *World Literature Today* 68 (1994): 261–71.

14. By comparison with the colonies, as Reed Way Dasenbrock and Feroza F. Jussawalla state, "The literature and culture of the dominions understandably demonstrate a much greater degree of continuity with that of Britain. After all, until very recently 'home' in these countries meant Britain, and even though this orientation towards Britain has inevitably weakened across time, the literature and culture of the dominions remain essentially European in form and spirit" (introduction to *Interviews with Writers of the Post-colonial World* [Jackson: University Press of Mississippi, 1992], 3–23). Similarly, Leela Gandhi observes: "There is a fundamental incommensurability between the predominantly cultural 'subordination' of settler culture in Australia, and the predominantly administrative and militaristic subordination of colonised culture in Africa and Asia" (*Postcolonial Theory,* 170). On the blurring of this distinction in "Commonwealth" literary studies, see Moore-Gilbert, *Postcolonial Theory,* 26–33. For a historically rich defense, see Diana Bryden and Helen Tiffin, "West Indian Literature and the Australian Comparison" in *Postcolonial Criticism,* ed. Bart Moore-Gilbert, Gareth Stanton, and Willy Maley (New York: Longman, 1997), 191–214. See also Stephen Slemon, "Unsettling the Empire: Resistance Theory for the Second World," *World Literature Written in English* 30, no. 2 (1990): 30–41.

15. On Ireland's postcoloniality, see Luke Gibbons, "Unapproved Roads: Ireland and Post-colonial Identity," *Transformations in Irish Culture* (Cork: Cork University Press, 1996), 171–80; Declan Kiberd, *Inventing Ireland* (London: Jonathan Cape, 1995); David Lloyd, *Anomalous States: Irish Writing and the Post-colonial Moment* (Durham, N.C.: Duke University Press, 1993); Edward Said, *Culture and Imperialism* (New York: Alfred A. Knopf, 1993); and David Cairns and Shaun Richards, *Writing Ireland: Colonialism, Nationalism and Culture* (Manchester: Manchester University Press, 1988).

16. Derek Walcott, "Meanings" (1970), in *Critical Perspectives on Derek Walcott,* ed. Robert D. Hamner (Washington, D.C.: Three Continents Press, 1993), 50.

17. On the "hybridity" model as depoliticizing and homogenizing, see, e.g., McClintock, "Angel of Progress"; Shohat, "Notes on the Postcolonial," 108–10; R. Radhakrishnan, "Postcoloniality and the Boundaries of Identity," *Callaloo* 16, no. 4 (1993): 750–71; and Aijaz Ahmad, *In Theory: Classes, Nations, Literatures* (London: Verso, 1995). For a critique of hybridity as a concept that perpetuates the racial categories it is meant to supplant, see Robert J. C. Young, *Colonial Desire: Hybridity in Theory, Culture and Race* (London: Routledge, 1995), 1–28. I discuss the critique of hybridity in the next chapter and in the coda. Susan Stanford Friedman distinguishes among varieties of hybridity theory according to "types (fusion/intermingling/always already syncretist), functions (routine/transgressive), orientations (spatial/temporal), and political modes (oppressive/oppositional/locational)" (*Mappings: Feminism and the Cultural Geographies of Encounter* [Princeton, N.J.: Princeton University Press, 1998], 82–93). I use the coinage "interculturation" to suggest mutuality and bricolage, avoiding the teleological implications of the related terms "transculturation" or "acculturation."

18. Said, *Culture and Imperialism;* Homi K. Bhabha, *The Location of Culture* (London: Routledge, 1994), and "Unpacking My Library . . . Again," in *The Post-colonial Question,* ed.

Iain Chambers and Lidia Curti (New York: Routledge, 1996), 199–211; Stuart Hall, "Cultural Identity and Diaspora," in *Identity: Community, Culture, Difference,* ed. Jonathan Rutherford (London: Lawrence & Wishart, 1990), 222–37, and "When Was 'the Postcolonial'?" in Chambers and Curti, eds., 242–60; James Clifford, *Routes: Travel and Translation in the Late Twentieth Century* (Cambridge, Mass.: Harvard University Press, 1997); Gayatri Chakravorty Spivak, *A Critique of Postcolonial Reason* (Cambridge, Mass.: Harvard University Press, 1999); and Mary Louise Pratt, *Imperial Eyes: Travel Writing and Transculturation* (New York: Routledge, 1992).

19. A. K. Ramanujan, "Where Mirrors Are Windows: Towards an Anthology of Reflections," in *The Collected Essays of A. K. Ramanujan,* ed. Vinay Dharwadker (New Delhi: Oxford University Press, 1999), 8. On the "ghostly mobility" and cultural interfusions of English India, see Sara Suleri, *The Rhetoric of English India* (Chicago: University of Chicago Press, 1992), 3.

20. Appiah, *In My Father's House,* 24; Paul Gilroy, *The Black Atlantic: Modernity and Double Consciousness* (Cambridge, Mass.: Harvard University Press, 1993), 3.

21. Edouard Glissant, *Caribbean Discourse: Selected Essays,* trans. J. M. Dash (Charlottesville: University Press of Virginia, 1989); Kamau Brathwaite, *The Development of Creole Society in Jamaica, 1770–1820* (Oxford: Oxford University Press, 1971). Drawing on Glissant and Brathwaite, the recent critical literature on Caribbean hybridity is especially rich; see, e.g., J. Michael Dash, *The Other America: Caribbean Literature in a New World Context,* New World Studies (Charlottesville: University Press of Virginia, 1998); Silvio Torres-Saillant, *Caribbean Poetics: Toward an Aesthetics of West Indian Literature* (Cambridge: Cambridge University Press, 1997); and Richard D. E. Burton, *Afro-Creole* (Ithaca, N.Y.: Cornell University Press, 1997).

22. M. M. Bakhtin, *The Dialogic Imagination: Four Essays,* ed. Michael Holquist, trans. Caryl Emerson and Michael Holquist (Austin: University of Texas Press, 1981), 298–362.

23. On North American poets as tourists after World War II, see Robert von Hallberg, *American Poetry and Culture, 1945–1980* (Cambridge, Mass.: Harvard University Press, 1985), 62–92. On the multilingual and multicultural "space" of postcolonial fiction, see Dasenbrock and Jussawalla, introduction to *Interviews with Writers,* 6–7.

24. Frantz Fanon, *The Wretched of the Earth,* trans. Constance Farrington (New York: Grove, 1963), 102.

25. Edward W. Said, *Orientalism* (New York: Vintage-Random House), 1–2.

26. Fanon, *The Wretched of the Earth,* 43, 250.

27. Ibid., 41, 38.

28. Ibid., 250.

29. Ibid., 210.

30. Derek Walcott, *Omeros* (New York: Farrar, Straus & Giroux, 1990), 136, 242.

31. Fanon, *The Wretched of the Earth,* 225.

32. Walcott, *Omeros,* 133.

33. Edward [Kamau] Brathwaite, *The Arrivants: A New World Trilogy* (Oxford: Oxford University Press, 1973), 124, 132.

34. Kofi Awoonor [formerly George Awoonor Williams], *Rediscovery and Other Poems* (Ibadan, Nigeria: Mbari Publications, 1964), 16.

35. Lenrie Peters, *Selected Poetry* (London: Heinemann, 1981), 27.

36. Jack Mapanje, "Your Tears Still Burn at My Handcuffs (1991)," in *The Chattering*

Wagtails of Mikuyu Prison (Oxford: Heinemann, 1993), 78–79. Decades before Mapanje's 1993 volume, Soyinka recalls his own imprisonment in *A Shuttle in the Crypt* (London: Rex Collings/Methuen, 1972), as does Awoonor in *The House by the Sea* (New York: Greenfield Press Review, 1978).

37. Christopher Okigbo, *Labyrinths, with Path of Thunder* (London: Heinemann, 1971), 66.

38. Walcott, *Omeros*, 289.

39. Agha Shahid Ali, *The Half-Inch Himalayas* (Middletown, Conn.: Wesleyan University Press, 1987), 1.

40. Bhabha, *The Location of Culture,* 9.

41. Ibid., 37. For the view that "all such clear-cut nostalgias for lost origins are suspect," see also Spivak, *Critique of Postcolonial Reason,* 306.

42. Grace Nichols, *Lazy Thoughts of a Lazy Woman* (London: Virago, 1989), 10. Compare Derek Walcott, "A Far Cry from Africa," in *Collected Poems, 1948–1984* (New York: Farrar, Straus & Giroux, 1986), 18; and Brathwaite, *The Arrivants,* 77.

43. Hall, "Cultural Identity and Diaspora," 226.

44. Martin Heidegger, "Letter on Humanism," trans. Frank A. Capuzzi with J. Glenn Gray, in *Basic Writings,* ed. David Farrell Krell (New York: Harper & Row, 1977), 193.

45. Gilles Deleuze and Félix Guattari, *Kafka: Towards a Minor Literature,* trans. Dana Polan (Minneapolis: University of Minnesota Press, 1986), 19, 17.

46. Eunice de Souza, "De Souza Prabhu," in *Ways of Belonging: Selected Poems* (Edinburgh: Polygon, 1990), 24.

47. R. Parthasarathy, "Homecoming 1," in *Rough Passage* (Delhi: Oxford University Press, 1977), 49.

48. Walcott, *Omeros,* 323.

49. Adil Jussawalla, *Missing Person* (Bombay: Clearing House, 1976), 14. See Homi Bhabha's reflections on the passage in *The Location of Culture,* 58–60.

50. Jussawalla, *Missing Person,* 15.

51. Ngugi wa Thiong'o, *Decolonising the Mind: The Politics of Language in African Literature* (London: James Currey, 1986).

52. Walcott continues, "It is the property of the imagination; it is the property of the language itself. I have never felt inhibited in trying to write as well as the greatest English poets" (*Conversations with Derek Walcott,* ed. William Baer [Jackson: University Press of Mississippi, 1996], 106).

53. Salman Rushdie, *Imaginary Homelands: Essays and Criticism, 1981–1991* (London: Granta-Penguin, 1991), 64.

54. John Agard, *Mangoes and Bullets: Selected and New Poems, 1972–84* (London: Pluto Press, 1985), 44.

55. Walcott, *Collected Poems,* 18; W. B. Yeats, *Later Essays,* ed. William H. O'Donnell (New York: Charles Scribner's Sons, 1994), 211.

56. Louise Bennett, *Aunty Roachy Seh,* ed. Mervyn Morris (Kingston: Sangster's Book Stores, 1993), 1.

57. Letter cited in *The Oxford India Anthology of Twelve Modern Indian Poets,* ed. Arvind Krishna Mehrotra (Calcutta: Oxford University Press, 1992), 4.

58. Brathwaite, *The Arrivants,* 192.

59. Wole Soyinka, *Idanre and Other Poems* (New York: Hill & Wang, 1967), 9.

60. Lorna Goodison, *Selected Poems* (Ann Arbor: University of Michigan Press, 1992), 55.

61. Brathwaite, *The Arrivants*, 270.

62. Derek Walcott, "What the Twilight Says: An Overture," in *Dream on Monkey Mountain and Other Plays* (New York: Farrar, Straus & Giroux, 1970), 9, 17, and "The Schooner Flight," in *Collected Poems*, 346.

63. A. K. Ramanujan, "Chicago Zen," in *Collected Poems* (Delhi: Oxford University Press, 1995), 186.

64. Okot told an interviewer he used the word "song" because "the word poem does not exist in my language" (Lee Nichols, "Okot p'Bitek," in *Conversations with African Writers*, ed. Nichols [Washington, D.C.: Voice of America, 1981], 250).

Chapter Two: W. B. Yeats

1. Edward Said, "Yeats and Decolonization," in *Culture and Imperialism* (New York: Alfred A. Knopf, 1993), 220–38; David Lloyd, "The Poetics of Politics: Yeats and the Founding of the State," in *Anomalous States: Irish Writing and the Post-colonial Moment* (Durham, N.C.: Duke University Press, 1993), 59–82; Declan Kiberd, *Inventing Ireland* (London: Jonathan Cape, 1995), 1–7, 115–29, 162–65, 199–217, 251–59.

2. Against the association of Yeats with the literature of decolonization, see Julian Moynahan, who cites Ireland's proximity and the 1800 Act of Union to claim that "colonialism . . . does not apply" to "Anglo-Irish Literature" (*Anglo-Irish: The Literary Imagination in a Hyphenated Culture* [Princeton, N.J.: Princeton University Press, 1995], xi–xiii). For Denis Donoghue, "not only is the postcolonial approach ill-suited to the Irish situation, it sacrifices literary understanding on the altar of politics" ("Fears for Irish Studies in an Age of Identity Politics," *Chronicle of Higher Education* [November 21, 1997], B4–B5). Some writers sympathetic to postcolonial studies also argue that Yeats isn't postcolonial but for different reasons; e.g., Joseph Chadwick believes that Yeats's "residual colonialism" as an Anglo-Irish writer disqualifies him ("Yeats: Colonialism and Responsibility," in *International Aspects of Irish Literature*, ed. Toshi Furomoto et al. [Gerrards Cross: Colin Smythe, 1996], 107–14).

3. Among many recent discussions of the meanings and problems of the term "post-colonial," see Ania Loomba, *Colonialism/Postcolonialism* (London: Routledge, 1998), 1–19; Deepika Bahri, "Once More with Feeling: What Is Postcolonialism?" *Ariel* 26, no. 1 (1995): 51–82; Tejumola Olaniyan, "On 'Post-colonial Discourse': An Introduction," *Callaloo* 16, no. 4 (1993): 743–49; Ella Shohat, "Notes on the Postcolonial," *Social Text* 31/32 (1992): 99–113; Anne McClintock, "The Angel of Progress: Pitfalls of the Term 'Post-colonialism,'" *Social Text* 31/32 (1992): 84–98.

4. Stuart Hall, "When Was 'the Post-colonial'? Thinking at the Limit," in *The Post-colonial Question*, ed. Iain Chambers and Lidia Curti (New York: Routledge, 1996), 242–60.

5. In Helen Tiffin's words, "Here the post-colonial is conceived of as a set of discursive practices, prominent among which is resistance to colonialism, colonialist ideologies, and their contemporary forms and subjectificatory legacies. The nature and function of this resistance forms a central problematic of the discourse" (introduction to *Past the Last Post: Theorizing Post-colonialism and Post-modernism*, ed. Ian Adam and Helen Tiffin [Calgary: University of Calgary Press, 1990], vii). In the same volume, Stephen Slemon writes of the "post-colonial" as "a network of disidentificatory traditions" ("Modernism's Last Post," 3).

6. W. B. Yeats, *The Poems*, rev. ed., ed. Richard J. Finneran (New York: Macmillan, 1989), 306–7. All further references to Yeats's poetry appear parenthetically in the text.

7. Conor Cruise O'Brien, "Passion and Cunning: An Essay on the Politics of W. B. Yeats," in *In Excited Reverie*, ed. A. N. Jeffares and K. G. W. Cross (London: Macmillan, 1965), 266. O'Brien also cites the letter quoted below (267).

8. W. B. Yeats, *The Letters of W. B. Yeats*, ed. Allan Wade (London: Rupert Hart-Davis, 1954), 881.

9. My discussion of Yeats's poetry within the postcolonial context is necessarily synchronic, but for finely grained diachronic accounts of Yeats's changing political identifications, see Elizabeth Cullingford, *Yeats, Ireland and Fascism* (New York: New York University Press, 1981); and R. F. Foster, *The Apprentice Mage*, vol. 1 of *W. B. Yeats: A Life* (New York: Oxford University Press, 1997).

10. W. B. Yeats, *Later Essays*, ed. William H. O'Donnell (New York: Charles Scribner's Sons, 1994), 210. References to this work will hereafter be cited parenthetically in the text as *Later Essays*.

11. Cullingford, *Yeats, Ireland and Fascism*, 99.

12. Yeats, quoted by Mark F. Ryan, *Fenian Memories*, 2d ed., ed. T. F. O'Sullivan (Dublin: Gill, 1946), 186. Elizabeth Cullingford cites and contextualizes this 1898 Centenary speech in *Yeats, Ireland and Fascism*, 38. Frantz Fanon, *The Wretched of the Earth*, trans. Constance Farrington (New York: Grove, 1963), 96.

13. Yeats, *The Letters*, 656.

14. W. B. Yeats, *Autobiographies*, ed. William H. O'Donnell and Douglas N. Archibald (New York: Scribner, 1999), 60–61. All further references to this work will be cited parenthetically in the text as *Autobiographies*.

15. Fanon, *The Wretched of the Earth*, 212–13; Seamus Deane, introduction to *Nationalism, Colonialism, and Literature*, ed. Seamus Deane (Minneapolis: University of Minnesota Press, 1990), 11–12. Yeats also worried, as he suggests in a 1914 speech, that hatred of the English could easily turn into hatred of one's own countrymen (see Foster, *Apprentice Mage*, 524).

16. See, e.g., Fanon, *The Wretched of the Earth*, 210–11; and Bill Ashcroft, Gareth Griffiths, and Helen Tiffin, *The Empire Writes Back: Theory and Practice in Post-colonial Literatures* (New York: Routledge, 1989), 4–6, 16–18.

17. Benedict Anderson, *Imagined Communities: Reflections on the Origin and Spread of Nationalism* (London: New Left, 1983). On Yeats and "imagined community," see, e.g., Said, "Yeats and Decolonization," 232; and Marjorie Howes, *Yeats's Nations: Gender, Class, and Irishness* (Cambridge: Cambridge University Press, 1996). Among recent discussions of Yeats and nationalism, see also Hazard Adams, "Yeats and Antithetical Nationalism," in *Yeats's Political Identities: Selected Essays*, ed. Jonathan Allison (Ann Arbor: University of Michigan Press, 1996), 309–24.

18. R. F. Foster, "Protestant Magic: W. B. Yeats and the Spell of Irish History," in *Yeats's Political Identities*, ed. Allison, 83. Foster seems to have moderated this view in his fine biography of Yeats.

19. Seamus Deane, "The Literary Myths of the Revival" and "Yeats and the Idea of Revolution," both in *Celtic Revivals* (London: Faber, 1985), 28–37, 38–50, respectively.

20. W. B. Yeats, *Explorations* (New York: Macmillan, 1962), 158.

21. W. B. Yeats, *Essays and Introductions* (London: Macmillan, 1961), 158. References to this work will hereafter be cited parenthetically in the text as *Essays*.

22. W. B. Yeats, *Uncollected Prose*, ed. John P. Frayne (New York: Columbia University Press, 1970), 1:164.

23. Yeats's characteristically equivocal feelings about the riots emerge in Foster's account (*Apprentice Mage*, 180–81). Also see Cullingford's description of Yeats's participation in the Jubilee protests and his influences on the Easter rebels (*Yeats, Ireland and Fascism*, 36–40, 85–100).

24. On the antinationalism of postcolonial poets, see Bruce King, "The Emergence of Post-independence Modern Nigerian and Indian Poetry," *World Literature Written in English* 26 (1986): 331–40. On "'native' breeds of colonization and oppression," see Bahri, "Once More with Feeling," 56.

25. Yeats, *Explorations*, 156.

26. I describe the erotics of this deferral in "'A Little Space': The Psychic Economy of Yeats's Love Poems," *Criticism* 35 (1993): 67–89.

27. Luke Gibbons, *Transformations in Irish Culture* (Cork: Cork University Press, 1996), 3, 171–80.

28. Said, "Yeats and Decolonization," 228; Kiberd, *Inventing Ireland*, 251.

29. Said, "Yeats and Decolonization," 228; Kiberd, *Inventing Ireland*, 251.

30. Said, "Yeats and Decolonization," 230, 234.

31. Kiberd, *Inventing Ireland*, 286.

32. Fanon, *The Wretched of the Earth*, 222. My use of the term "ironist" is indebted to Richard Rorty, *Contingency, Irony, and Solidarity* (Cambridge: Cambridge University Press, 1989).

33. Kiberd, *Inventing Ireland*, 251–53.

34. Among the many works on Yeats's relationships with Chatterjee, Tagore, and Shri Purohit Swami, as well as Indian thought more generally, see Ganesh N. Devy, "The Indian Yeats," in *International Aspects*, ed. Furomoto et al., 93–106; P. S. Sri, "Yeats and Mohini Chatterjee," *Yeats Annual* 11 (1994): 61–76; Sankaran Ravindran, *W. B. Yeats and Indian Tradition* (Delhi: Konark Publishers, 1990); Ramesh Chandra Shah, *Yeats and Eliot: Perspectives on India* (Atlantic Highlands, N.J.: Humanities Press, 1983); Sushil K. Jain, "Indian Elements in the Poetry of W. B. Yeats with Special Reference to Yeats's Relationship with Chatterji and Tagore," *Comparative Literature Studies* 7 (1970): 82–96; Naresh Guha, *W. B. Yeats: An Indian Approach* (Calcutta: Jadavpur University, 1968); Mary M. Lago, "The Parting of the Ways: A Comparative Study of Yeats and Tagore," *Mahfil* 3, no. 1 (1966): 32–57; Harbans Rai Bachchan, *W. B. Yeats and Occultism* (Delhi: Motilal Banarsidass, 1965), chaps. 2 and 4; Harold M. Hurwitz, "Yeats and Tagore," *Comparative Literature* 16 (1964): 55–64. In *Apprentice Mage*, Foster dates the first meeting with Chatterjee to April 1886 (552, n. 84) and connects Yeats's earliest Indian enthusiasm with an intellectual fashion of the 1880s (47).

35. Yeats first used *Crossways* as a descriptive heading for some of his earliest poems when he republished them in *Poems* (1895).

36. W. B. Yeats, *The Variorum Edition of the Poems of W. B. Yeats*, ed. Peter Allt and Russell K. Alspach, corrected ed. (New York: Macmillan, 1966), 837.

37. Ezra Pound, *Selected Letters, 1907–1941*, ed. D. D. Paige (New York: New Directions, 1971), 330.

38. Yeats, *The Variorum Edition*, 76–77.

39. See, e.g., R. Radhakrishnan, "Postcoloniality and the Boundaries of Identity," *Callaloo* 16, no. 4 (1993): 750–71; Shohat, "Notes on the Postcolonial," 108–10; McClintock, "Angel of Progress"; Bart Moore-Gilbert, *Postcolonial Theory: Contexts, Practices, Politics* (London: Verso, 1997), 193–96.

40. Yeats, *Explorations*, 82. On Protestant Ireland as having sold its Parliament to England, see *Autobiographies*, 311.

41. The Castle was the administrative center of British rule in Ireland. In the period 1909–10, when Yeats was considered for a possible professorship at Trinity, he moderated his antagonism toward this and other Irish Protestant institutions (Foster, *Apprentice Mage*, 429–31).

42. The quoted material is from Edward Baugh, *Derek Walcott* (Norfolk: Longman, 1978), 9.

43. A. K. Ramanujan, "Classics Lost and Found," in *The Collected Essays of A. K. Ramanujan*, ed. Vinay Dharwadker (New Delhi: Oxford University Press, 1999), 187.

44. See Said, "Yeats and Decolonization," 227; and Kiberd, *Inventing Ireland*, 163. Depending on his audience, Yeats at times championed the revival of the Irish language (see Foster, *Apprentice Mage*, 220, 226, 312).

45. Douglas Hyde, "The Necessity for De-Anglicizing Ireland" (1892), in *Irish Literature: A Reader*, ed. Maureen O'Rourke Murphy and James MacKillop (Syracuse, N.Y.: Syracuse University Press, 1987), 145; Ngugi wa Thiong'o, *Decolonising the Mind: The Politics of Language in African Literature* (London: James Currey, 1986), 9.

46. Yeats, *Uncollected Prose*, 1:256, 255.

47. Ibid., 255.

48. Yeats, *The Letters*, 834–35.

49. See Kiberd, *Inventing Ireland*, 269.

50. Yeats, *Uncollected Prose*, 1:269.

51. Deane, introduction to his *Celtic Revivals*, 13–15; Said, "Yeats and Decolonization," 225–26; Kiberd, *Inventing Ireland*, 119; George Bornstein, "Romancing the (Native) Stone: Yeats, Stevens, and the Anglocentric Canon," in *Yeats's Political Identities*, ed. Allison, 240. Bornstein explores Yeats's ambivalent literary nationalism, his "double allegiance both to his native land and to English literary tradition" (240).

52. Brendan O Hehir, "Kickshaws and Wheelchairs: Yeats and the Irish Language," *Yeats* 1 (1983): 93. Along with O Hehir's ironic discussion of Yeats's anglicizations (92–103), see also Hugh Kenner, *A Colder Eye: The Modern Irish Writers* (New York: Penguin, 1983), 111–19.

53. Lorna Goodison, *Selected Poems* (Ann Arbor: University of Michigan Press, 1992), 1–3; Derek Walcott, *Collected Poems, 1948–1984* (New York: Farrar, Straus & Giroux, 1986), 309.

54. Again, see O Hehir, "Kickshaws and Wheelchairs," 92–103, and Kenner, *A Colder Eye*, 111–19.

55. For an alternative reading of Yeats's gendering of his literary development as moving away from Celticism and toward an authentic nationalism, see Howes, *Yeats's Nations*, 17–18.

56. Patrick C. Power argues that Gaelic syllabic poetry influenced Yeats's meters (*The Story of Anglo-Irish Poetry, 1800–1922* [Cork: Mercier, 1967], 98–101). Bruce King argues for the influence on Yeats's prose style of Irish idiom, alliteration, and assonance, trisyllabic cadences, conversational strategies, allusiveness, and satire ("Yeats's Irishry Prose," in *W. B. Yeats, 1865–1965: Centenary Essays*, ed. D. E. S. Maxwell and S. B. Bushrui [Ibadan, Nigeria: Ibadan University Press, 1965], 127–35).

57. Helen Vendler, "Yeats at Sonnets," lecture at the Yeats International Summer School, Sligo, Ireland, August 1996.

58. Kenner, *A Colder Eye*, 107–08.

59. W. H. Auden, "The Public v. the Late Mr. William Butler Yeats," in *The English Auden*, ed. Edward Mendelson (London: Faber, 1986), 393.

60. "I have an ambition to be taken as an Irish novelist," the young Yeats wrote of his novel *John Sherman*, "not as an English or cosmepolitan [sic] one chosing [sic] Ireland as a background" (*The Collected Letters of W. B. Yeats*, vol. 1, ed. John Kelly and Eric Domville [New York: Oxford University Press, 1986], 274–75). But Yeats was attacked repeatedly by contemporaries, including Maud Gonne, for his cosmopolitianism (see Foster, *Apprentice Mage*, 297, 299).

61. Yeats, *Explorations*, 158.

Chapter Three: Derek Walcott

1. Derek Walcott, *Conversations with Derek Walcott*, ed. William Baer (Jackson: University Press of Mississippi, 1996), 59.

2. Derek Walcott, "Leaving School" (1965), in *Critical Perspectives on Derek Walcott*, ed. Robert D. Hamner (Washington, D.C.: Three Continents Press, 1993), 32.

3. Recalling Yeats's description of the Black and Tans as "drunken soldiery" ("drunken officer of British rule"), Walcott also transmutes Yeats's lines, "All men are dancers and their tread / Goes to the barbarous clangour of a gong," into a similarly bleak description of the compulsive brutality of "man": "Delirious as these worried beasts, his wars / Dance to the tightened carcass of a drum." See W. B. Yeats, *The Poems*, rev. ed., ed. Richard J. Finneran (New York: Macmillan, 1989), 207, 208; Derek Walcott, *Collected Poems, 1948–1984* (New York: Noonday-Farrar, Straus & Giroux, 1986), 17–18. Laurence A. Breiner dates the first publication of "A Far Cry from Africa" in *An Introduction to West Indian Poetry* (Cambridge: Cambridge University Press, 1998), 159; 247, n. 20.

4. Derek Walcott, *Omeros* (New York: Farrar, Straus & Giroux, 1990), 199. All further references to *Omeros* appear parenthetically in the text. Although Joyce is the more direct influence on *Omeros*, Yeats's presence is evident from the introduction of the two major female characters in the story: an Irishwoman notably named Maud and a local woman named Helen, who caribbeanizes a Greek paradigm as Yeats had earlier "irished" her.

Walcott has often been fruitfully discussed as a poet of "mixed" culture, "divided" inheritance, and "schizophrenic" allegiance; see Paul Breslin, "'I Met History Once, But He Ain't Recognize Me': The Poetry of Derek Walcott," *Triquarterly* 68 (1987): 168–83; Joseph Brodsky, "On Derek Walcott," *New York Review of Books*, 10 November 1983, 39–41; James Dickey, review of *Collected Poems, 1948–1984*, by Derek Walcott, *New York Times Book Review*, 2 February 1986, 8; Rita Dove, "'Either I'm Nobody, or I'm a Nation,'" review of *Collected Poems, 1948–1984*, by Derek Walcott, *Parnassus* 14, no. 1 (1987): 49–76; J. D. McClatchy, review of *Collected Poems, 1948–1984*, by Derek Walcott, *New Republic*, 24 March 1986, 36–38; James McCorkle, "'The Sigh of History': The Poetry of Derek Walcott," *Verse* ("Derek Walcott Feature Issue," ed. Susan M. Schultz) 11, no. 2 (1994): 104–12; J. A. Ramsaran, "Derek Walcott: New World Mediterranean Poet," *World Literature Written in English* 21, no. 1 (1982): 133–47; Rei Terada, *Walcott's Poetry: American Mimicry* (Boston: Northeastern University Press, 1992); Helen Vendler, "Poet of Two Worlds," review of *The Fortunate Traveller*, by Derek Walcott, *New York Review of Books*, 4 March 1982, 23+; Clement H. Wyke, "'Divided to the Vein': Patterns of Tormented Ambivalence in Walcott's *The Fortunate Traveller*," *Ariel* 20, no. 3 (1989): 55–71; and John Thieme, *Derek Walcott* (New York: Manchester University Press, 1999).

A biographical synopsis may be helpful for readers new to Walcott. He was born in Castries, Saint Lucia, on January 23, 1930. His father, a civil servant and amateur painter, died before he was a year old. His mother was the head teacher at a Methodist infant school on the predominantly Catholic island. His background was racially and culturally mixed. His grandmothers were of African descent, his white grandfathers a Dutchman and an Englishman. Speaking the Standard English that is the official language of the island, Walcott also grew up speaking the predominant French creole (or patois) that is the primary language of the street. At the age of fifteen, Walcott published a poem in the local newspaper, drawing a sharp rebuke in rhyme from a Catholic priest for his heretical pantheism and animism. A few years later, he borrowed money from his mother to print a booklet of twenty-five poems, hawking it on the streets to earn the money back. This book and his first major play, *Henri Christophe,* also met with disapprobation from the Catholic church.

In 1950 he left Saint Lucia to enter the University of the West Indies in Mona, Jamaica, where he was a vibrant literary entrepreneur among the university's first graduating class in liberal arts. Staying on in Jamaica, he made his living through teaching and journalism. He moved to Trinidad in 1958, still working as a reviewer and art critic but also pouring energy into directing and writing plays for the Trinidad Theater Workshop until 1976. His poetry began to receive international attention with *In a Green Night* (1962).

Since 1981, he has been teaching regularly at Boston University. He recently built a home on the northwest coast of Saint Lucia where he paints and writes. Among his major plays are *Ti-Jean and His Brothers* (1958), *Dream on Monkey Mountain* (1967), and *The Odyssey* (1993). He received the Nobel Prize for literature in 1992. See Bruce King, *Derek Walcott: A Caribbean Life* (New York: Oxford University Press, 2000); and Paul Breslin, *Nobody's Nation: Reading Derek Walcott* (Chicago: University of Chicago Press, in press).

5. In *Omeros* the name is spelled "Philoctete" and pronounced "Fee-lock-TET," in accordance with the French creole of Saint Lucia.

6. Edward [Kamau] Brathwaite, *The Arrivants: A New World Trilogy* (Oxford: Oxford University Press, 1973), 210, 249, 265; Walcott, "The Muse of History: An Essay," in *Is Massa Day Dead? Black Moods in the Caribbean,* ed. Orde Coombs (Garden City, N.Y.: Anchor-Doubleday, 1974), 3.

7. Walcott, "Tribal Flutes" (1967), in *Critical Perspectives,* ed. Hamner, 43, and "The Muse of History," 8, 2–3. Brathwaite and Walcott have often been compared; see, e.g., Patricia Ismond, "Walcott versus Brathwaite," in *Critical Perspectives,* ed. Hamner, 220–36; and J. Edward Chamberlin, *Come Back to Me My Language: Poetry and the West Indies* (Urbana: University of Illinois Press, 1993), 154–55.

8. Walcott, *Collected Poems,* 269, 286.

9. Ibid., 269, 270.

10. Walcott uses the Philoctetes type in his unpublished play *The Isle Is Full of Noises* (1982), but there the wound signifies indigenous political corruption, not inherited colonial injury. I am grateful to Paul Breslin for sharing with me the play's typescript.

11. C. L. R. James, *The Black Jacobins: Toussaint L'Ouverture and the San Domingo Revolution,* 2d ed. (New York: Vintage-Random House, 1989), 12.

12. Walcott complains bitterly that such "historical sullenness" results in "morose poems and novels" of "one mood, which is in too much of Caribbean writing: that sort of chafing and rubbing of an old sore." See Edward Hirsch, "The Art of Poetry" (1986 interview), in *Critical Perspectives,* ed. Hamner, 79.

13. D. J. Bruckner, "A Poem in Homage to an Unwanted Man" (1990 interview), in *Critical Perspectives*, ed. Hamner, 397.

14. Walcott, "Laventille," in *Collected Poems*, 88.

15. Anthony Milne, "Derek Walcott" (1982 interview), in *Critical Perspectives*, ed. Hamner, 62.

16. On Walcott's use of Crusoe instead of Friday, see his "The Figure of Crusoe" (1965 lecture), in *Critical Perspectives*, ed. Hamner, 33-40.

17. Walcott earlier belittles "exotic," cross-racial recasting of characters like Hamlet; see "Meanings" (1970), in *Critical Perspectives*, ed. Hamner, 47.

18. Other Greek-named characters in *Omeros* share a similar genealogy, but their looser affinities with their namesakes make them more independent characters than the allegorical Philoctete. On the relationships between Walcott's characters and their Homeric counterparts, see Robert Hamner, *Epic of the Dispossessed: Derek Walcott's "Omeros"* (Columbia: University of Missouri Press, 1997); Terada, *Walcott's Poetry*, 183-212; Geert Lernout, "Derek Walcott's *Omeros*: The Isle Is Full of Voices," *Kunapipi* 14, no. 2 (1992): 95-97; and Oliver Taplin, "Derek Walcott's *Omeros* and Derek Walcott's Homer," *Arion*, 3d ser., 1, no. 2 (1991): 213-26.

19. On the traditional fascination with Philoctetes' pain, see Oscar Mandel, *Philoctetes and the Fall of Troy* (Lincoln: University of Nebraska Press, 1981), 35-36. Mandel surveys Philoctetes' iconography (123-49).

20. Gotthold Ephraim Lessing, *Laocoön*, trans. Edward Allen McCormick (Baltimore: Johns Hopkins University Press, 1984), 29; Edmund Wilson, *The Wound and the Bow* (London: W. H. Allen, 1952), 257, 259; Seamus Heaney, *The Cure at Troy: A Version of Sophocles' "Philoctetes"* (New York: Noonday-Farrar, Straus & Giroux, 1991).

21. Terada, *Walcott's Poetry*, 188, 187.

22. Derek Walcott, "What the Twilight Says: An Overture," in *"Dream on Monkey Mountain" and Other Plays* (New York: Farrar, Straus & Giroux, 1970), 31, "The Figure of Crusoe," 36, and see also "The Muse of History," 4; Rob Nixon, "Caribbean and African Appropriations of *The Tempest*," *Critical Inquiry* 13 (1987): 557-78; and A. James Arnold, "Caliban, Culture, and Nation-Building in the Caribbean," in *Constellation Caliban: Figurations of a Character*, ed. Nadia Lie and Theo D'haen (Amsterdam and Atlanta, Ga.: Rodopi, 1997), 231-44, and other essays in the latter collection.

23. Shakespeare, *The Tempest*, 1.2.369-70. Walcott's remark about Timon of Athens and his script for *The Isle Is Full of Noises* indicate an additional Shakespearean prototype for the cursing Philoctete.

24. Walcott, "The Figure of Crusoe," 36.

25. Aimé Césaire, *A Tempest*, trans. Richard Miller (Paris: Editions du Seuil, 1986), 17, 18.

26. Walcott, "The Figure of Crusoe," 37, 35.

27. As an indication that Walcott closely associates Philoctetes and Crusoe, he gives the nickname "Crusoe" to the Philoctetes character in *The Isle Is Full of Noises*. Carol Dougherty argues for yet another Western prototype: Walcott introduces the scar-bearing Philoctete "as an Odysseus of sorts" ("Homer after *Omeros*: Reading a H/Omeric Text," *South Atlantic Quarterly* 96 [1997]: 339-47).

28. Walcott, "Necessity of Negritude," in *Critical Perspectives*, ed. Hamner, 20-23. On negritude and various conceptions of Africa in West Indian poetry, see Breiner, *An Introduction to West Indian Poetry*, 156-64.

29. Walcott, "The Caribbean: Culture or Mimicry?" (1974), in *Critical Perspectives*, ed. Hamner, 53.

30. Walcott, "The Muse of History, 7, 8.

31. At a more general level, Walcott follows the lead of negritude writers insofar as he, like them, dialectically inverts colonial stereotypes. Fanon, who worried about negritude's tendency to duplicate colonial views through such inversion, mentions as one of colonialism's dehumanizing terms the "stink" of the native. When Walcott stresses the foul "smell" of Philoctete's wound, he not only remembers the Greek prototype but also flouts a repressive stereotype (10). See Frantz Fanon, *The Wretched of the Earth*, trans. Constance Farrington (New York: Grove Press–Présence Africaine, 1963), 212–13, 42.

32. Walcott, "Necessity of Negritude," 21.

33. Aimé Césaire, *Cahier d'un retour au pays natal*, 2d ed. (bilingual), English trans. Emile Snyders (Paris: Présence Africaine, 1968), 40, 126.

34. Ibid.: "whip" (130), "brand" (114), "tom-toms" (94).

35. Jean-Paul Sartre, "Black Orpheus" (1948), trans. John MacCombie, reprinted in *The Black American Writer*, ed. C. W. E. Bigsby (Deland, Fla.: Everett/Edward, 1969), 2:13. The anthology in which Sartre's "Orphée Noir" was originally published is *Anthologie de la nouvelle poésie nègre et malgache de langue française*, ed. Léopold Sédar Senghor (Paris: Presses Universitaires de France, 1948).

36. Sartre, "Black Orpheus," 36; "Orphée Noir," 41.

37. Sartre, "Black Orpheus," 31–32; "Orphée Noir," 36.

38. Walcott, "The Antilles: Fragments of Epic Memory," reprinted in *Dictionary of Literary Biography Yearbook* (Detroit: Gale Research Co., 1992), 14.

39. Walcott, "The Muse of History," 27.

40. Yeats, "Crazy Jane Talks with the Bishop," in *Poems*, 260.

41. Walcott, *Collected Poems*, 346.

42. See Edward Kamau Brathwaite, *The Development of Creole Society in Jamaica, 1770–1820* (Oxford: Oxford University Press, 1971), and *Roots* (Ann Arbor: University of Michigan Press, 1993); Homi K. Bhabha, *The Location of Culture* (New York: Routledge, 1994); Edouard Glissant, *Caribbean Discourse: Selected Essays*, trans. J. Michael Dash (Charlottesville: University Press of Virginia, 1989); Roberto Fernández Retamar, *Caliban and Other Essays* (Minneapolis: University of Minnesota Press, 1989); and David A. Hollinger, *Postethnic America: Beyond Multiculturalism* (New York: Basic, 1995). The mixture in some models is primarily cultural, in others racial, and Walcott often conflates the two. Regarding the West Indies, "almost all contemporary approaches to Afro-Caribbean culture(s)," according to Richard D. E. Burton, "stress its (their) syncretistic or mosaic character," with significant differences in emphasis (*Afro-Creole: Power, Opposition, and Play in the Caribbean* [Ithaca, N.Y.: Cornell University Press, 1997], 3). On the hybridity of Caribbean literature, see Antonio Benítez-Rojo, *The Repeating Island: The Caribbean and the Postmodern Perspective*, trans. James Maraniss (Durham, N.C.: Duke University Press, 1992); Silvio Torres-Saillant, *Caribbean Poetics: Toward an Aesthetics of West Indian Literature* (Cambridge: Cambridge University Press, 1997); and J. Michael Dash, *The Other America: Caribbean Literature in a New World Context*, New World Studies (Charlottesville: University Press of Virginia, 1998).

43. Walcott, "Necessity of Negritude," 20.

44. Walcott, "The Caribbean," 52.

45. See Frantz Fanon's classic formulation of the three-stage "evolution" of native writing, from "unqualified assimilation" to nativist "exoticism" to "revolutionary," truly "national literature" (*The Wretched of the Earth,* trans. Constance Farrington [New York: Grove, 1963], 222–23). For a more recent example, see Bill Ashcroft, Gareth Griffiths, and Helen Tiffin, *The Empire Writes Back: Theory and Practice in Post-colonial Literatures* (New York: Routledge, 1989), 4–5: "Post-colonial literatures developed through several stages which can be seen to correspond to stages both of national or regional consciousness and of the project of asserting difference from the imperial centre." For Ashcroft, Griffiths, and Tiffin, as for many other critics, this literary historical narrative remains fundamental, despite a growing interest in "models of hybridity and syncreticity" (33–37).

46. According to John Barrell, the traditional image of Philoctetes, "with his wounded and unsupported foot, . . . express[es] the fear of castration," which "derives from the belief that the woman is castrated" and thus "produces the need for the companion representation" of a female figure (*The Birth of Pandora and the Division of Knowledge* [Philadelphia: University of Pennsylvania Press, 1992], 213).

47. Walcott, *Collected Poems,* 20. Joseph Farrell comments on the "unending succession whereby formerly enslaved and colonized peoples become oppressors in their own right" ("Walcott's *Omeros:* The Classical Epic in a Postmodern World," *South Atlantic Quarterly* 96 [1997]: 265).

48. Fredric Jameson, "Third-World Literature in the Era of Multinational Capitalism," *Social Text* 15 (1986): 69.

49. Elaine Scarry, *The Body in Pain: The Making and Unmaking of the World* (New York: Oxford University Press, 1985), 119; and see 121 for the ensuing quotation.

50. Arguably, even postcolonial novels such as Michelle Cliff's *No Telephone to Heaven* and J. M. Coetzee's *Waiting for the Barbarians,* which like *Omeros* allegorize the wound and scar, more readily satisfy the imperatives of much postcolonial criticism than poetry does.

51. Glissant, *Caribbean Discourse,* 65–66.

52. On the ambiguous historicity and positionality of trauma, see Cathy Caruth, introduction to *Trauma: Explorations in Memory,* ed. Cathy Caruth (Baltimore: Johns Hopkins University Press, 1995), 3–11; and Dori Laub, "Bearing Witness; or, The Vicissitudes of Listening," in *Testimony: Crises of Witnessing in Literature, Psychoanalysis, and History,* ed. Shoshana Felman and Dori Laub (Routledge: New York, 1992), 57–74.

Chapter Four: A. K. Ramanujan

1. Paul Ricoeur, *The Rule of Metaphor,* trans. Robert Czerny (Toronto: University of Toronto Press, 1977), 17, 18, 19. In my broad use of the term "metaphor," I follow Ricoeur and others for whom it is not merely a subspecies of trope, distinct from metonymy, synecdoche, or simile, but master trope for all such figural relations of resemblance.

2. I. A. Richards, *The Philosophy of Rhetoric* (Oxford: Oxford University Press, 1936), 94.

3. Paul Ricoeur, "The Metaphorical Process as Cognition, Imagination, and Feeling," in *Philosophical Perspectives on Metaphor,* ed. Mark Johnson (Minneapolis: University of Minnesota Press, 1981), 233.

4. Nelson Goodman, *Languages of Art: An Approach to a Theory of Symbols,* 2d ed. (Indianapolis: Hackett, 1976).

5. Ibid., 81, 72, 74, 72.

6. Ibid., 73, 74.

7. Ibid., 72.

8. Ibid., 77, 83, 83.

9. See George Lakoff and Mark Johnson, *Metaphors We Live By* (Chicago: University of Chicago Press, 1980); and George Lakoff and Mark Turner, *More Than Cool Reason: A Field Guide to Poetic Metaphor* (Chicago: University of Chicago Press, 1989).

10. In the deconstructionist critique, metaphor is said to disguise the distance, temporality, and contingency inherent within language. In my view, poetic metaphor, as instanced by Ramanujan's postcolonial practice, can highlight such spatiotemporal gaps in figuration even as it crosses them. See Paul de Man, *Allegories of Reading* (New Haven, Conn.: Yale University Press, 1979), 13–19, 60–63; and Jacques Derrida, "White Mythology: Metaphor in the Text of Philosophy," in *Margins of Philosophy*, trans. Alan Bass (Chicago: University of Chicago Press, 1982), 207–71.

11. Victor Shklovsky, "Art as Technique," in *Russian Formalist Criticism*, trans. Lee T. Lemon and Marion J. Reis (Lincoln: University of Nebraska Press, 1965), 12.

12. See Ricoeur, drawing on Roman Jakobson and W. Bedell Stanford ("The Metaphorical Process," 239–41).

13. Ricoeur, *Rule of Metaphor*, 256.

14. Pierre Reverdy's original phrase is "rapprochement de deux réalités . . . éloignées." "Plus les rapports des deux réalités rapprochées seront lointains et justes, plus l'image sera forte, plus elle aura de puissance émotive et de réalité poétique" (*Le gant de crin* [Paris: Plon, 1927], 32). Reverdy is cited in Albert Henry, *Métonymie et métaphore*, rev. ed. (Brussels: Palais des Académies, 1983), 82, 176, which is cited in turn in Ricoeur, *Rule of Metaphor*, 348, n. 26.

15. A. K. Ramanujan, "Where Mirrors Are Windows: Towards an Anthology of Reflections," in *The Collected Essays of A. K. Ramanujan*, ed. Vinay Dharwadker (New Delhi: Oxford University Press, 1999), 8—first published in *History of Religions* 28 (1989): 188–89— and "Classics Lost and Found," in *Collected Essays*, 187—first published in *Contemporary India: Essays on the Uses of Tradition*, ed. Carla Borden (New Delhi: Oxford University Press, 1989), 135.

16. A. K. Ramanujan, "Afterword," in *Poems of Love and War*, trans. Ramanujan (New York: Columbia University Press, 1984), 246, 287. In his own critical prose, Ramanujan sometimes characterizes Indian literature as "metonymic": "Both parts of the comparison . . . are part of one scene, one syntagm. . . . In Piercean semiotic terms, these are not symbolic devices, but indexical signs—the signifier and signified belong in the same context" ("Is There an Indian Way of Thinking? An Informal Essay," in *Collected Essays*, 43–44—first published in *India through Hindu Categories*, ed. McKim Marriott [New Delhi: Sage Publications, 1990], 50). Here, Ramanujan could as easily be describing his own poetry. Coining the oxymoron "metonymous metaphor" ("Afterword," 247), he indicates, however, the slipperiness of the metaphor/metonymy distinction. For the purposes of this essay, I circumvent the Jakobsonian distinction to avoid confusion, using "metaphor" inclusively.

17. Ramanujan translates and comments on this passage in his "Afterword," 243.

18. Ramanujan is often quoted as referring to himself as "the hyphen in Indian-American." For the sake of readers new to Ramanujan, I provide further brief biographical summary. Growing up in a Tamil Brahman family in Karnataka, Ramanujan moved among different languages in different levels of the house. Tamil was the language downstairs, associated with his mother and the kitchen. Upstairs, he spoke to his father in English, a math-

ematics professor at Mysore University. On the terrace at night, he learned from his father—both astronomer and astrologist—the English and Sanskrit names of the stars. Outside, Kannada was the language of the streets. These became the languages of his life's work as poet, translator, and linguist. After receiving a B.A. in English literature from Mysore University in 1949, Ramanujan taught English in Indian schools and became fascinated with Indian folklore. Beginning to study linguistics at Deccan College, he continued on a Fulbright grant at Indiana University in 1959, completing his dissertation in 1963. In 1961 he taught for the first time at the University of Chicago, where, with many trips to India and elsewhere, he taught linguistics, South Asian languages and civilizations, and creative writing until his death on 13 July 1993. A preeminent scholar of South Indian language and culture, Ramanujan, known as "Raman" among his friends, was honored in 1976 with the Padma Shri by the Indian government. With his wife Molly Ramanujan, he had two children, a son and a daughter. Along with his poetry and essays, his major works of translation include *The Interior Landscape: Love Poems from a Classical Tamil Anthology* (1967), *Speaking of Siva* (from Kannada, 1973), and *Hymns for the Drowning* (from Tamil, 1983).

19. R. Parthasarathy, "How It Strikes a Contemporary: The Poetry of A. K. Ramanujan," *Literary Criterion* 12, nos. 2–3 (1976): 196.

20. Gilles Deleuze and Félix Guattari, *Kafka: Towards a Minor Literature,* trans. Dana Polan (Minneapolis: University of Minnesota Press, 1986).

21. A. K. Ramanujan, "Telling Tales," in *Collected Essays,* 450 (first published in *Daedalus* 118, no. 4 [1989]: 241).

22. Cited in Parthasarathy, "How It Strikes a Contemporary," 197.

23. Ramanujan, "Afterword," 297. On Ramanujan as translator, see Vinay Dharwadker, "A. K. Ramanujan's Theory and Practice of Translation," in *Post-colonial Translation: Theory and Practice,* ed. Susan Bassnett and Harish Trivedi (New York: Routledge, 1999), 114–40.

24. Ramanujan, "Classics Lost and Found," 189.

25. Mary Louise Pratt coins "contact zone" "to refer to the space of colonial encounters" (*Imperial Eyes: Travel Writing and Transculturation* [New York: Routledge, 1992], 6–7). Homi K. Bhabha uses the term "Third Space" for the "*in-between* space" of "enunciation" and "hybridization" (*The Location of Culture* [London: Routledge, 1994], 36–39).

26. A. K. Ramanujan, *The Collected Poems* (Delhi: Oxford University Press, 1995), 189–90. All further references to Ramanujan's poetry are to this volume and are given parenthetically in the text. For a comparison between literary translation and the intercultural dynamics of postcolonial literature, see Maria Tymoczko, "Post-colonial Writing and Literary Translation," in *Post-colonial Translation,* ed. Bassnett and Trivedi, 19–40. For reflections on translation and the transnational, see Homi K. Bhabha, "Unpacking My Library . . . Again," in *The Post-colonial Question,* ed. Iain Chambers and Lidia Curti (New York: Routledge, 1996), 203–4.

27. Knowing that he is hardly "at a loss" in material terms, Ramanujan ironically alludes to the financial "change" in the fortune of the expatriate academic, who thinks in an American bank of the "dying children" of India.

28. Ramanujan, "Classics Lost and Found," 185. In a humorous anecdote about an American linguist who collected tribal songs in South India, Ramanujan recounts how, upon returning, the linguist found "to his great surprise they sang to him new songs about a white man who had collected songs among them several years earlier." Bruce King comments on the changeability and irrecuperability of the past in Ramanujan (*Three Indian Poets: Nissim*

Ezekiel, A. K. Ramanujan, Dom Moraes [Madras and New York: Oxford University Press], 74).

29. Frantz Fanon, *The Wretched of the Earth,* trans. Constance Farrington (New York: Grove Press-Présence Africaine, 1963), 210, 221–26.

30. A. K. Ramanujan, "A Conversation with A. K. Ramanujan," interview by Rama Jha, *Humanities Review* 3, no. 1 (1981): 7.

31. Rashmi Bhatnagar, "Uses and Limits of Foucault: A Study of the Theme of Origins in Edward Said's *Orientalism,*" *Social Scientist* 158 (1986): 5. Gayatri Chakravorty Spivak similarly warns against postcolonial "nostalgias for lost origins" in *A Critique of Postcolonial Reason* (Cambridge, Mass.: Harvard University Press, 1999), 306. See also Benita Parry, who cites Bhatnagar but offers a spirited defense of "nativism" in "Resistance Theory/Theorising Resistance; Or, Two Cheers for Nativism," in *Colonial Discourse/Postcolonial Theory,* ed. Francis Barker, Peter Hulme, and Margaret Iversen (Manchester: Manchester University Press, 1994), 172–96.

32. Ramanujan, "Classics Lost and Found," 184.

33. Ramanujan, "A Conversation," 7, 8.

34. Ramanujan, "Where Mirrors Are Windows," *History of Religions,* 215; in the *Collected Essays* version, the text reads "mirror in mirror" (32), no longer echoing Yeats's "The Statues" (*The Poems,* rev. ed., ed. Richard J. Finneran [New York: Macmillan, 1989], 337).

35. See Vinay Dharwadker's introduction to *The Collected Poems,* by Ramanujan, xxxvii.

36. Bhabha writes that in "flawed colonial mimesis," "to be Anglicized is *emphatically* not to be English" (*Location of Culture,* 87).

37. Michel Foucault, "Nietzsche, Genealogy and History," in *Language, Counter Memory, Practice,* ed. Donald F. Bouchard (Ithaca, N.Y.: Cornell University Press, 1977), 142–43.

38. Ramanujan, "Afterword," 314, 263, 246.

39. Dharwadker, introduction to *Collected Poems,* xxxiv. On "the plurality of identity in Ramanujan's poetry," see also Chirantan Kulshrestha, "The Self in A. K. Ramanujan's Poetry," in *Contemporary Indian English Verse,* ed. Chirantan Kulshrestha (Atlantic Highlands, N.J.: Humanities Press, 1981), 179; and P. K. J. Kurup, *Contemporary Poetry in English* (New Delhi: Atlantic, 1991), 189.

40. Salman Rushdie, *Imaginary Homelands* (London: Granta-Penguin, 1991), 394.

41. Ramanujan, "Is There an Indian Way?" 46.

42. Ibid., 40–41.

43. Ibid., 48. For a critical discussion of Ramanujan's distinctions, see Fred Dallmayr, "Western Thought and Indian Thought: Comments on Ramanujan," *Philosophy East and West* 44, no. 3 (1994): 527–42.

44. Ramanujan invites comparison between the Hindu myth of the god that "splits himself into male and female" with "the androgynous figure in Plato's *Symposium,* halved into male and female segments which forever seek each other and crave union" ("Some Thoughts on 'Non-Western' Classics, with Indian Examples," in *Collected Essays,* 122, 119—first published in *World Literature Today* 68 [1994]: 334, 332).

45. Ramanujan, "Afterword," 282.

46. According to M. K. Naik, the poem is about India's great creative synthesis of cults, cultures, and races ("A. K. Ramanujan and the Search for Roots," in *Living Indian English Poets,* ed. Madhusudan Prasad [New Delhi: Sterling Publishers Private Ltd., 1989], 18–19).

47. Ramanujan translates and discusses this poem from the *Taittiriya Upanishad* in

"Some Thoughts on 'Non-Western' Classics," 119–20, and "Food for Thought: Towards an Anthology of Hindu Food-Images," in *Collected Essays*, 74–75—first published in *The Eternal Food: Gastronomic Ideas and Experiences of Hindus and Buddhists*, ed. R. S. Khare [Albany: State University of New York Press, 1992], 222–23). See Bruce King's discussion of the allusion in his *Three Indian Poets*, 87.

48. Ramanujan, "Food for Thought," 75.

49. Ramanujan, "Where Mirrors Are Windows," 19–20.

50. See Yeats's "On a Picture of a Black Centaur by Edmund Dulac" and "Conjunctions" (*Poems*, 215, 288).

51. Musing in a later poem on the strange metamorphoses of the dead, Ramanujan writes that "Gandhi and King / . . . live and die / again and again" in shop photographs, coins and bills, and revisionist biographies ("A Report," in *Collected Poems*, 248).

52. For a critique of the family trope to signify postcolonial ethnicity, see Paul Gilroy, *The Black Atlantic: Modernity and Double Consciousness* (Cambridge, Mass.: Harvard University Press, 1993), 98–99.

53. Mark Turner, *Death is the Mother of Beauty: Mind, Metaphor, Criticism* (Chicago: University of Chicago Press, 1987), 12.

54. The conflict was one of cosmopolitanism (Bhabha) and indigeneity (Parthasarathy). See Homi K. Bhabha, "Indo-Anglian Attitudes," review of *Selected Poems*, by A. K. Ramanujan, *Rough Passage*, by R. Parthasarathy, and *Ten Twentieth-Century Indian Poets*, ed. R. Parthasarathy et al., *Times Literary Supplement* (3 February 1978), 136; see also R. Parthasarathy's critique (10 March 1978), 285; and Bhabha's reply (21 April 1978), 445. Parthasarathy's comment on the metaphor of the family appears in "How It Strikes a Contemporary," 189. On the family in Ramanujan, see also Shirish Chindhade, *Five Indian Poets* (New Delhi: Atlantic, 1996), 62–90; A. N. Dwivedi, *The Poetic Art of A. K. Ramanujan* (Delhi: B. R. Publishing Corp., 1995); Lakshmi Raghunandan, *Contemporary Indian Poetry in English* (New Delhi: Reliance, 1990), 150–202; and Emmanuel Narendra Lall, *The Poetry of Encounter: Three Indo-Anglian Poets* (New Delhi: Sterling, 1983), 42–64.

55. In a fascinating comparison between the Oedipus myth and Indian myths of the family, Ramanujan argues that "the *direction* of aggression or desire" is the opposite in the Indian myths: "most often we have fathers (or father-figures) suppressing sons and desiring daughters." Ramanujan speculates that, unlike modern Western culture, where the heroic quest is individuation "achieved through an overthrow of the father," "the Indian hero's quest is to fulfill his father, his family," in accordance with a traditional culture's need "to use and absorb the vitality of the young" ("The Indian Oedipus," in *Collected Essays*, 392, 394—first published in *Oedipus: A Folklore Casebook*, ed. Lowell Edmunds and Alan Dundes [Madison: University of Wisconsin Press, 1995], 252, 254–55).

56. Ramanujan continues: "One is often struck by the impression that Indian males repress their 'independence' as American males repress their 'dependence'" ("The Indian Oedipus," 393–94). In the poem "Highway Stripper," cross-gender identification is so powerful that it seems to obliterate distances not only between man and woman but also the cognate distance between one place and another, the speaker wondering finally if he is

> moulting, shedding
> vestiges,
> old investments,
> rushing forever

towards a perfect
coupling
with naked nothing
in a world
without places?
(166)

57. Ramanujan, "Is There an Indian Way?" 46, and "The Indian Oedipus," 394.

58. Ramanujan describes his father's appearance and thinking in "Is There an Indian Way?" 35. Edward C. Dimmock, Jr., and Krishna Ramanujan say that the poet was "both embarrassed and amused by the cover" ("Introduction: Two Tributes to A. K. Ramanujan," in *Collected Essays,* by Ramanujan, xv).

Chapter Five: Louise Bennett

1. Javed Majeed, "Amitav Ghosh's *In an Antique Land:* The Ethnographer-Historian and the Limits of Irony," *Journal of Commonwealth Literature* 30 (1995): 52, 54. This charge echoes the suspicion that celebrated postcolonial writers are Westernized, bourgeois, alienated from the politics and material realities of decolonizing societies; see Aijaz Ahmad, *In Theory: Classes, Nations, Literatures* (Oxford: Oxford University Press, 1992).

2. Wayne C. Booth, *A Rhetoric of Irony* (Chicago: University of Chicago Press, 1974), 29, citing Søren Kierkegaard, *The Concept of Irony, with Constant Reference to Socrates,* trans. Lee M. Capel (London: Collins, 1966), 265. On the view that irony is socially conservative, see Linda Hutcheon, *Irony's Edge: The Theory and Politics of Irony* (New York: Routledge, 1995), 29, 54.

3. Booth, *A Rhetoric of Irony,* 177.

4. Vaheed K. Ramazani, *The Free Indirect Mode: Flaubert and the Poetics of Irony* (Charlottesville: University Press of Virginia, 1988), 15, 26.

5. Linda Hutcheon, "'Circling the Downspout of Empire': Post-colonialism and Postmodernism," *Ariel* 20, no. 4 (1989): 161–62.

6. Ramazani, *The Free Indirect Mode,* 20.

7. D. C. Muecke, *The Compass of Irony* (London: Methuen, 1969), 19, 25–27.

8. Ibid., 29.

9. Booth, *A Rhetoric of Irony,* 40, 127.

10. Ramazani, *The Free Indirect Mode,* 24.

11. For an overview, see Hutcheon, *Irony's Edge,* 30–32.

12. Hutcheon, "'Circling the Downspout,'" 162.

13. Hutcheon's book on irony implicitly critiques the simpler view advanced in her essay on postcoloniality: "Irony's edge cuts many ways," she remarks (*Irony's Edge,* 176). "Irony's transideological politics," she adds, "complicate the theorizing of irony mightily, and part of the reason is irony's edge" (202).

14. Booth, *A Rhetoric of Irony,* 28, 29.

15. The fullest discussions of Bennett's work are Rex Nettleford's introduction and headnotes to *Jamaica Labrish,* by Louise Bennett (Kingston: Sangster's Book Stores, 1966), 9–24; Lloyd W. Brown, *West Indian Poetry* (Boston: Twayne-G. K. Hall, 1978), 100–101, 106–17; Mervyn Morris's introduction, as well as notes and comments, to *Selected Poems,* by Louise Bennett, ed. Mervyn Morris, corrected ed. (1982; reprint, Kingston: Sangster's Book Stores, 1983), iii–xix, 120–64, and "Louise Bennett in Print," *Caribbean Quarterly* 28, nos. 1, 2

(1982): 44–56; Carolyn Cooper, *Noises in the Blood: Orality, Gender and the "Vulgar" Body of Jamaican Popular Culture,* Warwick University Caribbean Series (London: Macmillan, 1993), chaps. 2, 3, and 9. I have benefited from Nettleford's placement of Bennett's work in its social and historical context; Brown's indications of the significance of her ironic rhetorical strategies; and Cooper's insights into the proverbial, oral, and gendered character of Bennett's poetry. I owe a pervasive debt to Morris's incisive and ample annotations, as well as to his argument for close literary readings of her work. See also Louis James, introduction to *The Islands in Between: Essays on West Indian Literature,* ed. Louis James (London: Oxford University Press, 1968), 15–17; Gordon Roehlehr, "The Folk in Caribbean Literature," *Tapia* 2 (24 December 1972): 8–11; George Panton, "Our Well-Known, Well-Beloved Poet," *Daily Gleaner,* 11 August 1974, 23; Barbara Gloudon, "The Hon. Louise Bennett, O.J.: Fifty Years of Laughter," *Jamaica Journal* 19, no. 3 (1986): 2–11; Bruce Woodcock, "'Long Memoried Women': Caribbean Women Poets," in *Black Women's Writing,* ed. Gina Wisker (New York: St. Martin's Press, 1993), 55–77; Elizabeth A. Wheeler, "Riddym Ravings: Female and National Identity in Jamaican Poetry," in *Imagination, Emblems and Expressions: Essays on Latin American, Caribbean, and Continental Culture and Identity,* ed. Helen Ryan-Hansom (Bowling Green, Ohio: Popular, 1993), 139–53; Angela Smith, "Long Memoried Women: Oodgeroo Noonuccal and Jamaican Poet, Louise Bennett," *Australian Literary Studies* 16, no. 4 (1994): 77–91; and Anita Haya Patterson, "Contingencies of Pleasure: Jamaican Women's Poetry," in *Feminist Consequences: Theory of the New Century,* ed. Elisabeth Bronfen (New York: Columbia University Press, in press).

Perhaps a bald recitation of events in Bennett's life would be helpful. She was born on 7 September 1919 in Kingston Jamaica. Her mother was a dressmaker, her father a baker who died when she was seven. While still in high school, she began to perform her creole poetry, making her debut performance in 1938 at the age of nineteen. She published her first book of poetry, *Dialect Verses,* in 1942, and in 1943 she began to publish poetry on a weekly basis in the *Sunday Gleaner.* She studied journalism, social work, and local folklore in Jamaica. From 1945 to 1947 she attended the Royal Academy of Dramatic Art in London on a British Council scholarship. Returning homesick to Jamaica to teach high school drama for two years, she went back to Britain to resume her acting career and her work on a special Caribbean program for the BBC. She lived in the United States from 1953 to 1955, performing on radio and the stage in New York and its environs. Marrying her long-time associate Eric Coverley in 1954, she returned to Jamaica in 1955. While writing and performing her poetry, she also gathered Jamaican folklore, traveled extensively in her work as drama specialist for the Jamaica Social Welfare Commission (1955–63), lectured on folklore and drama at the University of the West Indies (1959–61), and created her own radio and television programs. Her awards include the Order of Jamaica (1974) and the Musgrave Gold Medal of the Institute of Jamaica (1978). In recent years, she and her husband have been living in Canada.

16. Advertisement, *Jamaica Journal* 19, no. 3 (1986): 9.

17. See, e.g., the interpretation of the Yoruba trickster Esu-Elegbara and his African-American counterpart, the Signifying Monkey, in Henry Louis Gates, Jr., *The Signifying Monkey: A Theory of Afro-American Literary Criticism* (New York: Oxford University Press, 1988), chaps. 1 and 2.

18. Daryl C. Dance, *Folklore from Contemporary Jamaicans* (Knoxville: University of Tennessee Press, 1985), 12. See also Elisa Janine Sobo, *One Blood: The Jamaican Body* (Albany:

State University of New York Press, 1993): "Anansi, a folk-tale spider and a culture hero handed down from 'first time' slaves, is well known for getting things free through hilarious tricks that 'disadvantage' those who would control him. A trickster-hero, he does and says things real people, especially those ruled by others, cannot" (93).

19. On the reimagining of Anancy by various writers, see Helen Tiffin, "The Metaphor of Anancy in Caribbean Literature," in *Myth and Metaphor,* ed. Robert Sellick (Adelaide: Centre for Research in the New Literatures in English, 1982), 15–52. Not all West Indian writers have conceived of Anancy as a positive model for the artist. Glossing the figure of Anancy in Brathwaite's *Arrivants,* e.g., Gordon Roehlehr writes, "Here Ananse represents the atrophied and self-evasive sensibility of early Caribbean artists" (*Pathfinder: Black Awakening in "The Arrivants" of Edward Kamau Brathwaite* [Tunapuna, Trinidad: Gordon Roehlehr, 1981], 182).

20. In childhood, writes Bennett, "we would swap stories about Anancy, the 'trickify' little spider man who speaks with a lisp and lives by his wits. He is both comic and sinister, both hero and villain of the folk stories. Bra'nancy, as he is affectionately called, is a lovable rascal who has magical powers and his stories make it quite plain that he is able to get away with tricks which ordinary mortals can't. Every existing custom is said to have been started by Anancy (is Anancy meck it)" (introduction to *Poetry in the Caribbean,* by Julie Pearn [London: Hodder & Stoughton, 1985], iii). According to Jeremy Poynting, "It was not really until the work of Louise Bennett and Andrew Salkey . . . that the [Anancy] tradition was fully recuperated as an adult one" ("From Ancestral to Creole: Humans and Animals in a West Indian Scale of Values," in *Monsters, Tricksters, and Sacred Cows: Animal Tales and American Identities,* ed. A. James Arnold, New World Studies [Charlottesville: University Press of Virginia, 1996], 208).

21. Carolyn Cooper, "That Cunny Jamma Oman: Representations of Female Sensibility in the Poetry of Louise Bennett," in *Noises in the Blood,* 47–48.

22. Dance, *Folklore from Contemporary Jamaicans,* 12.

23. F. G. Cassidy and R. B. Le Page, eds., *Dictionary of Jamaican English,* 2d ed. (Cambridge: Cambridge University Press, 1980), xxxvii–xliii. See also R. B. Le Page and Andrée Tabouret-Keller, *Acts of Identity: Creole-Based Approaches to Language and Ethnicity* (Cambridge: Cambridge University Press, 1985). On Jamaican language and class, see Lisa Douglass, *The Power of Sentiment: Love, Hierarchy, and the Jamaican Family Elite* (Boulder, Colo.: Westview Press, 1992), 80–83. Jamaican English or creole is also referred to as "patois" (the local term), "dialect" (now seen as pejorative), and a variety of "nation language" (Kamau Brathwaite's honorific term, especially for the "the *submerged*" or "African" aspects of the language). See Edward Kamau Brathwaite, *History of the Voice: The Development of Nation Language in Anglophone Caribbean Poetry* (London: New Beacon Books, 1984), 13. For an introduction to the issue of West Indian creole as a literary language, see the essays by R. B. Le Page, Gerald Moore, Mervyn Morris, John Figueroa, and Gordon Roehlehr in pt. 4, "A Language of One's Own," in *Critics on Caribbean Literature,* ed. Edward Baugh (London: George Allen & Unwin, 1978), 123–61. With regard to poetry, see also Laurence A. Breiner, *An Introduction to West Indian Poetry* (Cambridge: Cambridge University Press, 1998); J. Edward Chamberlin, *Come Back to Me My Language: Poetry and the West Indies* (Urbana: University of Illinois Press, 1993); and Paula Burnett, introduction to *The Penguin Book of West Indian Verse in English,* ed. Paula Burnett (New York: Penguin, 1986), xxiii–lxiv.

24. Morris, introduction to *Selected Poems,* by Bennett, xiii.

25. Cited in Dance, *Folklore from Contemporary Jamaicans*, 12.

26. "Why People Now Eat Rabbit" exemplifies periphrasis: when Rabbit's magic mounds kill anyone who counts to ten, Anancy counts "Nine, Plus One," inducing Rabbit to kill himself with the word "Ten" in "Why People Now Eat Rabbit" (Louise Bennett, *Anancy Stories and Dialect Verse* [1950; reprint, Kingston: Pioneer Press, 1957], 36–37). "Anancy an' Crab" offers an example of phonemic distortion: Anancy heightens the strangeness of his speech as a ruse to fool Crab, saying "'Tank yuh sar, but me ish not from dese parts an me doan tink me wi se' yuh again, but ah wi memba yuh promish.' (Anancy tongue tie.)" (Bennett, *Anancy Stories,* 17, and *Anancy and Miss Lou,* ed. Mervyn Morris (Kingston: Sangster's Book Stores, 1979), 12).

27. Bennett, introduction to *Poetry in the Caribbean,* by Pearn, iv; Louise Bennett, "Bennett on Bennett," interview by Dennis Scott, *Caribbean Quarterly* 14, nos. 1, 2 (1968): 97.

28. Brathwaite, *History of the Voice,* 27.

29. Brown, *West Indian Poetry,* 101.

30. She says, "wat me cross out gawn like storm / An wat me lef kean wrong" (Louise Bennett, "Votin' Lis'," in *Jamaica Labrish,* 134).

31. Rex Nettleford's headnote to the poem (in ibid., 133).

32. Bennett, "Rightful Way," in *Jamaica Labrish,* 134–35.

33. Roger D. Abrahams, *The Man-of-Words in the West Indies: Performance and the Emergence of Creole Culture* (Baltimore: Johns Hopkins University Press, 1983), 57. Abrahams's account derives, in part, from Peter J. Wilson's discussion of West Indian "reputation" in *Crab Antics: A Social Anthropology of English-Speaking Negro Societies in the Caribbean* (New Haven, Conn.: Yale University Press, 1973). Among the recent adaptations of Wilson and Abrahams, see Richard D. E. Burton, *Afro-Creole* (Ithaca, N.Y.: Cornell University Press, 1997), 156–73. Jean Besson modifies Wilson's thesis to indicate that West Indian women participate not only in a Euro-Caribbean mode of "respectability" but in the Afro-Caribbean system of "reputation" as well ("Reputation and Respectability Reconsidered: A New Perspective on Afro-Caribbean Peasant Women," in *Women and Change in the Caribbean: A Pan-Caribbean Perspective,* ed. Janet H. Momsen [Kingston: Ian Randle Publishers; Bloomington: Indiana University Press, 1993], 14–37).

34. Bennett, "Jamaica Oman," in *Selected Poems,* 21–23. All further references to this edition appear parenthetically in the text.

35. Abrahams, *The Man-of-Words in the West Indies,* 58.

36. Bennett, "Bennett on Bennett," 100.

37. Abrahams, *The Man-of-Words in the West Indies,* 86.

38. Bennett, "Bennett on Bennett," 98.

39. Ibid., 97.

40. Ibid., 99.

41. Derek Walcott, "Fiddle, Chac Chac and Drum Take Over," *Sunday Guardian* (Trinidad), 26 July 1964, 4. Living in Jamaica, Walcott, like Bennett, deplored "execrable" Jamaican poetry written in Victorian English and promoted by the Poetry League, but in his articles surveying Jamaican poetry, he is unable to recognize Bennett as a poetic alternative ("Some Jamaican Poets," pts. 1 and 2, *Public Opinion* [Jamaica], 3 August 1957, 7, and 10 August 1957, 7, respectively).

42. In his 1979 discussion of Bennett (published in 1984), Brathwaite is generally appreciative but regrets "the tyranny of the pentametre" in her poetry (*History of the Voice,* 26–30).

43. Mikhail Bakhtin, *Rabelais and His World,* trans. Hélène Iswolsky (Bloomington: Indiana University Press, 1984), 89.

44. Silvio Torres-Saillant urges that the Caribbean "has produced its own metadiscourse with which to speak about its own cultural artifacts" (*Caribbean Poetics: Toward an Aesthetic of West Indian Literature* [Cambridge: Cambridge University Press, 1997], 29).

45. Morris, "Louise Bennett in Print," 45, 49.

46. Bennett, "Bennett on Bennett," 98.

47. Bennett, "Jamaica Language," in *Aunty Roachy Seh,* ed. Mervyn Morris (Kingston: Sangster's Book Stores, 1993), 1.

48. Cassidy and Le Page, eds., *Dictionary of Jamaican English,* lxii.

49. Katherine Wiggan, "Comedy and Creole in Selvon's London Stories," in *The Comic Vision in West Indian Literature,* ed. Roydon Salick (Marabella, Trinidad: Printex Converters, 1993), 20.

50. Although M. M. Bakhtin is describing the novel, his analysis bears on poetry by Bennett and other postcolonial writers (*The Dialogic Imagination: Four Essays,* ed. Michael Holquist, trans. Caryl Emerson and Michael Holquist [Austin: University of Texas Press, 1981], 360–61).

51. See the entries for these words in Cassidy and Le Page, eds., *Dictionary of Jamaican English;* and Morris's notes to *Selected Poems,* by Bennett, 120.

52. Ramazani, *The Free Indirect Mode,* 25. On mimicry and postcolonial ambivalence, see Homi K. Bhabha, *The Location of Culture* (New York: Routledge, 1994), 85–92.

53. Wole Soyinka, *Death and the King's Horseman* (1975; reprint, New York: Noonday, 1989), 37–39.

54. Morris's note, *Selected Poems,* by Bennett, 121. For Smith, too, the phrase instances Bennett's "celebration of the vitality and ingenuity of the language" ("Long Memoried Woman," 88).

55. Morris's note, *Selected Poems,* by Bennett, 121.

56. On code switching, see Le Page and Tabouret-Keller, *Acts of Identity* 94–96, 100–102, 156–57; Bill Ashcroft, Gareth Griffiths, and Helen Tiffin, *The Empire Writes Back: Theory and Practice in Post-colonial Literatures* (New York: Routledge, 1989), 46–48, 72–77; and Breiner, *Introduction to West Indian Poetry,* 180–85.

57. Hutcheon, *Irony's Edge,* 54–55, 94. See the discussion of how both creole and ethnic humor unify through separation, reinforcing "in-group/out-group boundaries," in Bryan Bott, Robin Bott, and Barbara Fennell, "Titas, Blalahs, and Haoles: Linguistic Markers of In-Group/Out-Group Status in Hawaiian Ethnic Humor," *Essays in Arts and Sciences* 24 (October 1995): 77–100.

58. Hutcheon, *Irony's Edge,* 98, 91.

59. According to Lisa Douglass, "Jamaicans make reference to color in their daily practices, but they claim that what they call 'color prejudice,' whether black or white, is a rare and unfortunate individual trait, or they view it as a thing of the past" (*The Power of Sentiment,* 8). "The prevalence of dark skin notwithstanding, whiteness is a valued characteristic here and most Jamaicans consider it insulting to be called black by fellow islanders. African heritage is often denied or submerged. . . . Color prejudice . . . is still prevalent"; "The Jamaican social system has been characterized as a color and class system in which people rank each other, both conceptually and practically (as in hiring practices and marriage preferences), according to skin color" (Sobo, *One Blood,* 21, 22).

60. Bennett, "Class an Colour Debate," in *Aunty Roachy Seh*, 29.

61. Hutcheon, *Irony's Edge*, 60; Ramazani, *The Free Indirect Mode*, 25, citing Lionel Duisit.

62. See Bennett's discussion of the abundant onomatopoeia in Jamaican English in "Jamaica Language," 2.

63. Bennett, "Colour-Bar," in *Jamaica Labrish*, 211.

64. Cassidy and Le Page, eds., *Dictionary of Jamaican English*, 317.

65. Bakhtin, *Rabelais*, 11–12.

66. Susan Willis, "Caliban as Poet: Reversing the Maps of Domination," *Massachusetts Review* 23 (1982): 615–30.

67. My account is indebted to the discussion of the *Windrush* and governmental reaction in Kathleen Paul, "Keeping Britain White," in *Whitewashing Britain: Race and Citizenship in the Postwar Era* (Ithaca, N.Y.: Cornell University Press, 1997), 111–30.

68. Ibid., 121.

69. *Oxford English Dictionary*, 2d ed., s.v. "populate."

70. As Lloyd Brown observes, "The rambunctious Jamaican self-esteem is skillfully interwoven with a pointed self-criticism to create an impressively ambiguous image of the poet's subject" (*West Indian Poetry*, 115).

71. For another reading of this poem, see Cooper, *Noises in the Blood*, 175–77.

72. Fanon, *The Wretched of the Earth*, 88.

73. Ibid., 89.

74. Bennett, *Jamaica Labrish*, 511.

75. See Morris's note in Bennett, *Selected Poems*, 159. Brown sees the poem as a "spirited attack on British colonialism" (*West Indian Poetry*, 114).

76. Cooper calls Bennett's use of proverbs in this "potentially explosive context . . . an excellent example of linguistic subterfuge, indirection as a strategy to preserve psychic equilibrium" (*Noises in the Blood*, 60).

77. Edouard Glissant, *Caribbean Discourse: Selected Essays*, trans. J. Michael Dash (Charlottesville: University Press of Virginia, 1989), 125.

78. Ibid., 21, 128.

79. Bennett, "Jamaica Language," 2.

80. Walter DeSouza, "This Is My Land," *Sunday Gleaner,* 5 August 1962, 32.

81. "Midnight Tonight—a Date with Destiny," *Sunday Gleaner,* 5 August 1962, 1.

82. *Sunday Gleaner,* 5 August 1962, page 33.

83. Jay Munroe, "Your World and Mine: When the Flag Goes Up," *Sunday Gleaner,* 5 August 1962, 8.

84. Later, Louise Bennett pointed to this collection as the first anthology to include her poetry ("Bennett on Bennett," 98); but the inclusion remained remarkably exclusionary: Bennett's poetry was grouped not in the section for poetry proper but with other "miscellaneous" and implicitly subpoetic pieces.

85. Emphasizing the anti-imperial dimension of the independence poems, Cooper reads them as instances of satire and parody (*Noises in the Blood*, 177–82). For more on the historical issues, see Gordon Lewis, "The Challenge of Independence in the British Caribbean," in *Caribbean Freedom: Society and Economy from Emancipation to the Present,* ed. Hilary Beckles and Verene Shepherd (Kingston: Ian Randle Publishers, 1993), 511–18; and Rex Nettleford, "Race, Identity and Independence in Jamaica," in *Caribbean Freedom,* ed. Beckles and Shepherd, 519–27.

86. Bennett, "Is Me," in *Jamaica Labrish,* 140.

87. Elleke Boehme, *Colonial and Postcolonial Literature* (New York: Oxford University Press, 1995), 184.

88. Morris glosses "capture" as "ironic, as though Jamaica is being captured again, as by the Spanish in 1494, and the English in 1655. The word also carries a resonance from Rastafarian usage: to 'capture' land is to occupy it illegally" (*Selected Poems,* by Bennett, 161).

89. Charles Wolfe, "The Burial of Sir John Moore," in *The Poems of Charles Wolfe* (London: A. H. Bullen, 1903), 1, lines 1–4. Morris notes, "In the parody of 'The Burial of Sir John Moore at Corunna,' a British piece much recited by Jamaican schoolchildren in the colonial period, it is as if the colonizer is being buried while a new nation is born" (*Selected Poems,* by Bennett, 161–62).

90. Bennett, "Dear Departed Federation," in *Jamaica Labrish,* 168–69.

91. Brown, *West Indian Poetry,* 115.

92. "Independence Finds a Ready Jamaica," *Sunday Gleaner,* 5 August 1962, 9.

93. "I Know You Will Respond to the Challenge," *Daily Gleaner,* 8 August 1962, 1.

94. Willis, "Caliban as Poet," 615–30.

95. Bahktin, *Rabelais,* 6, 90, 92, 123.

96. David Dabydeen, "On Not Being Milton: Nigger Talk in England Today," in *The State of the Language,* ed. Christopher Ricks and Leonard Michaels (London: Faber & Faber, 1990), 6, 11–12.

Chapter Six: Okot p'Bitek

1. Charles R. Larson, *The Emergence of African Fiction* (Bloomington: Indiana University Press, 1972), 44.

2. Christopher L. Miller, *Theories of Africans: Francophone Literature and Anthropology in Africa* (Chicago: University of Chicago Press, 1990), 6, 4.

3. Kwame Anthony Appiah, *In My Father's House: Africa in the Philosophy of Culture* (New York: Oxford University Press, 1992), 68. Appiah directly criticizes Miller's views (62–64) and briefly discusses *Song of Lawino* (66–67).

4. Ibid., 62–72.

5. Amitav Ghosh, "The Imam and the Indian," *Granta* 20 (1986): 136–46; David Scott, "Locating the Anthropological Subject: Postcolonial Anthropologists in Other Places," *Inscriptions* 5 (1989): 75–85; James Clifford, *Routes: Travel and Translation in the Late Twentieth Century* (Cambridge, Mass.: Harvard University Press, 1997), 1–2, 4–6.

6. "Acoli" is pronounced and sometimes spelled "Acholi." The Acoli language was also known by the broader designation "Luo" or "Lwo," and *Song of Lawino* itself uses "Luo."

7. Chinweizu, Onwuchekwa Jemie, and Ihechukwu Madubuike, *Toward the Decolonization of African Literature* (Washington, D.C.: Howard University Press, 1983), 163, 259. On the pivotal influence of *Song of Lawino* on East African writing, see Michael R. Ward, "Okot p'Bitek and the Rise of East African Writing," in *A Celebration of Black and African Writing,* ed. Bruce King and Kolawole Ogungbesan (Ibadan, Nigeria: Oxford University Press Nigeria, 1975), 217–31.

8. Ngugi wa Thiong'o, introduction to *Africa's Cultural Revolution,* by Okot p'Bitek (Nairobi: Macmillan, 1973), xi.

9. Bernth Lindfors, "The Songs of Okot p'Bitek," in *The Writing of East and Central Africa,* ed. G. D. Killam (London: Heinemann, 1984), 144, 146.

10. Nkem Okoh, "Writing African Oral Literature: A Reading of Okot p'Bitek's *Song of Lawino,*" *Bridges* (Dakar, Senegal) 5, no. 2 (1993): 51.

11. G. A. Heron, introduction to *"Song of Lawino" and "Song of Ocol,"* by Okot p'Bitek (Oxford: Heinemann, 1984), 1, 8. All quotations from these poems will be cited parenthetically in the text.

12. Okot, *Africa's Cultural Revolution,* vii.

13. Ibid., 1–2.

14. Ibid., 2–3.

15. Ibid., 3.

16. Kirsten Petersen, "Okot p'Bitek: Interview," *Kunapipi* 1, no. 1 (1979): 89; Bernth Lindfors, "An Interview with Okot p'Bitek," *World Literature Written in English* 16 (1977): 282–83.

17. Lindfors, "Interview with Okot," 283.

18. Okot remarked to an interviewer, "The tradition I grew up in had love songs, funeral songs and so on and so forth to be danced, to celebrate particular important occasions, birth and circumcision and so on and so forth," in contrast to his "long, long, long songs," which are generically "a new thing altogether" (Lee Nichols, "Okot p'Bitek" [1978], in *Conversations with African Writers,* ed. Lee Nichols [Washington, D.C.: Voice of America, 1981], 250). Studies of the influence of Acoli oral traditions on Okot's poetry include Charles Okumu, "The Form of Okot p'Bitek's Poetry: Literary Borrowing from Acoli Oral Traditions," *Research in African Literatures* 23, no. 3 (1992): 53–66; Okoh, "Writing African Oral Literature," 35–53; and Gerald Moore, "The Horn of the Grasslands," in *Twelve African Writers* (London: Hutchinson University Library for Africa, 1980), 174–76. But Okumu observes that "Okot's songs can neither be sung nor fitted into the thematic classification of Acoli oral songs. Oral songs are composed in response to an immediate event or as a means of reflecting a localized issue within the village or clan" ("Form of Okot's Poetry," 55).

19. Lindfors, "Interview with Okot," 282; Petersen, "Okot: Interview," 89; Nichols, "Okot p'Bitek," 245.

20. Henry Wadsworth Longfellow, *The Song of Hiawatha* (1855; reprint, New York: Federal Book Co., 1902), 10–11.

21. To fill in further the biographical details, Okot p'Bitek was born in 1931 in Gulu, Uganda. His father was a Protestant schoolteacher but also an accomplished dancer and storyteller from the Patiko chiefdom, his mother a famous composer of songs and a dancer. He attended Gulu High School, King's College, Budo, and the Mbara Teachers Training College. In 1953 he published his first book, a novel in Acoli entitled *Lak tar,* later translated as *White Teeth,* and in 1956 an early Acoli version of *Wer pa Lawino* was rejected by a publisher's agent. As a schoolteacher, he played for several years on the Ugandan national soccer team, which eventually led to his studies in Britain. In the wake of Ugandan independence in 1962, Okot returned to teach and work in the extramural department at Makerere University in Kampala in 1963, also serving as the director of the Uganda National Cultural Centre (1966–68), before being forced out of this post for political reasons. During eleven years of enforced exile from Uganda, Okot taught in African studies, sociology, and literature at the University of Nairobi, Kenya, with brief visiting appointments at the University of Texas and the University of Iowa's writing program. Under the tyrannical and murderous rule of Idi Amin (1971–79), many of Okot's relatives in Uganda were killed. In the last few years of his life, Okot taught at the University of Ife, Nigeria, and at Makerere University, where he died in 1982. Along with *Song of Lawino* and *Song of Ocol,* Okot published the poetic monologues *Song of*

Prisoner (1971) and *Song of Malaya* (1971). Author of several books of anthropology, Okot also collected and translated folk songs in *The Horn of My Love* (1974), folktales in *Hare and Hornbill* (1978), and *Acholi Proverbs* (1985). For more on Okot's life, see G. A. Heron, *The Poetry of Okot p'Bitek* (London: Heinemann, 1976), 1–5; Lubwa p'Chong, "A Biographical Sketch," in *Artist, the Ruler,* by Okot p'Bitek (Nairobi: Heinemann, 1986), 1–12; Monica Nalyaka Wanambisi, *Thought and Technique in the Poetry of Okot p'Bitek* (New York: Vantage Press, 1984), 1–2.

22. Okot, *Africa's Cultural Revolution,* 98.

23. Ibid., 33.

24. Okot p'Bitek, *African Religions in Western Scholarship* (Kampala: East African Literature Bureau, 1971), 9–10.

25. Sally Falk Moore, "Changing Perspectives on a Changing Africa: The Work of Anthropology," in *Africa and the Disciplines,* ed. Robert H. Bates, V. Y. Mudimbe, and Jean O'Barr (Chicago: University of Chicago Press, 1993), 10.

26. Ibid., 3.

27. Clifford, *Routes,* 21.

28. Moore, "Changing Perspectives," 3.

29. My references to different versions of the poem are indebted to Heron's account; Heron also discusses this shift in voice (*Poetry of Okot p'Bitek,* 33–45).

30. Moore, "Changing Perspectives," 12.

31. Okot p'Bitek, "Table of Nilotic Religious Concepts," in *Religion of the Central Luo* (Nairobi: East African Literature Bureau, 1971), unpaginated.

32. Heron, *Poetry of Okot p'Bitek,* 37.

33. Okot, *Religion of the Central Luo,* 160.

34. Godfrey Lienhardt, *Divinity and Experience: The Religion of the Dinka* (Oxford: Clarendon Press, 1961), 13; E. E. Evans-Pritchard, *Nuer Religion* (Oxford: Clarendon Press, 1956), 39.

35. For a searching critique of nativism, see Appiah, "Topologies of Nativism," chap. 3 of *In My Father's House,* 47–72.

36. Okot, *African Religions,* viii–ix.

37. Ibid., vii–viii, 44–45. Ensuing references to this work appear parenthetically in the text.

38. Cited by Lubwa p'Chong, "A Biographical Sketch," 7.

39. Talal Asad, introduction to *Anthropology and the Colonial Encounter,* ed. Talal Asad (London: Ithaca Press, 1973), 16, 17. Asad makes no direct reference to Okot; in his comment about "wild remarks," he is paraphrasing a view dismissed by Victor Turner.

40. Edward Said, "Representing the Colonized: Anthropology's Interlocutors," *Critical Inquiry* 15 (1989): 220.

41. Ibid., 225.

42. Ibid., 212. The long quotation above is from Okot's *Africa's Cultural Revolution,* 90–91.

43. Clifford, *Routes,* 69.

44. Kirin Narayan, "How Native Is a 'Native' Anthropologist?" *American Anthropologist* 95 (1993): 671.

45. Clifford, citing Kamela Visweswaran, *Routes,* 85.

46. Narayan, "How Native Is a 'Native' Anthropologist?" 671; Clifford, *Routes,* 77. See Gayatri Chakravorty Spivak's comparable skepticism about the "native informant" in "How

to Read a 'Culturally Different' Book" in *Colonial Discourse/Postcolonial Theory*, ed. Francis Barker, Peter Hulme, and Margaret Iverson (New York: Manchester University Press, 1994), 126–50, and *A Critique of Postcolonial Reason* (Cambridge, Mass.: Harvard University Press, 1999).

47. Lindfors, "Interview with Okot," 284. Angela Smith notes the authorial "self-mockery" implicit in Lawino's complaint that books have smashed the testicles of Acoli men (*East African Writing in English* [London: Macmillan, 1989], 89).

48. Florence Stratton has "denounced" Okot for "following the model provided by Senghor," which "analogizes woman to the heritage of African values, an unchanging African essence" (*Contemporary African Literature and the Politics of Gender* [New York: Routledge, 1994], 50, 41, 43).

49. Okot, *Africa's Cultural Revolution*, 61. For an interesting recent attempt to defend Tempels, see V. Y. Mudimbe, *The Invention of Africa: Gnosis, Philosophy, and the Order of Knowledge* (Bloomington: Indiana University Press, 1988), 50–54, 136–42.

50. Okot, *Africa's Cultural Revolution*, 62.

51. Mary Louise Pratt states, "If ethnographic texts are those in which European metropolitan subjects represent to themselves their others (usually their subjugated others), autoethnographic texts are representations that the so-defined others construct *in response to* or in dialogue with those texts." It should be noted, however, that by "ethnography" (or the counterdiscursive "autoethnography") Pratt means not the historically specific discipline of ethnography per se but any metropolitan representation of "others." See her "Transculturation and Autoethnography: Peru, 1615/1980," in *Colonial Discourse/Postcolonial Theory*, ed. Barker, Hulme, and Iverson, 28, and *Imperial Eyes: Travel Writing and Transculturation* (New York: Routledge, 1992), 7.

52. As Michael R. Ward observes, "Okot p'Bitek avoids the tone of anthropological description . . . by speaking directly to the audience (using the second person)" ("Okot p'Bitek and the Rise of East African Writing," 224). On Okot's use of dramatic monologue and apostrophe, see Heron, *Poetry of Okot p'Bitek*, 12–25, 60–61; Moore, "Horn of the Grasslands," 176; Ogo A. Ofuani, "Digression as Discourse Strategy in Okot p'Bitek's Dramatic Monologue Texts," *Research in African Literatures* 19 (1988): 312–340; and Okoh, "Writing African Oral Literature," 48–50. On anaphora and apostrophe in Okot's "Songs," see Wanambisi, *Thought and Technique*, 103–11. On apostrophe more generally, see Paul de Man, "Autobiography as De-Facement," in *The Rhetoric of Romanticism* (New York: Columbia University Press, 1984), 67–81; and Jonathan Culler, "Changes in the Study of the Lyric," in *Lyric Poetry: Beyond New Criticism*, ed. Chaviva Hošek and Patricia Parker (Ithaca, N.Y.: Cornell University Press, 1985), 40.

53. Gayatri Chakravorty Spivak, "Can the Subaltern Speak?" in *Marxism and the Interpretation of Culture*, ed. Cary Nelson and Lawrence Grossberg (Urbana: University of Illinois Press, 1988), 271–313, subsequently revised in chap. 3 of her *Critique of Postcolonial Reason*.

54. Herbert Tucker, "Dramatic Monologue and the Overhearing of Lyric," in *Lyric Poetry*, ed. Hošek and Parker, 228.

55. On exotic monologues, see Alan Sinfield, *Dramatic Monologue* (New York: Barnes & Noble, 1977), 44–45.

56. Loy D. Martin, *Browning's Dramatic Monologues and the Post-Romantic Subject* (Baltimore: Johns Hopkins University Press, 1985), 106.

57. Frantz Fanon, *Black Skin, White Masks*, trans. Charles Lam Markmann (New York: Grove Wiedenfeld, 1967), 141–54, 190–203. Referring to African history and culture, Ocol says:

> Smash all these mirrors
> That I may not see
> The blackness of the past
> From which I came
> Reflected in them.
>   (129)

On "self-hatred" and the "inferiority complex" in Okot's poetry, see J. O. J. Nwachukwu-Agbada, "Okot p'Bitek and the Story of a Paradox," *Commonwealth Essays and Studies* 12 (Autumn 1989): 95–107.

58. Okot, *African Religions*, 59.

59. Moore, "Changing Perspectives," 12.

60. Okot, *African Religions*, 62; see also Petersen, "Okot: Interview," 91.

61. Heron adds that these "deliberately odd translations giv[e] a totally new effect in the translation from that given in the original, where the Christian meanings of the words would be accepted without any strangeness by now" (*Poetry of Okot p'Bitek*, 56–57).

62. Okot, *African Religions*, 87–88.

63. Ibid., 67.

64. Ibid., 9.

65. Lindfors, "Songs of Okot," 150.

66. Mudimbe, *Invention of Africa*, 19.

67. Okot, *African Religions*, 14.

68. K. L. Goodwin, *Understanding African Poetry* (London: Heinemann, 1982), 161.

69. Moore, "Horn of the Grasslands," 175.

70. For reflections on glossed and untranslated words in postcolonial texts, see Bill Ashcroft, Gareth Griffiths, and Helen Tiffin, *The Empire Writes Back: Theory and Practice in Post-colonial Literatures* (New York: Routledge, 1989), 61–66; and Maria Tymoczko, "Post-colonial Writing and Literary Translation," in *Post-colonial Translation: Theory and Practice*, ed. Susan Bassnett and Harish Trivedi (New York: Routledge, 1999), 25.

71. Michael C. Onwuemene, "Limits of Transliteration: Nigerian Writers' Endeavors toward a National Literary Language," *PMLA* 114 (1999): 1057, 1058. See also the discussion of "relexification" in Chantal Zabus, "Language, Orality, and Literature," in *New National and Post-colonial Literatures: An Introduction*, ed. Bruce King (Oxford: Clarendon Press, 1996), 35–36; and of nonstandard lexemes due to literal translation in Tymoczko, "Post-colonial Writing and Literary Translation," 26.

72. Taban lo Liyong, *The Last Word: Cultural Synthesism* (Nairobi: East African Publishing House, 1969), 140, 141.

73. Heron, *Poetry of Okot p'Bitek*, 55–58.

74. Wole Soyinka, *Myth, Literature and the African World* (1976; reprint, Cambridge: Cambridge University Press, 1990), vii.

75. A. K. Ramanujan, *The Collected Poems* (Delhi: Oxford University Press, 1995), 139–40.

Coda: On Hybridity

1. See Anne McClintock, "The Angel of Progress: Pitfalls of the Term 'Post-Colonialism,'" *Social Text* 31/32 (1992): 84–98; R. Radhakrishnan, "Postcoloniality and the Boundaries of Identity," *Callaloo* 16, no. 4 (1993): 750–71; Ella Shohat, "Notes on the Post-colonial," *Social Text* 31/32 (1992): 108–10; Robert J. C. Young, *Colonial Desire: Hybridity in Theory, Culture and Race* (London: Routledge, 1995), 1–28; Aijaz Ahmad, *In Theory: Classes, Nations, Literatures* (London: Verso, 1995); and Bart Moore-Gilbert, *Postcolonial Theory: Contexts, Practices, Politics* (London: Verso, 1997), 193–96.

INDEX

A

Abacha, Sani, 11
Abrahams, Roger D., 109, 138–39
Achebe, Chinua, 1, 40, 177
    Things Fall Apart, 26, 141
    Yeats's influence on, 22
Acoli, 209n. 6
    and Okot's poetry as record of village culture of, 146
    and use of language and genre by Okot, 16, 144, 176
    and use of songs of by Okot, 1–2
Act of Union of 1800, 22, 23
Africa
    and negritude, 59
    poetry of and Okot, 143–76
    and political violence, 10–11
    postcolonial and language, 15
Agard, John, "Listen Mr. Oxford don," 15
Ali, Agha Shahid
    and metaphor, 69
    "Postcard from Kashmir," 11–12
    and use of Urdu sounds in English-language poetry, 16, 38
allegory, national, 65
Amin, Idi, 11, 210–11n. 32
Anancy (Anansi), 107–8, 111, 139, 204–5n. 18, 205n. 20, 206n. 26
Anderson, Benedict, and "imagined community," 27–28
anthropology, 141–78
    and complicity with colonialism, 154–56
    and ethnocentrism, 169
    imperialism of, as pictured in *Song of Ocol,* 171–72
    and native rejection of Western ways, 147
    and problem of observer, 157–58
    religious bias of, 156, 163–66
    similarity to discourse of in *Song of Lawino,* 148–51, 153, 154, 174
    and standard of "controlled empathy," 157, 159
    use of and conflict with by postcolonial writers, 141–43, 177–78
anticolonialism, 23–24, 36
Appiah, Kwame Anthony, 7, 141
Aristotle, 72, 73
Asad, Talal, *Anthropology and the Colonial Encounter,* 156, 211n. 39
Ashcroft, Bill, 198n. 45, 207n. 56, 213n. 70
assimilationism, 33, 110
Auden, W. H., 47

Awooner, Kofi, 10
    and hybridization of oral and literary, 18
    "Songs of Sorrow," 18
    "The Weaver Bird," 10, 18

B

Bakhtin, Mikhail
    and carnival, 110, 139
    and "folk laughter," 124
    and intentional and organic hybridity, 7, 17, 113
Banda, Hastings, 11
Barrell, John, 198n. 46
Beattie, John, 155
Bennett, Louise, 105–40
    and Anancy, 107–8, 205n. 20
    as a performer, 111
    biographical synopsis of, 203–4n. 26
    and "broad talk," 109, 111, 114, 138–39
    chronological publication of her work, 6, 183
    and comic hybridity, 113–14, 116, 122, 124
    and community-building irony, 113, 114–15
    and creole and use of language, 1, 15–16, 38, 107–18, 123, 130, 140, 182
    cultural prominence of in Jamaica, 106
    and emigration, 124–30
    and ethnography, 109, 178
    and hybridization of forms, 18, 113
    and independence, 130–39
    and irony as correlative for biculturalism, 19
    and "labrish" or gossip, 116–17
    and "Miss Lou's Views" (radio show), 106, 107
    and poems on Jamaican racism and classism, 27
    and poetry that resembles speech, 46
    as postcolonial, 5
    and race, 118–24
    and reciprocal violence, 128–29
    and "Ring Ding" (television show), 106
    and transformation of past by colonialism and modernity, 10
    and Walcott, 110, 179, 206n. 41
    works
        Anancy and Miss Lou, 107
        Anancy Stories and Dialect Verse, 107
        "Back to Africa," 110, 120–21
        "Bans a Killin," 111–12
        "Bed-Time Story," 116–17
        "Colonization in Reverse," 125–28
        "Colour-Bar," 122
        "Dear Departed Federation," 135–36
        "Dry-Foot Bwoy," 113–15
        "Independance," 136–38

Eliot, T. S., 2, 75
Waste Land, The, 2, 58
emigration, 125–30
English language
abandonment of in favor of native tongue, 14–15, 37–38
ambivalence of postcolonial poets toward, 13–15
as a creole, 111–12, 182
creolization of by postcolonial poets, 15–17, 38
and its use to rail against English in *Song of Lawino*, 161
postcolonial appropriation and transformation of, 14–15
and Walcott, 14, 189n. 52
and Walcott's versus Bennett's, 179
West Indian, 15–16
See also creole
ethnographic and antiethnographic discourse, 19, 141–43, 177–78, 212n. 51
and antiethnographic discourse in *Song of Lawino*, 154–62
and Okot, 142–76
Evans-Pritchard, E. E., 155
and definition of tribe, 171
Nuer Religion, 146, 150–51, 154
religious bias of, 156, 163
Ezekiel, Nissim, 75

F
family and metaphor, 97–101
Fanon, Franz, 26, 40
Black Skin, White Masks, 162
and criticism of postcolonial state, 29
and historical recovery process, 9, 10
and memory, 80
and negritude's tendency to duplicate colonial views, 197n. 31
and phases of colonial history and culture, 32, 33, 198n. 45
and reciprocal violence between colonizer and colonized, 128–29
Wretched of the Earth, The 8
Farrell, Joseph, 198n. 47
fiction, postcolonial, compared to poetry, 1–2, 183–84, 198n. 50
Fisher King, 58, 59
food, 92, 93, 95
Foster, R. F., 28
Foucault, Michel, 87
Frazer, James, 58
Friedman, Susan Stanford, 187n. 17

G
geography
and cartography, 137
language of, 73

and metaphor, 74, 99–100
and place names, 41–43
Gandhi, Leela, 186n. 11, 187n. 14
Ghosh, Amitav, 47, 103, 178
and anthropology in "The Imam and the Indian," 142
in comparison with Okot, 142–43
Gibbons, Luke, 32
Gilroy, Paul, 7
Gleaner (newspaper), 106, 130–38
Glissant, Edouard, 7, 63, 69, 129–30
globalization of anglophone poetry, 1, 183
Golden Dawn, 21
Gonne, Maud, 28
Goodison, Lorna, 2, 22, 183–84
"On Becoming a Mermaid," 17
and intercultural place names, 42
"To Us, All Flowers Are Roses," 42
Goodman, Nelson, *Languages of Art*, 73–74
Goodwin, K. L., 175
Graves, Robert, 58
Greenberg, Joseph H., 147
Griffiths, Gareth, 198n. 45, 207n. 56, 213n. 70
Guattari, Félix, 13, 77

H
Hall, Stuart, 7, 13, 23
Hardy, Thomas, 124–25
Harris, Wilson, 63, 107
Heaney, Seamus, *The Cure at Troy*, 55
Heidegger, Martin, 13
Heron, G. A., 143, 176, 213n. 61
home
and homelessness, 11–13
image of, 10–11
Hughes, Langston, 139, 145
Hutcheon, Linda, 103–4, 104–5, 203n. 13
hybridity, 36, 37, 179–84, 187n. 17
of anglophone canon, 182–83
and charge of its replication of binary model, 181
and criticism of false symmetry, 36, 38, 180
and critique that all cultures are hybrid, 36, 181–82
definition of, 6, 36
in form, 16–18
of Indian and Western poetics, 88
and insights it affords, 182
intentional and organic, 7, 17, 18, 113
and irony, 104
in language, 2, 15–17, 175–77
in metaphor, 16, 69, 72–75
of "native" cultural artifacts, 175, 182
and sociopolitical context, 180–81
of Western literary and non-Western oral traditions, 18, 46, 180
Hyde, Douglas, 37